The Special Criminal Court, 1922–2005

To the memory of

Commandant Frank Davis, Irish Free State Army

and

Timothy Cullinane, G Company, 1st Cork Brigade, Old IRA

The History and Development of the Special Criminal Court 1922–2005

Fergal Francis Davis

FOUR COURTS PRESS

Set in 11 on 12.5 Ehrhardt for
FOUR COURTS PRESS LTD
7 Malpas Street, Dublin 8, Ireland
e-mail: info@fourcourtspress.ie
http://www.fourcourtspress.ie
and in North America
FOUR COURTS PRESS
c/o ISBS, 920 N.E. 58th Avenue, Suite 300, Portland, OR 97213.

ISBN 978–1–84682–013–7

Printed in England by
Antony Rowe Ltd, Chippenham, Wilts.

Contents

Acknowledgments

Thanks are due to the staff of the School of Law, Trinity College, Dublin, the National Library of Ireland and the British Library, Boston Spa Reading Room. I am deeply indebted to the friendly and professional staff of the Irish National Archives.

To the staff of the School of Law, University of Sheffield, thank you for your kind words and support over the past years. Particular thanks are due to Professor Douglas Lewis, Dr Richard Kirkham, Sorcha MacLeod and Paul J. Cardwell.

I would also like to thank Professor Maurice Bric and the Irish Research Council for the Humanities & Social Sciences for their financial and academic support during my PhD studies; Professor Clive Walker, University of Leeds; Professors Sean Doran and John Jackson, Queen's University, Belfast; Professor Alex Stein, Hebrew University, Jerusalem; Professor Mark Tushnet, Harvard Law School; David Walker, Security & Northern Ireland Division, Department of Justice, Equality and Law Reform; and Hala Khoury-Bisharat, for their invaluable assistance on a variety of points.

My sincerest appreciation is extended to Dr Gerard Hogan of the School of Law, Trinity College Dublin. Despite an extremely busy schedule he has provided expert supervision and guidance throughout – from helping me develop and frame an understanding of the role of the Special Criminal Court to the point of correcting footnotes when I had been sloppy. Thank you for your patience and encouragement.

My interest in history stems from a childhood surrounded by those with a deep passion for Ireland and its past – as well as its future. My parents have been hugely influential in this respect, but appreciation is also due to Bill Wall and Br. Tim of Presentation Brothers College, Cork.

I would like to thank my family for their unwavering support, financial, emotional and academic. You have acted as counsellors and librarians, archivists and friends. Your influence is upon every page. Go raibh míle maith agaibh go léir.

To my wife, Dr Tessa Davis, thank you for everything. I know I could not have done this without you. If nothing else, I now have a somewhat greater understanding of the importance of the semicolon. Your proof-reading skills are unparalleled but I love you for much more than that.

Finally, to Michael Adams and all the staff of Four Courts Press, I apologize for the delays and thank you for all your help and encouragement. Your commitment has been outstanding and is greatly appreciated.

If I have forgotten anyone, I can only apologize. Although the help of everyone is greatly appreciated, I alone claim responsibility for any and all errors contained within.

Abbreviations

AG	Attorney General
Cmnd	Command (as in Command Paper)
DPP	Director of Public Prosecutions
ECOSOC	The Economic & Social Council
EPA	Emergency Powers Act
EPO	Emergency Powers Order
FARC	Revolutionary Armed Forces of Columbia
HRC	Human Rights Committee
ICC	International Criminal Court
ICCPR	International Covenant of Civil & Political Rights
ICTR	International Criminal Tribunal for Rwanda
ICTY	International Criminal Tribunal for the Former Yugoslavia
IRA	Irish Republican Army
JI	Jemaah Islamiah
JRA	Japanese Red Army Faction
MAK	Maktab-al-Khidarrat
MIA	Missing in action
MK	Member of the Knesset
NGO	Non-Governmental Organization
OAS	Offences against the State
POW	Prisoner of war
PSA	Public Safety Act
RIC	Royal Irish Constabulary
RUC	Royal Ulster Constabulary
SPA	Special Powers Act
TD	Teachta Dála (member of the Irish parliament)
WRA	War Relocation Authority

1

Trial by jury

This book is primarily concerned with the evolution of the Special Criminal Court and the legitimacy of its use. To place that evolution in context I shall begin by considering the role of trial by jury. In the adversarial, common law system employed in Ireland, trial by jury is the norm in serious cases, and the abolition of trial by jury for defendants in trials related to a threat to security is therefore a deviation from this norm.

1.1 Trial by jury internationally

While trial by jury is the norm in many parts of the common law world, it is not the only trial process; and beyond the common law world, variations upon trial by jury and exceptions to it are frequently to be found. In the Netherlands, criminal trials are conducted by three judges without a jury.[1] Spain employs a non-jury system and has a special court, the Audiencia Nacional, for cases involving 'crimes against the crown, the high organs of the nation, or the government in the form of counterfeit and monetary crimes, drug trafficking, food and drugs crimes … terrorism, extradition of prisoners' and so forth.[2] This court sits in Madrid and essentially removes the case from the Audiencia Provincial; it takes it from the local to the national level, thereby reducing local involvement. Similarly, the courts in France have accepted the use of non-jury courts in terrorist cases; in 1986 the Chirac government introduced the Lois Pasqua in an attempt to combat terrorism. 'The loi sought to create a non-jury court for terrorist offences of seven judges, rather than the normal three judges sitting with nine jurors. This was done to prevent jury intimidation.'[3] The Counseil recognized that the right to an unbiased court is part of due process but rejected the proposition that the removal of jury trial breached this principle; indeed, it noted that 'since the independence of the ordinary judiciary is guaranteed by Article 64 of the [French] Constitution … judges themselves are seen as constituting a guarantee of this aspect of due process'.[4]

It is also significant that the International Military Tribunal at Nuremberg did not employ a jury. It was composed of four members[5] appointed by the

1 *Report of the Committee to review the Offences against the State Acts, 1939–1998 and related matters* (Dublin, 2002), para. 9.34 citing Charleton & McDermott. 2 E. Merino-Blanco, *The Spanish legal system* (1996), p. 87. 3 J. Bell, *French constitutional law* (1992), p. 315. 4 Ibid., p. 195. 5 Article 2, *Charter of the International Military Tribunal*, http://usa.usembassy.de/etexts/ga4-trials.htm, accessed 8 August 2005.

four signatories of the Charter of the International Military Tribunal.[6] The presence of all four members, or their appointed alternates, was required in order to constitute a quorum.[7] The tribunal, which did not require a jury despite the fact that it was trying the most serious of offences,[8] has been criticized as being an example of 'victors' justice'. While Article 16 of its charter did give guarantees of a fair trial, the issues it addressed were largely procedural, focusing on means of ensuring that the defendant could understand the charges and proceedings.[9]

> It has been argued that the Tribunal cannot be regarded as a court in the true sense because, as its members represent the victorious Allied Nations, they must lack that impartiality which is an essential in all judicial procedure. According to this view only a court consisting of neutrals, or, at least, containing some neutral judges, could be considered to be a proper tribunal. As no man can be a judge in his own case, so no allied tribunal can be a judge in a case in which members of the enemy government or forces are on trial.[10]

These criticisms of the tribunal's independence are legitimate. If the tribunal had employed a jury, or if it had employed judges drawn from neutral states rather than judges appointed by the governments of the victorious nations, it would also have benefited from a higher level of legitimacy. Any lack of legit-

6 The four signatories were the government of the United States of America, the provisional government of the French Republic, the government of the United Kingdom of Great Britain and Northern Ireland and the government of the Union of Soviet Socialist Republics. Article 1, *Charter of the International Military Tribunal.* 7 Article 4, *Charter of the International Military Tribunal.* 8 The Tribunal had jurisdiction to prosecute, crimes against peace, war crimes and crimes against humanity. Article 6, *Charter of the International Military Tribunal.* 9 In order to ensure fair trial for the defendants, the following procedure shall be followed:

(a) The indictment shall include full particulars specifying in detail the charges against the defendants. A copy of the Indictment and of all the documents lodged with the indictment, translated into a language which he understands, shall be furnished to the defendant at reasonable time before the trial.
(b) During any preliminary examination or trial of a defendant he will have the right to give any explanation relevant to the charges made against him.
(c) A preliminary examination of a defendant and his trial shall be conducted in, or translated into, a language which the defendant understands.
(d) A defendant shall have the right to conduct his own defense before the Tribunal or to have the assistance of counsel.
(e) A defendant shall have the right through himself or through his counsel to present evidence at the trial in support of his defence, and to cross-examine any witness called by the prosecution.

Article 16, *Charter of the International Military Tribunal.* 10 A.L. Goodhart, 'The legality of the Nuremberg trials', *Juridicial Review,* April 1946, http://www.nizkor.org/hweb/imt/, accessed 8 August 2005.

imacy stemmed from the nature of the judicial appointments and not from the lack of a jury.

Since Nuremberg, other international criminal tribunals have been established for the Former Yugoslavia and for Rwanda, neither of which utilizes trial by jury. The International Criminal Court (ICC) provides for the prosecution of the most serious of offences before a panel of international jurists without a jury;[11] there is a significant difference between this new court and that of the Nuremberg tribunal – namely, that the ICC employs a panel of international jurists rather than a panel appointed by the four Potsdam powers. The judges, therefore, benefit from a greater level of independence and as such the court can be said to be more legitimate.

So, although it has been stated that 'trial by jury is a cornerstone of the criminal justice system',[12] it is not necessarily indispensable. There is a long history of interference with the right to trial by jury within the common law. Cornish refers to a series of examples where it was felt necessary to remove the jury in order to guarantee justice:

> In places such as the first West African colonies, the jury was introduced for the whole populace, but such foreseeable obstacles to success as anti-African prejudices, inter-tribal partisanship and extensive bribery of jurors led to its abandonment in the later nineteenth century for civil cases, and to severe curtailment or supersession by trial with assessors in criminal cases.[13]

Furthermore, in 1958 the Law Commission of India recommended the removal of trial by jury due to bribery of jurors.[14] The state of Israel has also adopted a system of criminal trial which does not employ a jury: lesser offences are tried by a single judge sitting alone, while appeals and more serious offences are heard by a panel of three judges. Article 37 of the Courts Law [Consolidated Version], 5744 – 1984 states that trials concerning an offence that demands the death penalty or ten years' imprisonment as punishment should be conducted by a panel of three judges. Moreover, Article 37(3) allows the president or vice-president of the District Court to order that any other issue be heard by three judges. This is particularly interesting for two reasons. Firstly, Israel has adopted a common law, adversarial, system and yet does not employ trial by jury; and, secondly, the choice of three judges is based on a Talmudic source from the Pirkei Avot (Ethics of the

11 Rome Statute of the International Criminal Court, 17 July 1998, Part IV. http://www.un.org/law/icc/statute/romefra.htm, accessed on 4 August 2005. 12 *Committee to review the Offences against the State Acts, 1939–1998*, para. 9.88. 13 W.R. Cornish, *The Jury* (1968), pp 15–16. 14 Ibid., p. 17.

Fathers),[15] which states that, 'Rabbi Yishmael . . . used to say: Do not act as a judge alone, for none judges alone except One.'[16]

1.2 A brief history of the right to trial by jury

In England juries began to be employed more frequently during the reign of Henry II. Trial by jury replaced

> trial by ordeal of fire or water. [This] jury consisted of 12 persons in the neighbourhood, *witnesses,* who swore to the truth of what they knew. It was not until much later that they emerged as a body of strangers to the case whose task was to decide it rationally upon evidence put before them.[17]

Thus, the jury began as an 'evidentiary and investigative rather than a decision making body'.[18] The shift to a jury system during the Middle Ages was caused not by an overwhelming desire to defend the individual against the excesses of the state but rather to increase speed and efficiency. For example, land disputes tended to be lengthy affairs; the ultimate decision in such cases rested with God, who would decide the case through the ordeal of battle, 'a judicial duel introduced by the Normans, through the Grand Assize of 1179; [later] Henry [II] gave the defendant in such actions the option of having the matter determined conclusively by a jury of 12 knights'.[19] The early jury was utilized specifically for their local knowledge, the function of the modern jury is to base their decision on the facts presented in court and not on personal knowledge or prejudices.[20]

The jury has developed greatly since the time of Henry II. In 1956 Lord Devlin proclaimed:

> The first object of any tyrant in Whitehall would be to make parliament utterly subservient to his will; and the next to overthrow or diminish trial by jury, for no tyrant could afford to leave a subject's freedom in the hands of twelve of his countrymen. So that trial by jury is more than an instrument of justice and more than one wheel of the constitution: it is the lamp that shows that freedom lives.[21]

15 'Pirkei Avot transmits the favourite moral advice and insights of the leading rabbinic scholars of different generations.' See Rabbi J. Telushkin, *Jewish literacy: the most important things to know about the Jewish religion, its people, and its history* (2001), p. 526. 16 Chapter 4, verse 10. Rabbi N. Scherman (trans.), *The complete artscroll siddur: ashkenaz* (2001), p. 567. 17 Lord Justice Robin Auld, *Review of the criminal courts of England & Wales,* (London, 2001), chapter 5 para. 7, henceforth *Auld Review,* http://www.criminal-courts-review.org.uk/ccr-00.htm, accessed 4 August 2005. 18 Ann Lyon, *Constitutional history of the United Kingdom* (London, 2003), p. 33. 19 Ibid. 20 Cornish, *The Jury,* p. 10. 21 Sir Patrick Devlin, *Trial by jury* (1966), p. 164.

Historically, this assertion can be easily challenged: rather than abolishing trial by jury it has been more convenient for any would-be tyrant to intimidate the jury. Thus, in 1535 a jury which declared the bishop of Rochester guilty of treason said afterwards that they had been fearful 'for the safety of their goods and lives which they were all well assured they would lose, in case they acquitted him'.[22] In *Bushell's Case*, in 1670, the jury failed to convict and was swiftly imprisoned by the trial judge who disagreed with their verdict; this judicial power was removed shortly thereafter[23] (the fear of jury intimidation has been key to the introduction of the Special Criminal Court, as we shall see later). It is also worth noting that, despite widespread belief to the contrary, there is no 'right' to trial by jury in England and Wales; the Magna Carta does not guarantee any such right.[24] Therefore, there is no historic right to trial by jury, and the mere existence of the jury has not been capable of safeguarding liberty.

In 1768, William Blackstone famously declared that the jury was the bulwark of liberty;[25] but is such a position a truly accurate depiction of the role of the jury in law? Early examples of trial by jury are unrecognizable to the modern eye. Jury tampering by the authorities was common, and the role of the jury has been altered dramatically, from that of informed witness to one of independent stranger. To state that 'the jury' is the light which shows that freedom lives, begs the question: Which jury?

1.3 The 'democratizing' effect

The current justification for trial by jury can be summed up as being that the jury, as an institution, incorporates a 'democratizing' effect. Thus, the belief has emerged that the jury should contain 'a representative cross-section of a community'.[26] In *de Búrca v. Attorney General*[27] the Supreme Court held that sections of the Juries Act, 1927, 'which excluded from jury service all those who were without a minimum rating qualification in respect of a house or land, and exempted women from service subject to an individual woman's right to apply to serve', were unconstitutional.[28] In a telling passage Henchy J stated:

> it is incompatible with the necessary diffusion of rights and duties in a modern democratic society that important decisions such as voting, or jury verdicts involving life or liberty should be made by male citizens only. What is missing in decisions so made is not easy to define; but reason and experience show that such decisions are not calculated to lead to a sense of general acceptability, or to carry an acceptable degree

22 Cornish, *The Jury*, p. 128. **23** Ibid., p. 129. **24** *Auld Review*, chapter 5, para. 7. **25** Cornish, *The Jury*, p. 126. **26** G. Hogan & G. Whyte, *Kelly: the Irish Constitution* (2003), para. 6.5.393. **27** [1976] IR 38. **28** Hogan & Whyte, *Kelly*, para. 6.5.393.

> of representativeness, or to have the necessary stamp of responsibility and involvement on the part of the community as a whole.[29]

Therefore, for Henchy J at least, the role of the jury is to increase the legitimacy of verdicts through the involvement of a representative sample of the community.

Lord Devlin is of a like mind, describing the jury as a 'little parliament'.[30] This view of the modern jury is key to the democratization theory. It sees the jury as representing society at large in much the same way as parliament represents the people in a representative democracy. This argument is overly romantic. The ability of any given jury to represent the public is derived from the randomness of its selection. This point was key in *de Búrca*. A jury should consist of 'twelve individuals chosen at random from the appropriate panel';[31] however, the jury system consistently struggles to deliver this randomness. The Diplock Report in Northern Ireland identified the problem of partisan juries within the context of that sectarian conflict; at the time of the report, 'the property qualifications for jury service [were] more likely to be possessed by Protestants than Catholics'[32] and, as such, the system contained an in-built bias in favour of the Protestant population. Such a system could not be described as representative. While it is possible to distinguish Northern Ireland as an example of a dysfunctional jury system, research in England and Wales as recently as 1993 has also shown that women and non-whites remained under-represented on juries in that jurisdiction.[33] The view of the random jury as democratically representative is open to question.

Despite these criticisms it must be conceded that the democratizing effect of the jury remains an attractive argument. De Tocqueville summarizes the position eloquently:

> Using juries for the suppression of crime appears to me the introduction of a predominately republican institution into government ... The jury may be aristocratic or democratic according to the class which supplies the juries, but it always retains a republican character in that it entrusts the actual control of society into the hands of the ruled, or some of them, rather than into those of the rulers.[34]

29 [1976] IR 38, 77. 30 Devlin, *Trial by jury*, p. 164. 31 Lord Chief Justice's practice direction; see Peter Thornton, 'Trial by jury: 50 years of change', [2004] *Criminal Law Review*, 683–701 at 686. 32 Lord Diplock, *Report of the commission to consider the legal procedures to deal with terrorist activities in Northern Ireland*, Cmnd. 5185 (London, 1972), para. 36, henceforth *Diplock Report*. 33 Thornton, 'Trial by jury', 685. 34 A. de Tocqueville, *Democracy in America & two essays on America*, trans. G.E. Bevan (2003), pp. 317–18.

For de Tocqueville the jury is an element of the sovereignty of the people;[35] significantly, however, he is not overly interested in the judicial efficiency of juries. He states, 'I do not know whether juries are much use to litigants but I am sure that they are of great use to those who judge the case. They are ... one of the most effective means available to society for educating the people.'[36] This argument might be summarized as advocating the educative rather than the democratizing effect of jury service. Interestingly, recent reforms in Japan appear to be predicated, in part at least, upon this argument. The Japanese have recently decided to introduce a form of mixed jury system in which jurors and judges will hear cases together. 'What commonly underlies these reforms is the will that each and every person will break out of the consciousness of being a governed object and will become a governing subject'.[37]

It is difficult to assess how tangible this educative effect is. After all, a civilized state like the Netherlands has a strong functioning democracy without trial by jury. What is clear, however, is that this line of argument sees the jury as a political rather than a judicial tool. Indeed, de Tocqueville concedes that 'if it were a question of knowing how far the jury ... serves the good administration of justice, I would admit that its usefulness could be challenged'.[38] If that position is accepted, the attractiveness of trial by jury rests on its involvement of the population in the administration of justice.

1.4 Jury failure

Despite the philosophical advantages of trial by jury, one cannot ignore its judicial function. The primary role of the jury is not to involve the public or educate the citizenry: it is to deliver justice. If it can succeed in doing this while at the same time delivering these additional benefits, then that is ideal. However, when trial by jury fails to secure the effective administration of justice, one is forced to consider whether or not these benefits are outweighed by that failure. In recent years a debate has emerged concerning the suitability of the jury system in complex trials. In particular, academic comment has focused on the issue of juries understanding of forensic evidence and their ability to cope with serious fraud cases. In the case of forensic science, a perception has emerged that juries might be incapable of understanding the complex nature of the evidence presented. It seems logical to assume that jurors, randomly selected from the population at large, might have some difficulty interpreting and understanding scientific evidence. Research has found that jurors' 'main impediment to understanding proceedings was the use of

35 Ibid., p. 319. 36 Ibid., p. 321. 37 Robert M. Bloom, 'Jury trials in Japan' (March 16, 2005), Boston College Law School Research Paper No. 66, http://ssrn.com/abstract+688185, accessed 17 August 2005. 38 De Tocqueville, *Democracy*, p. 316.

legal terminology'.[39] However, technical evidence also poses a problem as table 1.1 illustrates:

Table 1.1
Jury understanding[40]

Aspects difficult to understand	*Number of responses*
The legal terminology	43
Legal or factual information	16
Technical evidence	15
Information on the nature of the charges	12
The order of proceedings, the opening statements and address	8
Summing up	7
Use of exhibits, physical evidence, visual aids etc. (maps/photos)	4
Evidence	5
Total	110

It is important to note that this research was based upon jurors' own perceptions and individual juror understanding was not objectively assessed. This approach is of questionable benefit since a juror may claim to understand something of which he or she, in fact, has but little comprehension.[41] One difficulty in the field of forensic science concerns the issue of cross-examining experts. It has been suggested that any questioning of the reputation of a witness automatically damages his or her credibility in the eyes of the jury, even where such questioning is without basis.[42] In the absence of further research it is impossible to say whether or not juries can cope with forensic science evidence. 'It is highly likely that the number of cases which depend on complex forensic evidence will increase'; so it is important that research be conducted as a matter of urgency.[43] What can be said with certainty is that any jury unable to understand the evidence placed before it is incapable of delivering justice.[44]

39 R. Matthews, L. Hancock & D. Briggs, 'Juror's perceptions, understanding, confidence and satisfaction in the jury system: a study in six courts' (Home Office Online Report 05/04), p. 37, http://www.homeoffice.gov.uk/rds/pdfs2/rdsolr0504.pdf, accessed on 22 August 2005. **40** Ibid. This research is based on contacts with 361 jurors. Table 1.1 is based on responses to question 28 of the questionnaire. Question 28 begins with a filter: 'Did you find any aspects of the trial difficult to understand?' If 'yes', the respondents are given the above list of options. It is unclear how many respondents answered 'yes' to the initial filter question. Therefore, while it is clear that question 28 elicited 110 responses it is unclear how many actual respondents account for the 110 responses. See Matthews, Hancock & Briggs, 'Juror's perceptions, understanding, confidence and satisfaction in the jury system: a study in six courts' (Home Office online report 05/04), appendix A, p. 82. **41** House of Commons science & technology committee, *Forensic science on trial, seventh report of sessions 2004–05*, HC 96–1 (2005), para. 165. **42** Ibid., para. 165. **43** Ibid., para. 167. **44** The evidence placed before the jury needs to be of a high quality. In the

The second area of recent controversy has to do with serious fraud trials. The Auld Report (2001) has identified a series of problems associated with trial by jury in complex fraud trials. As with forensic science evidence, there are concerns about the ability of juries to understand complicated evidence. However, further difficulties arise due to the length of these trials. It 'is not just a matter of expense and toil flowing from the use of procedures peculiar to jury trial in such difficult cases. The remorseless increase in the length of such trials over recent years has become a severe intrusion on jurors' working and private lives.'[45] The length of these trials 'has the effect of making juries even less representative of the community than they are already, since the court excuses many who would otherwise be able and willing to make short-term arrangements to do their civic duty'.[46] If juries are not representative, then the benefits of trial by jury identified in *de Búrca* and by de Tocqueville no longer apply. Lord Justice Auld, therefore, recommended the abolition of trial by jury in such cases and its replacement: 'the nominated trial judge should be empowered to direct trial by himself sitting with lay members or, where the defendant has opted for trial by judge alone, by himself alone'.[47] 'Auld's scepticism as to the attractiveness of jury trial ... is not unique. It is timely and consistent when an overall decline in the frequency of juries in other common law jurisdictions.'[48]

1.5 The issue of jury bias

The single greatest difficulty in any analysis of trial by jury results from the fact that researchers are denied the right to question and interview jurors, so it is impossible to collect data on their reasoning, prejudices and understanding. There is, however, no doubt that people (and therefore jurors) do have personal prejudices. The Diplock Report identified the potential problem of bias within the context of sectarian violence in Northern Ireland. Since then, Canadian researchers have identified four categories of bias: *interest prejudice,* where a juror may have a vested interest in a particular outcome; *specific prejudice,* where a juror may have a pre-existing opinion about the case in hand; *generic prejudice,* which arises when a jurors pre-existing opinion causes that juror to stereotype the defendant, victim or crime; and *conformity prejudice,* where the juror may feel pressure to conform to a particular view. These categories can arise either due to an individual juror's pre-existing opinions, interests or prejudices, or as a result of a juror's

field of expert scientific evidence cases exists where the jury has been given inaccurate or misleading evidence. Such evidence is in and of itself bad evidence, and the jury, as an institution, cannot be held liable for that failure. For example, recent cases in the UK surrounding convictions based on the evidence of Prof. Sir Roy Meadows. Ibid., para. 168. **45** *Auld Review*, para. 173. **46** Ibid., para. 181. **47** Ibid., para. 206. **48** David Corker, 'Trying fraud cases without juries' (2002) *Criminal Law Review*, 283–94 at 284.

opinion about a given case, consequent on pre-trial publicity or some other factor.[49]

Article 6 of the European Convention on Human Rights (ECHR) demands that everyone be entitled to trial by an 'independent and impartial tribunal established by law'.[50] In *Sander v. the United Kingdom* the European Court of Human Rights stressed that 'a tribunal, including a jury, must be impartial',[51] so the issue of jury bias is one of fundamental importance and can directly impede a defendant's right to a fair trial. The European Court has established a two-part test for dealing with issues of bias. Firstly, 'there is a presumption that all tribunals are free from bias unless otherwise proven and secondly, once an allegation of bias is made it must be investigated unless it is "manifestly devoid of merit"'.[52] *Remli, Sander* and *Gregory*[53] all involved situations where one or more jurors were alleged to have displayed racist views. The ability of the court to investigate such allegations and the procedure to be followed in such instances has been laid down by the European Court of Human Rights; but the significant factor is that the potential for such jury bias has been established.

DPP v. Haugh[54] focused upon the issue of pre-trial publicity and its potential effect on the defendant's right to a fair trial. *Haugh* is a rather peculiar case in that it involved the trial of a former Taoiseach, Charles Haughey, and the pre-trial publicity arose from the publication of the report of the Moriarty Tribunal. Thus, this was not merely the kind of publicity that might surround any normal trial. Mr Haughey was concerned that the publicity generated by the McCracken and Moriarty tribunals would prejudice his right to a fair trial.[55] In the cases of

> *D v. DPP*[56] and *Z v. DPP*[57] ... the Supreme Court acknowledged that it would be naïve in modern society to hope to empanel a jury which had not heard anything about a case of considerable notoriety. However, the mere fact that an offence had received significant publicity does not itself mean that the trial of that offence would be unfair.[58]

49 Katie Quinn, 'Jury bias and the European Convention on Human Rights: a well kept secret?' (2004) *Criminal Law Review*, 998–1014 at 999. 50 Article 6, European Convention on Human Rights. See also *Holm v. Sweden* (1994) 18 EHRR 79 and the High Court of Australia decision in *Webb v. the Queen* (1993–1994) 181 CLR 41. 51 (2001) 31 EHRR 44, para. 22. 52 Quinn, 'Jury bias and the European Convention on Human Rights: a well kept secret?', 1001–2, citing *Remli v. France* (1996) 22 EHRR 253, para. 48. 53 *Gregory v. the United Kingdom* (1997) 25 EHRR 577. 54 [2000] 1 IR 184. 55 John L. O'Donnell, 'The jury on trial: reflections on *DPP v. Haugh*' (July, 2000) *Bar Review*, 470–75 at 470. 56 [1994] 2 IR 465. 57 [1994] 2 IR 476. 58 O'Donnell, 'The jury on trial: reflections on *DPP v. Haugh*', 471.

In *Haugh* the trial judge sought to alter the procedure in order to guarantee a fair trial.[59] Specifically, Haugh J, the trial judge, sent a questionnaire to potential members of the jury.[60] In the view of the High Court, the decision to alter the procedures by sending out a questionnaire was without jurisdiction;[61] furthermore, Carney J saw no reason for establishing a special set of rules in this case; such rules would in fact be offensive to the 'constitutional imperative that all citizens should be equal before the law'.[62] The conclusion in *Haugh* was that the trial judge may not alter the procedures simply on the grounds of the notoriety of the accused; rather, he must employ warnings and so forth during the course of the trial in order to ensure fair procedures.[63] Similarly, in the case of *Gregory* the European Court accepted that where the trial judge discussed the alleged racial bias with counsel and then delivered a strict warning to the jury he had discharged his duty.[64] The court's decision in *Sander* differed from that in *Gregory:* here an allegation of bias was made by one juror; the trial judge told the jury of the complaint and reminded them of their oath; the next day he received two letters: the first was from the entire jury, denying any prejudice; the second from an individual juror, admitting making racist jokes but denying racial prejudice. Under the circumstances, the European Court of Human Rights was of the opinion that, although no evidence of subjective bias existed, it could be argued that the second letter provided evidence of objective bias; therefore the court held that the trial had breached Article 6.[65] *Haugh, Gregory* and *Sander* confirm the complexity of determining how to respond to jury bias. The Irish and European case law makes it clear that courts must react to allegations of or concerns about jury bias; relying on the random selection process is insufficient. Therefore, while it is presumed that bias does not exist, if an allegation of bias arises the court must investigate it and act accordingly.

While the above cases provide some guidance that might help to reduce the problem of jury bias, these measures are only effective if the alleged bias emerges before sentence; where allegations of bias are made after the trial, it is obviously not possible to issue a warning to the jury. The jurisprudence in such cases is somewhat unclear. The European Court of Human Rights has not directly considered the issue and the UK courts have failed to reach a conclusive decision.[66] In the conjoined UK appeals of *Conor* and *Mizra,*[67] the House of Lords held that the rules governing secrecy of jury deliberations were compatible with the ECHR and that none of the defendants had received an unfair trial despite allegations of jury bias.[68] The dissenting

59 Ibid. **60** [2000] IEHC 178. **61** [2000] 1 IR 184, 208. **62** [2000] 1 IR 184, 194. **63** O'Donnell, 'The jury on trial: reflections on *DPP v. Haugh*', 474. **64** Quinn, 'Jury bias and the European Convention on Human Rights: a well kept secret?', 1002. **65** Ibid., 1003. **66** For further discussion on this point see Quinn, 'Jury bias', 1004–6. **67** [2004] 1 AC 1118. **68** [2004] 1 AC 1118, 1119.

judgment of Lord Steyn is illuminating; he posited two hypothetical scenarios: in the first it emerges after the verdict that a number of the jurors belonged to a neo-nazi group and had advocated conviction on the basis that the defendant was a black immigrant; in the second the jurors refused to deliberate and reached their verdict by spinning a coin. Lord Steyn contended that such a verdict would be perverse,[69] concluding that

> it would be an astonishing thing for the ECHR to hold ... that a miscarriage of justice may be ignored in the interests of the general efficiency of the jury system. The terms of Article 6(1) of the European Convention, the rights revolution, and fifty years of development of human rights law and practice, would suggest that such a view would be utterly indefensible.[70]

The rationale behind Lord Steyn's view is that the jury is a judicial tribunal and is therefore bound by the same rules as all other judicial tribunals. He argues that 'a jury is not above the law. As a judicial tribunal it must comply with the requirements of article 6(1) of the European Convention on Human Rights.'[71] It is this emphasis on the judicial, rather than the political, role of the jury which distinguishes Lord Steyn from de Tocqueville.

1.6 Juries and perverse verdicts

Lord Justice Auld has commented that many 'fervently support what they regard as the right of the jury to ignore their duty to return a verdict according to the evidence and to acquit where they disapprove of the law or of the prosecution in seeking to enforce it'.[72] This issue is clearly highlighted by the decision of the UK courts in *R v. Ponting*.[73] Clive Ponting, a senior civil servant, had drafted a response to Mr Tom Dalyell MP's parliamentary questions about the sinking of the *Belgrano*. The minister, Michael Heseltine, chose not to use these responses and instead sent his own brief replies. Ponting then took it upon himself to leak two documents to Mr Dalyell.[74] The point of law in *Ponting* rested upon the definition of 'in the interests of the state' within the UK's Official Secrets Act, 1911.

> Clive Ponting admitted in court passing two official documents to Tom Dalyell but pleaded 'not guilty' to communicating them unlawfully. His defence was based on the ground that it was his duty 'in the

69 [2004] 1 AC 1118, 1129. 70 [2004] 1 AC 1118. 1136. 71 [2004] 1 AC 1118, 1130. 72 *Auld Review*, para. 99. 73 (1985) Central Criminal Court, 11 February. 74 Rosamund M. Thomas, 'The British Official Secrets Acts 1911–1939 and the Ponting case' (1986) *Criminal Law Review*, 491–510 at 492.

> interests of the state' to inform parliament (via Tom Dalyell) because it had been misled about the Belgrano affair by ministers.[75]

Significantly, the trial judge directed the jury that the words 'interests of the state' referred to 'the policies of the state ... at the time of the disclosure and [that] they [the jury] should not consider whether they agreed with the policies of the government'.[76] Based on this direction it is clear that Ponting's defence would fail in law. However, the jury refused to return a guilty verdict, and Ponting was acquitted against the evidence. The case highlighted the absence of a public interest defence in the Official Secrets Acts, 1911–1939 and became something of a cause célèbre.

Lord Devlin supported the jury's right to dispense with the law in such circumstances by arguing that 'it as a protection against laws that the ordinary man might regard as "harsh and oppressive" and an insurance "that the criminal law will conform to the ordinary man's idea of what is fair and just".'[77] The power of the jury to dispense with unpopular or harsh law could be seen as the exercise of the democratic function by these twelve randomly selected individuals and is in keeping with Devlin's view of the jury as a 'little parliament'. On the other hand, Auld LJ questions whether the jury has, in fact, any 'right' to dispense with the law in such a fashion; he argues that 'although juries may have the ability to dispense with or nullify the law, they have no right to do so', and notes that such action is contrary to their oath.[78] In *The People v. O'Shea*[79] Henchy J considered this point. He asserted that

> both judges and legislators have accepted that while a jury, properly instructed by the trial judge, have no *right* to bring in a verdict for the accused which is against the evidence, yet they have the *power* to do so; and that the risks inherent in any efforts at controlling the exercise of that power would not be warranted. The use of the power to err in favour of the accused is left to the conscience of the jurors.[80]

Like Lord Devlin, Henchy J also sees the jury as fulfilling the role of a mini-parliament, noting that 'what may seem to judges to be a perverse verdict of acquittal may represent the layman's rejection of a particular law ... So it is that such verdicts have often led to reform of the criminal law.'[81] As such, juries do not possess the right to dispense with the law; however, they have retained the ability or power to do so. The problematic nature of the dispensing power is highlighted by the possibility of perverse convictions. While the right of a jury to acquit an individual because they do not agree

75 Ibid., 497. 76 Ibid. 77 *Auld Review*, para. 99, citing Devlin, *Trial by jury*, p. 160. 78 *Auld Review*, para. 101. 79 [1982] IR 384. 80 [1982] IR 384, 438. 81 Ibid.

with the law is one thing, few would claim that juries have any right to convict a defendant in the absence of evidence. Furthermore, while some perverse acquittals (such as in *Ponting*) have the attractive nature of being a 'blow for freedom', others might be based on less defensible jury prejudice.[82]

The apparent power of perverse acquittal has no basis in law; it is a power which juries have developed largely because they are never called upon to justify their decisions. Furthermore, despite pronouncements to the contrary, it is not democratic. Representative democracy operates on the basis that the public select representatives who then legislate and govern on their behalf. Low voter turn-out, the party system and the complex nature of modern election manifestos have cast some doubts over the ability of representative democracy to reflect the views of the populous. However, the difference between representative democracy and jury selection is that in democratic elections the public have the opportunity to select their rulers and those who govern derive their legitimacy from the selection process. Juries, however, are randomly selected to act as a trier of fact and are not entitled to legislate. The fact that juries are made up of lay people does not in and of itself qualify them to represent the public at large. The Boy Scouts, the Women's Institute and the Orange Order are all made up of lay people but that does not entitle them to legislate on behalf of the entire population. I concur with Auld LJ in rejecting the right of the jury to deliver perverse verdicts.

1.7 A mature response

It has been argued that

> most of the great pronouncements on constitutional liberty, from the eighteenth century onwards, have been the work of judges, either sitting in appellate courts or giving directions to juries. The assumption that political liberty at the present day depends upon the institution of the jury … is in truth merely folklore.[83]

Despite this, civil libertarians tend to be protective of the right to trial by jury: possibly because they instinctively support the kind of egalitarian agenda which, in the eyes of de Tocqueville, is encapsulated by the jury; so, any attempt at limiting the right to trial by jury tends to be roundly criticized. Indeed, it might be argued that 'the fate of the socialist-minded activist in modern democratic politics is that of the perpetual bemoaner, lamenting the reactionary zeal of the Right or the betrayals of the governing Left, as the case may be'.[84] Gearty argues that part of the difficulty arises from the over

82 *Auld Review*, para. 100. 83 *Auld Review*, para. 102, citing Dr Glanville Williams. 84 C. Gearty, 'Reflections on civil liberties in an age of counterterrorism' (2003) 41 *Osgoode Hall Law Journal*, 185–208 at 186.

use of the phrase 'civil liberties'.[85] He advocates a reassessment of its core values: 'The core of the subject lies in the protection of political freedom. Civil liberties [are] concerned with making representative democracy work.'[86] Therefore, civil libertarians should emphasize the significance of the rights to liberty, expression, association and assembly.[87] A functioning representative democracy does not require trial by jury; however, the right to a fair trial can be seen as a facet of the right to liberty. Attention must be refocused on the protection of the right to a fair trial rather than the retention of juries in all cases.

Since this book focuses on the curtailment of the right to trial by jury in emergency cases, the question arises as to how to limit the exercise of emergency powers. There are two traditional controls on the executive power, namely, the separation of powers and judicial review. 'Both mechanisms aim to ensure that the national government exercises its powers responsibly – with sufficient vigour to meet the nation's challenges, but, without intruding on protected liberties.'[88] Both of these mechanisms will be considered in detail in Chapter 8, which will examine the role of the courts and the legislature in reviewing executive actions. At this stage two points are worth considering. Firstly, in the US context, a historicist analysis identifying a certain trend of 'social learning', suggests that

> the threat to civil liberties posed by government actions has diminished in successive wartime emergencies. We ratchet down our reaction to what we perceive to be a threat each time we observe what we think in retrospect were exaggerated reactions to threats. To take the obvious example, nothing on the scale of the Japanese internment has yet been proposed during the current situation.[89]

This analysis might also be said to apply to the Irish scenario. The gradual improvement from the Public Safety Act (PSA), 1927 to the Offences against the State Act (OAS), 1939 will be examined in Chapter 3. The 'social learning' thesis is problematic, however, since it merely involves an observation of previous behaviour. Tushnet accepts that he does not 'have any structural account of why there might be systematic tendencies towards this sort of learning'.[90] So, while the social learning thesis provides an interesting observation worth bearing in mind when considering the history of the Special Criminal Court, it will not be a theme to which this work will return.

The second point of interest concerns the debate surrounding the consti-

85 Ibid., 187. **86** Ibid., 208. **87** Ibid., 193. **88** M. Tushnet, 'Replies: controlling executive power in the war on terrorism' (2005) 118 *Harvard Law Review*, 2673–2682 at 2673. **89** M. Tushnet, 'Defending Korematsu?: reflections in civil liberties in wartime' (2003) *Wisconsin Law Review*, 273–307 at 294–5. **90** Tushnet, correspondence with the author, 31 August 2005.

tutionalization of emergency powers. As we shall see, the Special Criminal Court is constitutionally anticipated.[91] Such a method is not entirely uncontroversial.

> Constitutional provisions dealing with emergency powers place regimes of exception within the constitutional order. Constitutional provisions dealing with emergency powers provide a language of justification for the invocation of emergency powers, even though the precise language used in the constitution may be inapt for the occasion on which emergency powers are invoked.[92]

Thus, incorporating emergency provisions into the Constitution may offer justification or at least the language of legitimacy to the illegitimate. Such concerns can be set aside for two reasons. Firstly, as will be seen in Chapter 2, Irish experience suggests that it is better to bring the executive under constitutional control than to leave it unrestrained. The PSA, 1927 and Article 2A effectively amended every Constitutional provision that they contravened. Thus, while legislating the government was free from constraints; the results were draconian. The OAS, 1939 was drafted within constitutional parameters and was a more considered and restrained piece of legislation.[93]

The second reason for setting aside concerns surrounding constitutionalization is that the alternatives are unclear. If one accepts that the state has an inherent right to protect itself from both internal and external threats, then emergency measures will inevitably be necessary. Tushnet advocates the use of 'emergency powers outside the Constitution'.[94] He argues that 'it is better to have emergency powers exercised in an extraconstitutional way, so that everyone understands that the actions are extraordinary, then to have the actions rationalized away as consistent with the Constitution and thereby normalized'.[95] To the constitutional lawyer there is a certain attractiveness to this argument since it allows the Constitution to remain unsullied, standing head and shoulders above the executive, while allowing the latter to get on with the business of defending the state from threat. Tushnet rejects suggestions that this leaves the executive free from control arguing that 'the exercise of executive power is to be controlled, not by courts, but by legislatures and the people acting in their constitutional capacities'.[96] The UK Human Rights Act (HRA) 1998 employs a mechanism which is similar to that anticipated by Tushnet; s.4 provides the courts with the power to make a declaration of

91 See in particular Chapter 3. 92 Tushnet, 'Defending Korematsu?', 304. 93 The drafting of the Offences against the State Act, 1939 will be considered in detail in Chapter 3. 94 Tushnet, 'Defending Korematsu?', 304. 95 Ibid., 305. 96 Tushnet, correspondence with the author, 31 August 2005.

incompatibility rather than granting them the power to declare legislation void. This is the result of peculiarly British sensitivities about the need to maintain parliamentary sovereignty. S.4(6)(a) states that such a declaration 'does not affect the validity, continuing operation or enforcement of the provision in respect of which it is given' and as such the impugned provision continues in force until the Houses of Parliament or a minister of the crown[97] choose to alter it. This reliance on parliament and public action to hold the executive to account appears optimistic.[98] The courts require a controlling role.

97 by means of s.10 of the UK Human Rights Act, 1998, a minister may amend legislation which has been declared incompatible. See Fergal Davis, 'Extra-Constitutionalism, the Human Rights Act and the "Labour rebels": applying Prof. Tushnet's theories in the UK' (2006) 4 *Web Journal of Current Legal Issues*, http://webjcli.ncl.ac.uk/ 2006/issue4/davis4.html, accessed 4 October 2006. 98 The inherent weakness of relying upon the Dáil to hold the executive in check arises from the fact that the executive, by definition, has a majority in the Dáil. Therefore, in order for the Dáil to control the executive members of the governing parties must vote against the government. While this is not unheard of, it is rare.

2

From military tribunals to the Special Criminal Court

2.1 The birth of the Irish Free State

The history of emergency legislation in Ireland is both interesting and lengthy; unfortunately, it is not possible to consider that history in any depth here. In a revealing passage Arthur Balfour declared that Cromwell's failure in Ireland was due to his reliance on coercion alone and he was determined not to repeat that mistake: 'I shall be as relentless as Cromwell in enforcing obedience to the law, but, at the same time, I shall be as radical as any reformer in redressing grievances.' In other words, 'contrary to popular belief the process of "killing home rule with kindness" began with Arthur, not Gerald Balfour'.[1] This combination of coercion and conciliation is illustrated by the events of 1881. In that year

> the Land League was proclaimed illegal, meetings were broken up by the batons of the police, *habeas corpus* was suspended and over one thousand men were imprisoned, including Parnell, John Dillon (his chief lieutenant) and Michael Davitt; at the same time a more or less conciliatory Land Act was passed.[2]

The use of repression was a response to the violence of the land wars;[3] for example, in 1882 the murders of Lord Frederick Charles Cavendish, the chief secretary, and Thomas Henry Burke, the under-secretary, in the Phoenix Park was the trigger for the introduction of the Crimes Act, 1882, which gave considerable powers to the police, provided for detention

1 L. Perry Curtis, *Coercion & conciliation in Ireland, 1880–1892* (1963), pp 178–9. 2 D. Macardle, *The Irish Republic* (1968), p. 48. 3 The land wars had been characterised by sectarian violence where Catholics boycotted farms and led violent assaults on landlords and Orange Emergency Committees attempted to provide 'emergency men', mostly from Ulster, to work on the boycotted properties. R.V. Comerford, 'The Land War & the politics of distress, 1877–1882' in W.E. Vaughan (ed.), *A new history of Ireland* vi (1996), p. 46. It is said that Edward Carson, the Ulster unionist leader, witnessed agrarian violence during the Land War and as a result he 'knew how vulnerable unionists were outside the north-east corner of the island, and for him, therefore the essence of the matter was that the connection with Britain must never be broken': F.S.L. Lyons, 'The developing crisis, 1907–1914' in Vaughan (ed.), *A new history of Ireland,* vi, p. 130. This concern about Protestant vulnerability ensured that as nationalist demands for Home Rule grew, unionist opposition strengthened. Finally, on 24 and 25 April 1914 Ulster Unionists landed weapons at three harbours in Ulster and on 26 July 1914 the Irish Volunteers responded by landing arms at Howth. Lyons, 'The developing crisis, 1907–1914', p. 141.

without trial and allowed for juries to be replaced by commissions of judges in certain cases.[4] Although some were critical of the repressive legislation used in Ireland,[5] it remained a fundamental part of British policy. In April 1889 the prime minister, Lord Salisbury, referred to a need for 'a long spell of firmly and impartially administered law',[6] and such governmental responses were common;[7] indeed, the Crimes Act, 1882 'was the fifty-seventh special Act for dealing with disaffection in Ireland passed since the [Act of Union, 1801]'.[8]

The effect of harsh government responses may have been counterproductive. For example, although the Easter Rising of 1916 did not appear to have initial popular support, a mere two years later Sinn Féin, the party most closely associated with it, was to attain seventy-three seats in the Westminster elections.[9] 'The executions, the heroic demeanour of the leaders, the fear of conscription and the dislike of "England's War" made a dangerous mixture',[10] which assisted Sinn Féin in dramatically overtaking the Irish Parliamentary Party.[11] The growth of Sinn Féin was to be of great significance. The Sinn Féin candidates elected in 1918 refused to take their seats in Westminster and declared a republic, describing themselves as Dáil Éireann. The two and a half years of violence that followed would become known as the War of Independence or Anglo-Irish War.[12] This conflict can be broken down into three phases: 1919 and the early months of 1920 saw isolated incidents which in time escalated in size and frequency occurred; this was followed, from March through December 1920, by a more intensive guerrilla-style campaign; the final period, January to July 1921, was one of truce and negotiation.[13] One of the responses of the British government to the unrest in Ireland during the third period was to impose martial law in Munster and parts of Leinster; this resulted in two systems of law operating within miles of each other; predictably, the army lacked control, because they were unable to prevent rebels moving in and out of the martial law areas.[14] The truce and the negotiations referred to above, led to the Treaty, which in turn provided for the creation of the Irish Free State. The pattern

4 Macardle, *Irish Republic*, p. 49. 5 Joseph Chamberlain described the system of governance in Ireland as, 'a system which is founded on the bayonets of thirty thousand soldiers encamped permanently as in a hostile country. It is a system as completely centralised and bureaucratic as that with which Russia governs Poland, or as that which prevailed in Venice under the Austrian rule'. See Macardle, *Irish Republic*, p. 49, citing Mr Chamberlain at Holloway, 1885. 6 *The Nation*, 27 April 1889; see A. Mitchell & P. Ó Snodaigh (eds), *Irish political documents: 1869–1916* (1989), p. 76. 7 For example see, the Irish habeas corpus suspension acts and coercion acts of 1797, 1803 and 1833, Leo Kohn, *The Constitution of the Irish Free State* (1932), p. 138. 8 Macardle, *Irish Republic*, p. 49. 9 F.S.L. Lyons, 'The new nationalism, 1916-1918' in Vaughan (ed.), *A new history of Ireland, vi: Ireland under the Union, ii: 1870-1921* (1996), p. 239. 10 Tom Garvin, *The evolution of Irish nationalism* (1981), p. 114. 11 The Irish Parliamentary Party collapsed from eighty-six seats to six, while Sinn Féin had grown from seven to seventy-three seats. Lyons, 'The new nationalism, 1916–1918', p. 239. 12 T.E. Hachey, *Britain & Irish separatism* (1977), p. 259. 13 Ibid., chapter 10. 14 J.M. Curran, *The birth of the Irish Free State, 1921–1923* (1981), p. 28.

of guerrilla conflict followed by coercive legislation was to be maintained by the new Irish government.

2.2 Anarchy and civil war

In 1922 Ireland was on the verge of anarchy. Nation-building is always a difficult business, but in 1922

> there was no state and organized forces. The provisional government was simply eight young men in the City Hall standing amidst the ruins of one administration, with the foundations of another not yet laid, and with wild men screaming through the keyhole.[15]

At this stage the Free State had four main objectives: the reconstruction of the machinery of government; the assertion of the status of the nation in the Commonwealth; the regeneration of the nation's economy; and, 'the restoration ... of a respect for law and order, the demonstration, *ruthless if need be,* that here at last was a government prepared to govern'.[16] The fulfilment of these none too modest aims was severely hampered by the prevailing conditions. As Cosgrave noted, at the time of the creation of the state there existed a brief window of opportunity: 'last December Ireland was in a position of power and influence of great promise for the country. Foreign nations expressed their appreciation of the settlement, and for a short period there was a boom in business. The actions of the opposition destroyed that boom.'[17] The outbreak of civil war made the attainment of these goals even more distant.

The restoration of law and order was problematic due to the national experience prior to the creation of the Free State. One effect of British rule in Ireland, including the coercive legislation referred to earlier, was that the Irish had become indifferent, if not hostile, to government; this meant that it would take time to develop a sense of civic responsibility.[18] During the War of Independence Sinn Féin had promoted a policy of hostility toward the Royal Irish Constabulary (RIC) arguing that it was a military organization which brutally enforced British rule. Eamon de Valera had urged the people to ostracize members of the force in order that they 'be shown and made feel how base are the functions they perform and how vile is the position they occupy'.[19] Such animosity toward the RIC prior to independence meant that it was difficult for the fledgling state to secure public support for the new police force. The divisions caused by the Anglo-

15 Tom Garvin, *1922: The birth of Irish democracy* (1996), p. 94, citing Kevin O'Higgins. 16 F.S.L. Lyons, *Ireland since the Famine* (1973), p. 480. 17 W.T. Cosgrave, Dáil Éireann, 11 September 1922; see Michael McLoughlin (ed.), *Great Irish speeches of the twentieth century* (1996), p. 121. 18 C. Townshend, *Political violence in Ireland: government & resistance since 1948* (1983), p. 365. 19 Hachey, *Britain & Irish separatism*, p. 259.

Irish Treaty of 1921 and the creation of the Free State made that even more difficult.

The Treaty brought about an end to the conflict with Britain, but it was not universally welcomed. In many respects none of Ireland's dreams had been fulfilled,

> not the Gaelic League's Irish speaking nation, nor Yeats's literary-conscious people, nor the republic of the IRA, nor the worker's republic of Connolly, nor Griffith's economically self-sufficient dual monarchy, nor Redmond's home rule within an empire which the Irish had helped to build, nor Carson's United Kingdom.[20]

Opposition to the Treaty split the Dáil[21] and led to outbreak of Civil War in July 1922.

2.3 The Constitutional framework of the Irish Free State

To assess the government's later actions we need to consider the relevant constitutional provisions. 'Unlike democracies, which are subject to civil libertarian, humanitarian, and constitutional limitations, tyrannical regimes can employ the most brutal counter-measures against terrorists.'[22] The Irish Free State was struggling to establish a democracy, and its Constitution could, at the very least, be described as 'liberal'. Of course, 'no state, however liberal, has abandoned its residual power of suspending the rule of law in time of emergency',[23] but the Free State was severely restricted. Despite Ireland's recent turbulent history, its Constitution did not provide for any special courts; in fact, Article 70 expressly provided that 'extraordinary courts shall not be established'. This provision seems to have been a response to previous over-use of extraordinary powers, much resented by the population; however, given the level of opposition to the new state Article 70 was somewhat optimistic if not legislatively naïve. In compensation, the Article did allow for the extension of the jurisdiction of military courts over the civilian population during times of war or armed rebellion, but it excluded such jurisdiction from any area 'in which all civil courts are open or capable of being held'.[24] This formula had previously been employed by the courts of the United States. In *Ex parte Milligan* Davis J stated that 'martial rule can never exist where the courts are open, and in proper and unobstructed exercise of their jurisdiction';[25] Chase CJ,

20 D. McCartney, 'From Parnell to Pearse (1891–1921)' in T.W. Moody & F.X. Martin (eds), *The course of Irish history* (1967), p. 312. 21 64 to 57 in favour. 22 A. Dershowitz, *Why terrorism works: understanding the threat, responding to the challenge* (New Haven, 2002), p. 106. 23 Kohn, *The Constitution of the Irish Free* State, p. 128. 24 Hogan & Whyte, *Kelly* (2003), para. 6.5.317. 25 71 US (4 Wall) 2, 127; see Ten Broek et al., *Prejudice war & the constitution* (1975), p. 230.

in the same case, stated that military government was only acceptable 'in time of insurrection or invasion ... within districts or localities where ordinary law no longer adequately secures public safety and private rights'.[26] Unfortunately, *Milligan* was not applied by the US Supreme Court during World War II. In *Hirabayashi*,[27] Chief Justice Stone articulated a 'rule of reason' test. This test was far more accommodating and defined the military power as 'including any steps needed to wage war successfully'.[28] The restrictive Article 70 of the Constitution of the Irish Free State was to face a fate similar to that of the doctrine in *Milligan.* Indeed, the ineffectiveness of Article 70 in tackling the threat now faced by the Free State was to have a detrimental impact upon the development of its Constitution.

2.4 The Civil War

The circumstances that resulted in civil war and the response of the government of the Irish Free State to it were outlined succinctly by Kevin O'Higgins in a speech to the Irish Society at Oxford University in 1924. He was of the opinion that when one considers that a

> guerrilla territorial force, which had been the Irish Volunteers, was divided on the issue of the Treaty and ... throughout the country, supplementing the frenzied eloquence of Mr De Valera, the fair were inciting the brave to sanguinary wadings in defence of what was called 'the existing Republic' ... the problem which confronted the provisional government emerges ... This new tyranny had to be met and smashed. The right of the people to found a state on the basis of the Treaty which had been signed by their plenipotentiaries and endorsed by their parliament had to be vindicated beyond question.[29]

These challenges were certainly faced down by the Free State, and Kevin O'Higgins would play a central role in that process.

The opening act of the Civil War was the occupation of the Four Courts by anti-Treaty forces. This was a serious affront to the provisional government – a symbolic act designed to mirror the example of 1916.[30] The

26 71 US (4 Wall) 2, 142; see Ten Broek et al., *Prejudice war*, p. 230. 27 *Hirabayashi v. United States*, (1943) 320 U.S. 81. 28 E.V. Rostow, 'The Japanese American cases: a disaster', (1945) 54 *Yale Law Journal*, 489–533 at 524. 29 T. de Vere White, *Kevin O'Higgins: strong man in the Free State government, 1922–27* (1966), pp 100–1. 30 Townshend, *Political violence in Ireland*, p. 137. It should be noted that one theory of the civil war suggests that it had in fact begun long before the seizure of the Four Courts. Fitzpatrick's research in IRA engagements in Co. Clare between 1919 and 1921 led him to conclude that GHQ had little or no control and that these actions were, in effect, land seizures. While Sinn Féin led a middle class struggle for national liberation, those in the poorer rural districts were engaged in a land struggle. These groups were enaged in a

leaders of the occupation would have stood a better chance had they 'preserved their freedom of manoeuvre instead of cooping themselves up in the city centre',[31] yet, it is irrefutable that the occupation of the Four Courts was highly disruptive to the running of the country and the administration of justice.[32] The response of the government was to grant extra-judicial powers to the military and this led to a position of great constitutional delicacy. By threatening the insecure basis of the state the anti-Treatyites arguably ensured the anglicization of Irish politics: Collins was forced to borrow British artillery, and O'Higgins resorted to English legal doctrine to assert civil control.[33] Furthermore, the fledgling state became indebted, financially, to Great Britain; as 'the Lord of the Treasury stated in the House of Commons on 20 February [1923], the Free State had made payments on account during the financial year amounting to approximately £1,000,000 for guns, arms, ammunition, aeroplanes, motor vehicles and other munitions of war handed over by the British government'.[34]

Because the provisional government was unsure if its provisional status entitled it to those prerogative powers that had enabled its predecessor to act, it adopted a two-pronged approach, relying on the general power of executive authority to take exceptional measures to restore public order, and seeking the sanction of the provisional parliament.[35] The Special Powers resolution of September 1922 granted the army more discretionary powers than the British proclamation of martial law had done. Furthermore, it is undeniable that these powers were abused by the army. The events of 7 March 1923 in Kerry provide some evidence of this abuse: on that day, nine prisoners were taken from Tralee prison to Ballyseedy Cross by soldiers of the Free State; the prisoners were tied in a ring with an explosive mine in the centre; the mine was then detonated, killing them all. On the same day five prisoners were taken from Killarney prison to Countess Bridge in similar circumstances; again a mine was detonated by soldiers, killing four of the five; only Tadhg Coffey survived. These gruesome reprisals were in response to the IRA killings of three officers in Knocknagashel, Co. Kerry, who had been killed by an exploding mine.[36] However, O'Higgins' defence of the Free State actions 'under the maxim *salus populi suprema lex* –

struggle against the 'Apparatus of the English State' which would survive independence rather than against English domination. As a result it is suggested that the Civil War in the West had begun before the truce, let alone the Treaty. For a more detailed analysis of this point, see Townshend, *Political violence in Ireland*, pp 370–1. 31 J. J. Lee, *Ireland, 1912–1985: politics & society* (1989), p. 63. 32 For example, it resulted in the Chief Justice having to hear some cases in his own private residence. Gerard Hogan, 'Hugh Kennedy, the Childers habeas corpus application and the return to the Four Courts' in C. Costello (ed.), *The Four Courts: 200 years* (1996), pp 179–83. 33 Townshend, *Political violence in Ireland*, p. 373. 34 Macardle, *Irish Republic*, p. 763. 35 Kohn, *The Constitution of the Irish Free State*, p. 143. 36 Macardle, *Irish Republic*, p. 765.

'Ultimately all government is based on force, must meet force with greater force if it is to survive' – met with a public acceptance which no British government had obtained'.[37] Public acceptance was one thing; however, the legal uncertainty referred to above guaranteed that these provisions would be challenged in the courts.

2.5 A riddle in the sands

Erskine Childers, the English-born son of an Irish mother, spent much of his youth in Ireland and had gradually developed an interest in Irish politics. He owned and navigated the yacht which had landed weapons for the Irish Volunteers at Howth. A member of the first Dáil and a signatory of the Treaty, he has been compared to Byron and Lafayette in that his adoption of the Irish cause was at times a sort of romantic adventure; and it is fair to say that he was not universally trusted.[38] Importantly, although a signatory of the Treaty, Childers was an anti-Treatyite. He was arrested in Wicklow for carrying a loaded revolver and was sentenced to death by military tribunal.[39] Perhaps 'it did not occur to him that his capture in possession of a lethal weapon would rank as a capital charge, and that the military court would be bound to find him guilty, whether he chose to recognize its legality or not'.[40] The validity of this claim is difficult to assess; after all, the first executions under the special powers had been carried out on 17 November 1922. In that case four youths had been captured in Dublin carrying loaded revolvers, and although they had shown 'no disposition to use' the guns, they had been executed by firing squad.[41] The case of Childers appears similar, and whether it was expected or not he was sentenced by military tribunal to death.

Childers challenged the jurisdiction of the military tribunal before the Master of the Rolls. Article 70 of the Constitution of the Free State, as we have seen, allowed for the extension of military law to the civilian population during times of war or armed rebellion when the ordinary courts could not function; and the measures under which Childers was tried were introduced by the provisional government and parliament. The Master of the Rolls accepting that a state of war existed which made the functioning of the ordinary courts impossible, upheld the jurisdiction of the military tribunal. He said:

> An affidavit was filed on behalf of the provisional government showing the appalling condition to which the country has been

37 Townshend, *Political violence in Ireland*, p. 373. 38 de Vere White, *Kevin O'Higgins*, pp 60–1. 39 Ibid., pp 127–8. 40 A. Boyle, *The riddle of Erskine Childers* (1977), p. 299. 41 de Vere White, *Kevin O'Higgins*, p. 127.

> brought – so appalling as to present a picture which might well describe the seat of great war between France and Germany. But if there was no affidavit at all, I would be bound to take judicial notice of the fact that for months this country has been enduring a state of war.[42]

This judgment had a number of consequences. It resulted in the execution of Childers[43] and in the judicial acceptance that the nation was at war, although the comparison with the Great War may have been far-fetched. Finally, it confirmed the judicial acceptance of the extension of military law to civilian populations and the role of military tribunals in Irish law.

The establishment of the military tribunal in 1922 set an important precedent. Just at the time when the Free State Constitution which severely restricted the use of special trial procedures was being introduced, the provisional government was utilizing the old tool of military tribunal. This contradiction must be viewed in light of the level of civil unrest. The tactics of the anti-Treatyites were designed to prevent the legislature and judiciary from functioning through intimidation and assassination. They sought to drive the landowning classes from the country by arson and plunder, and they attempted to destroy the nation's economy. In short, they wished to make the country ungovernable.[44] An illustration of these attempts occurred on 7 December 1922, when the IRA assassinated Seán Hales, a pro-Treaty TD, and wounded Pádraic Ó'Máille, the Deputy Speaker of the Dáil.[45] In such a climate it is not surprising that draconian measures were introduced and utilized:

> The cabinet was called, and General Mulcahy, as Minister for Defence and the Army representative in the government, asked that four republicans who were in custody should be taken out and shot without trial as a deterrent to further assassinations of Deputies. When he had given his reasons, the majority of the executive council agreed.[46]

42 *R. (Childers) v. the Officer Commanding the Troops, Portobello Barracks, in the County of Dublin, and the Adjutant General of the Forces of the Irish Provisional Government* [1923] 1 IR 5, 13 43 Childers was in fact executed while an appeal had been lodged against the decision of the master of the rolls. Hogan, 'Hugh Kennedy, the Childers habeas corpus application and the return to the Four Courts', p. 194. 44 D. O'Sullivan, *The Irish Free State & its Senate* (New York, 1972), p. 99. 45 de Vere White, *Kevin O'Higgins*, p. 131. 46 'O'Higgins, upon whom the responsibility of this horrific deterrent is laid, was in fact the last but one to consent to it. He did so only after he heard Eoin MacNeill giving his agreement in the gravity of the crisis. The last to agree – and it took an amount of persuading – was Joseph McGrath'. This account is based on the diary of Patrick Hogan and the confirmation of Ernest Blythe. See de Vere White, *Kevin O'Higgins*, p. 131.

The executions attracted some condemnation. Tom Johnson, the leader of the Labour Party and as such the *de facto* leader of the opposition, described the executions as murder, noting that the four had been in jail for months and had nothing to do with Hales' assassination (a stark illustration of the tragedy of civil war is that one of those executed, Rory O'Connor, had been O'Higgins' best man a year earlier).[47]

> Opinions differ on whether the executions shortened the war, and thus saved innocent lives, or prolonged it by reinforcing the resolve of the anti-Treaty forces. There were no more assassinations of Dáil Deputies. But relatives of leading Treaty supporters, including an uncle of Cosgrave and the father of Kevin O'Higgins, Minister for Home Affairs, were murdered.[48]

In the words of Winston Churchill, the members of the government, 'although deeply troubled in their souls, were courageous and hot-blooded, and driven as they had been into a corner with their lives at stake – and much more than their lives, the cause they had conducted so far – they hit back with primordial freedom'.[49]

It has generally been accepted that 'in times of national danger, or in the interests of general public safety, necessary measure of precaution may be taken by the legislature to restrict ... fundamental rights'.[50] To that end, the establishment of military tribunals was justified. The powers of a non-reviewable tribunal to sentence an accused to death may have been less acceptable, however. Certainly, the execution of Childers while an appeal had been lodged against the decision of the Master of the Rolls,[51] and execution without trial of four leading republicans in what was officially described as an act of reprisal,[52] would appear intolerable. However, 'republican atrocities ... had the effect of making people ... indifferent to Free State ruthlessness and the electorate seem to have consented quietly to the executions'.[53] This complicity seems to have continued after the Civil War, possibly because the public recognized that the 'menace of the renewal of civil war persisted so long as the republican deputies refused to take their seats in the Dáil'.[54] Draconian responses to civil unrest became the norm.

47 Curran, *The birth of the Irish Free State*, pp 265–6. 48 Lee, *Ireland, 1912–1985*, p. 67. 49 Ibid. 50 *per* Hanna J, *The A.G. v. McBride* [1928] IR 451, 454. 51 Hogan, 'Hugh Kennedy, the Childers habeas corpus application and the return to the Four Courts', p. 194. 52 C. Campbell, *Emergency law in Ireland, 1918–1925* (1994), pp 166–7. 53 Garvin, *1922: the birth of Irish democracy*, p. 103. 54 D. R. Gwynn, *The Irish Free State 1922–1927* (1928), p. 153.

2.6 Assassination and the Public Safety Act, 1927

The Civil War can be said to have ended with a whimper. The IRA never formally surrendered and no arms decommissioning occurred.[55] Individual instances of violence were frequent. Between 1923 and 1924, for example, there were 738 cases of arson in Ireland.[56] The government's response was predictable. In November 1926, following a series of raids upon Civic Guard barracks, it sought extra powers and a Public Safety (Emergency Powers) Bill was introduced. Interestingly, Cosgrave stated that the Act was to be permanent in nature and would be activated only during times of emergency;[57] this model of a standing piece of legislation capable of activation when necessary was to be employed again in the future. One of the most striking examples of violence during the post-Civil War period was the assassination of Kevin O'Higgins, one of the most significant, if at times under-rated, figures in the history of the Free State. Vice-President, Minister for Justice and Minister for External Affairs in the Cosgrave administration,[58] he had led the Irish delegation to the Imperial Conference of 1926 and helped pave the way for what would later become the Statute of Westminster.[59] He had taken a hard line during the Civil War and had, on one occasion, argued for executions in every county, since those in Dublin had only limited local impact.[60] After the Civil War, he did not relax, and took steps to obtain powers under the Public Safety Act, 1923.[61] He was assassinated on his way to church on 10 July 1927.

The government responded swiftly with the Public Safety Act, 1927.[62] This draconian legislation decreed severe penalties for the membership of unlawful organizations, granted drastic search powers, and provided for a special court that could impose death or life imprisonment for the unlawful possession of fire arms.[63] The Department of An Taoiseach files relating to the 1927 Act show that the drafters were determined to impose severe penalties. For example, an early document has a suggestion of a maximum sentence of five years' penal servitude for membership of an unlawful organization; the figure five is crossed out and the figure ten is substituted.[64] This initial draft also refers to a possible power of exile; it suggests that the Minister for Justice should have the power to order any person to depart from, and remain outside, the Free State.[65] (This power appears to have caused much concern in the United Kingdom since it was presumed that expelled individuals were bound to go there.)[66]

55 Garvin, *1922: the birth of Irish democracy*, p. 121. 56 Lee, *Ireland, 1912–1985*, p. 172. 57 Gwynn, *The Irish Free State, 1922–1927*, p. 154. 58 J.A. Murphy, *Ireland in the twentieth century* (1989), p. 70. 59 de Vere White, *Kevin O'Higgins*, p. 219. 60 Lee, *Ireland, 1912–1985*, p. 98. 61 Lyons, *Ireland since the Famine*, p. 481. 62 hereinafter PSA, 1927. 63 Ibid. 64 Department of An Taoiseach file S5486, 'Suggestions for a bill towards more effectual suppression of treasonable and seditious activities', para. 3. 65 Ibid., para. 7. 66 Department

During the Civil War, the executive employed a military tribunal in an attempt to effectively tackle the threat posed by Irregular, or Anti-Treaty, forces. Most interestingly, early drafts of the Public Safety Act, 1927 proposed a special court to be set up consisting of three judges of the High Court sitting without a jury.[67] A later, more advanced, version of the bill includes a proposed Part IV which provides for the 'Establishment of Special Criminal Courts'. Section 22 of this draft is quoted in full since it is considered to be extremely instructive:

> 22(1) As soon as may be after every occasion on which this Part of this Act comes into force there shall be established by the executive council one or more tribunals (in this Part of the Act referred to as special courts) consisting of at the option of the executive council either –
>
> (a) of three members of whom one shall be an ordinary judge of the Supreme Court and two shall be judges of the High Court, or
> (b) of three members of whom one (who may or may not be an officer in the Defence Forces of Saorstát Éireann) shall be a person certified by the Attorney-General to have legal knowledge and experience and the others shall be officers of the Defence Forces not below the rank of commandant.[68]

Firstly, the text provides for the establishment of special courts and uses the term 'Special Criminal Court'. Secondly, it gives the attorney-general, and thereby the executive, a central role in selecting the members of the court – a matter which may cause some concern vis-à-vis the separation of powers and the independence of the court. Finally, it retains the suggestion that ordinary members of the judiciary sit as members of these courts. However, a later draft proposes the possibility of members of the Defence Forces sitting in judgment. This shifts the court in the direction of military tribunal rather than special court. Perhaps more significantly, the word 'delete' is handwritten in the margin next to s.22(1)(a). This is the last reference to members of the judiciary sitting on the special courts and subsequent versions simply replace s.22(1)(a) with a more compact s.22(1).[69] Cosgrave later admitted that at least two judges of the Supreme

of An Taoiseach file S5486, 'Letter of 2 November, 1927, signed LOVAT (for the Secretary of State)'. The letter makes it clear that while the British government was concerned by any such developments it did not want to interfere. **67** Department of An Taoiseach file S5486, 'Suggestions for a bill towards more effectual suppression of treasonable and seditious activities', para. 1. **68** Department of An Taoiseach file S5486, Public Safety Bill, 1927. Part IV. **69** The later draft reads; '22 – (1) As soon as may be after every occasion on which this Part of this Act

Court had informed him that they would relinquish their office if called upon to act as a special court under the PSA, 1927.[70] Their reluctance must have influenced the drafters.

The draconian nature of the Act is reinforced by a series of other provisions. S.3 provided that, while the Act was in force, any provisions of the Act which were repugnant to the Constitution would operate as amendments of the Constitution.[71] This is an extraordinary measure: it meant that an ordinary piece of legislation could amend the Constitution despite the fact that the Act's long title made no reference to its being for that purpose. Furthermore, rather than amending a specific provision of the Constitution, s.3 operated as a 'catch-all' provision: it would now be virtually impossible to know which constitutional provisions had been amended and since the amendment lasted only for as long as the Act was in force, the Constitution would be a permanent state of flux. The Act provided for the detention of children under the age of 16 'under such conditions as the Minister for Justice may direct'; any such child was held at the pleasure of the Minister, and its parent or guardian was also liable to a sentence of six months' imprisonment.[72] Most seriously, the Act granted extensive powers to the Special Courts but stated that,

> No appeal shall lie from any conviction, sentence, order or judgment of a special court and no special court shall be liable to be restrained in the execution of its powers under this Part of this Act by any other Court.[73]

Draconian the legislation may have been, but the government was convinced of its necessity. The bill was sent to the governor general for his signature despite the fact that the usual seven-day period between the passing of a bill and its signing into law had not passed.[74]

The PSA, 1927 was repealed in 1928, and the special courts were never actually established;[75] however, it did provide the model for the later Article

comes into force there shall be established by the executive council one or more tribunals (in the Part of this Act referred to as special courts) consisting of three or more members of whom one (who may or not be an officer in the Defence Forces of Saorstát Éireann) shall be a person certified by the Attorney-General to have legal knowledge and experience and the others shall be officers of the Defence Forces of Saorstát Éireann not below the rank of commandant'. **70** O'Sullivan, *The Irish Free State & its Senate*, p. 261. **71** Kohn, *The Constitution of the Irish Free State*, p. 153. **72** s. 8(1) The Public Safety Act, 1927. **73** s. 25(5) The Public Safety Act, 1927. **74** Department of An Taoiseach file S5486, Letter dated 10 August 1927, to TM Healy Esq., KC, Governor General of the Irish Free State, signed M, Secretary to the executive council. **75** In fact it appears that the PSA, 1927 was not widely utilized. Seán McBride was certainly detained under suspicion of having been involved in the murder of O'Higgins, but it was established that he was out of the country on the day in question and he was eventually released. In February 1928, two

2A of the Constitution and many elements of the early drafts of the PSA, 1927 can be seen in the Offences against the State Act, 1939. A second legislative response to the death of O'Higgins was contained in an Electoral Amendment Bill, designed to combat the abstentionist policies of Fianna Fáil and Sinn Féin. Candidates for nomination were required to swear an affidavit to the effect that, if elected, they would take the Oath.[76] The bulk of republican, anti-Treaty deputies decided to stand in elections and take their seats in the Dáil. On 10 August 1927, Fianna Fáil declared that the oath was an 'empty political formula' and intimated that they would take it.[77] 'The forty-three members of the Fianna Fáil Party took their seats in the Dáil on the 12th August 1927.'[78]

2.7 Article 2A – the background

The period between 1928 and 1931 appears, at first glance, to have seen a step in the direction of constitutionalism. The PSA, 1927 had been repealed and its most worrisome sections never implemented. However, Fianna Fáil were not exactly committed to the constitutional process. They were a 'slightly constitutional party' whose stated objective was to establish a Republic. Seán Lemass made it clear that they would attempt to achieve that objective by constitutional means, but this was seen as a pragmatic and not a principled decision.[79] Furthermore, the facts show that even after Fianna Fáil chose the 'slightly constitutional' route, outrages continued.

Following the repeal of the PSA, 1927, 'crimes and violence and intimidation – particularly of juries – began to increase'.[80] Illegal drilling took place and a number of murders were committed. A table of murders said to arise 'directly or indirectly from political motives, labour disputes or rent agitation' from 1927 to 1931 is provided at page 195 below; it includes a reference to the outcome of each case and it will be noted that only one

'middle-aged ladies' were arrested for distributing leaflets inciting the murder of the governor general. The accused refused to recognize the Court and as such incurred 'such drastic penalties that the jury refused to convict'. It was the view of one contemporary commentator that the draconian nature of the Act prevented the successful prosecution. See Gwynn, *The Irish Free State, 1922–1927*, p. 163. **76** O'Sullivan, *The Irish Free State & its Senate*, p. 215. **77** Ibid., pp 216–17. **78** Ibid., 219. **79** Lemass's remarks are open to misinterpretation. He did not imply that Fianna Fáil was ready to re-embrace violent means but he was rather circumspect in his comments stating, 'we have adopted the method of political agitation to achieve our end, because we believe, in the present circumstances, that method is best in the interests of the nation and of the republican movement, and for no other reason'. This should probably be seen as a political statement designed to keep republican sympathies 'on-side', however it can hardly be described as a ringing endorsement of constitutional politics and it is undeniably ambiguous on the issue of a future return to violence. Clearly, the statement expresses the Fianna Fáil view that the Irish Free State was illegitimate. See, Dáil Éireann, *Parliamentary Debates*, 21 March 1928, vol. 22, col. 1615, also see McLoughlin (ed.), *Great Irish speeches*, pp 144–45. **80** Lyons, *Ireland since the Famine*, p. 497.

conviction is recorded; and the comment column shows that these murders were largely associated with disrupting the organs of the state. Individuals were targeted because they gave evidence in court, because they were suspected police agents or because they were active against the IRA. Richard More O'Farrell attempted to prevent a mob from tarring and feathering his father, a land agent, and was shot; Vice-Admiral Henry Boyle Sommerville helped boys to join the British Navy, and was shot; and the unfortunate Mrs Frances McGoy died one week after the IRA blew up her house in revenge for her son's giving information to the police.[81] Upon introducing the legislation which was to provide for Article 2A President Cosgrave stated:

> Political pressure in the Dáil,[82] combined with the fact that there had been an absence of serious political crime for a considerable period, induced the government in December, 1928, to consent to repeal special legislation ... and within two months of the repeal one witness (Armstrong) was murdered and a juror (White) was gravely wounded in Dublin ... This signalled the breakdown of the jury system.[83]

By 1931 the ordinary courts were no longer capable of dealing with the situation.[84] Eventually, an interview by Frank Ryan of the IRA caused the government to act. Ryan justified three killings and claimed the IRA was capable of more. Gerald Boland later said that it was this interview that caused the Department of Justice to advise Cosgrave to introduce military tribunals.[85]

A secondary reason for the introduction of Article 2A was a concern that communist elements[86] were operating within the state. Members of Saor Éire, a new organization with which the IRA's name was linked, were said to have been trained in the communist gospel in Soviet Russia and were now attempting to pervert Irish youth. A joint pastoral letter was released by Catholic bishops referring to the dangers of communism[87] and Cosgrave stated:

81 Department of An Taoiseach, file S 9249, see Appendix 1. 82 It is presumed that this refers to the new-found opposition in the form of Fianna Fáil. 83 President W.T. Cosgrave, 'Constitution (Amendment No. 17) Act, 1931. Summary of opening statement made by the President in Dáil Éireann, on 14th October, 1931'. Department of An Taoiseach file S2267. 84 T.P. Coogan, *De Valera: long fellow, long shadow*, (London, 1993), p. 409. A detailed, though not exhaustive, account of the level of unrest in the nation in 1931 is given by O'Sullivan, *The Irish Free State & its Senate*, pp 258–60. The statement of President Cosgrave, above note 183, is also instructive. 85 Coogan, *De Valera*, p. 409. 86 The fear of the spread of Communism must be seen in light of the events in Russia thirteen years earlier, the events unfolding in Spain at the time, coupled with the conservative nature of both Irish society and the Cosgrave government. 87 Department of An Taoiseach file S2267, 'Joint Pastoral issued by His Eminence, Cardinal

> The situation which the present Act was intended to meet was definitely much more serious than that which we had to face after the murder of Mr Kevin O'Higgins. Murder had become one of the normal and expected elements of the present situation, and the new teachings of communism which are accepted to a greater or lesser extent by these organizations had greatly increased the danger of the permanent perversion of the youth of the country.[88]

Given the importance of O'Higgins to the Irish Free State, this reference is clear hyperbole; however, it does give a sense of the gravity of the situation. These statements were not mere propaganda for public consumption; the situation was serious enough for Minister for Justice Fitzgerald-Kenny to tell the chief justice that 'the forces making for anarchy are stronger than men dream of'.[89] As a result of these dangers to the state, the government responded by introducing fresh emergency legislation. That legislation, the Constitution (Amendment No. 17) Act, 1931 would be known as Article 2A.

2.8 Article 2A – the provisions

Like the PSA, 1927, the Constitution (Amendment No. 17) Act, 1931 was an amendment to the Constitution. One of the unusual features of the earlier act was that its long title did not acknowledge the Act's role as an amendment upon the Constitution; furthermore, the Act was capable of amending any section of the Constitution. In contrast, the Constitution (Amendment No. 17) Act, 1931 was an identifiable amendment, namely, the new Article 2A. Note: the original provision allowing for Constitutional amendment by means of ordinary legislation was due to expire in December 1930.

> On March 13, 1929 the Dáil debated the second stage of the Consitution (Amendment No. 16) Bill, 1928. The object of this bill was to extend the eight year transitional period for a further eight years from December 1930 until December 1938. While the debate in the Dáil was perfunctory, the bill subsequently passed all stages in the Seanad without debate.[90]

During this period amending the Constitution by way of ordinary legislation was not unusual and twenty-five acts were passed between 1923 and

MacRory, and the Archbishops and Bishops of Ireland', (October 1931). **88** Department of An Taoiseach file S 2267 statement of President Cosgrave, above note 183. **89** Hogan, 'Hugh Kennedy, the Childers habeas corpus application and the return to the Four Courts', p. 214. **90** G. Hogan, 'A desert island case set in the silver sea: *The State (Ryan) v. Lennon* (1934)' in E. O'Dell (ed.) *Leading cases of the twentieth century* (Dublin, 2000), pp 80–103, p. 83.

1936 for that purpose. 'Virtually every page was cluttered with deletions, additions and amendments: forty-one of its eighty-three articles had been amended.'[91] Remarkably, Article 2A was a very detailed amendment containing thirty-four sections and an appendix. It was in reality an elaborate anti-terrorism law.[92]

Like its predecessor, Article 2A provided that all subsequent Articles of the Constitution were to be construed in light of Article 2A and, where any inconsistency arose, 2A would prevail.[93] The Article provided for the creation of a five-member military tribunal, which would have considerable powers[94] – such as the power to impose any penalty, including death, greater than that provided for by law, if the tribunal felt that such penalty was necessary or expedient.[95] These powers were especially severe given that the only appeal against a decision of the tribunal was to the executive and not the courts.[96] This attempt to limit the right of appeal to the courts was unsuccessful; but it remains significant that the legislature sought to interfere with the role of the judiciary in this way.[97] Article 2A also granted extensive powers of arrest[98] and allowed the executive to order the banning of public meetings,[99] and the military tribunal could order the closing of any building for six months upon an application from the Garda Siochána.[1] An appendix to the Act covered crimes of a violent and subversive nature which could be tried by the military tribunal, but, members of the executive council were also empowered to order the transfer of any trial to the military tribunal where to the best of the minister's knowledge the offence was committed 'with the object of impairing or impeding the machinery of government or the administration of justice'.[2] The legislation, therefore, granted considerable powers both to the executive and the tribunal. In spite of any concerns on 20 October 1931 the governor general duly appointed five members of the Defence Forces to the tribunal (a notice of their appointment appeared in *Iris Oifiguil* on Friday 23 October). In an interesting aside, a handwritten note asks whether 'the members of the Tribunal should be sworn before anybody and if so in what form?' The response is unequivocal; 'the Attorney General says "definitely *no*"'.[3] It seems that,

91 B. Farrell, 'From First Dáil through Irish Free State' in B. Farrell (ed.), *De Valera's Constitution & ours* (1988), p. 30. 92 G. Hogan, 'The constitutional review group of 1934' in F. Ó Muircheartaigh (ed.) *Ireland in the coming times: essays to celebrate T.K. Whitaker's 80 years* (Dublin, 1997) pp 342–69, p. 345. 93 s. 2 Constitution (Amendment No. 17) Act, 1931. 94 s. 4(2) Constitution (Amendment No. 17) Act, 1931. 95 s. 7(1) Constitution (Amendment No. 17) Act, 1931. 96 s. 12(1) Constitution (Amendment No. 17) Act, 1931. 97 See *The State (O'Duffy) v. Bennett* [1935] IR 70; *The State (Hughes) v. Lennon* [1935] IR 128. 98 s. 13 Constitution (Amendment No. 17) Act, 1931. 99 s. 24(1) Constitution (Amendment No. 17) Act, 1931. 1 s. 27 Constitution (Amendment No. 17) Act, 1931. 2 Appendix, Constitution (Amendment No. 17) Act, 1931. Hogan & Whyte, *Kelly*, para. 6.5.321. 3 Signed 21.10.31 (that is 21 October 1931); Department of An Taoiseach file S2433.

although the executive felt that this extraordinary tribunal was necessary, they did not want to attract undue attention to it and therefore sought to avoid all pomp and ceremony.

2.9 Article 2A – the legal challenges

Given the nature of this constitutional amendment it is not surprising that it caused quite an amount of controversy. A serious challenge to the validity of the legislation came in the form of *The State (Ryan & Others) v. Lennon & Others.*[4] The constitutionality of the Act was upheld; however in a dissenting judgment Kennedy CJ attacked the provision quite forcefully, noting that the defenders of the Act had 'opened their argument by an apology and an appeal saying that they were in the unenviable and very difficult position of having to stand over an Act which was repellent to the instincts of every lawyer'.[5] Having started in this manner, he continued in a similar vein. The provisions of Article 2A were, he said, 'the antithesis of the rule of law, and are, within their scope, *the rule of anarchy*'.[6] In an often-quoted passage he concluded that:

> I find it impossible to reconcile as compatible with the Natural Law the vesting in three military servants of the executive, power to impose as punishment for any offence within the indefinite, but certainly extensive, ambit of the Appendix, the penalty of death, whenever these three persons are of the opinion that it is expedient.[7]

This passage identifies some of the most objectionable elements of the legislation. Firstly, the tribunal was extremely political in nature: it tried political offences, it was staffed by the Defence Forces (who are servants of the executive), and the only appeal against its decisions was to the executive. Secondly, it could impose the most severe penalty, namely death, in a wide variety of cases and solely because three officers of the Defence Forces believed it to be expedient. For an amendment to the Constitution to attract such a damning verdict from the most senior judge in the nation is, surely, close to being without precedent.

The judgment of Kennedy CJ has attracted much praise and has been cited internationally,[8] but it was a dissenting judgment. Ultimately, Article 2A was upheld by the Supreme Court and remained part of the Constitution of the Irish Free State for the next six years. Chief Justice Kennedy's dissent has been described as a magnificent but personal judicial response to the draconian nature of this Constitutional Amendment.[9] The

4 [1935] IR 170. 5 Ibid., 194. 6 Ibid., 198, my emphasis. 7 [1935] IR 170, 204–5. 8 See the decision of the Indian Supreme Court in *Kesavandra v. State of Kerala* [1973] AIR 1461 (S.C. India) and Hogan, 'A desert island case set in the silver sea', p. 90. 9 Hogan, 'A desert island

judgments of the majority of the High Court and Supreme Court which have attracted far less attention are, by definition, more reflective of the prevailing judicial attitude. The essential issue in *Ryan* was whether or not the Constitution had been validly amended. It was noted earlier that legislation such as the PSA, 1927 had been allowed to act as an amendment of the Constitution.

> The constitutionality of such legislation was upheld in a series of cases, chiefly on the remarkable ground that during the initial eight year period following the entry into force of the Constitution, any legislation enacted by the Oireachtas which was found to be in conflict with the Constitution had the effect, *ipso facto,* of amending that Constitution, whether on a permanent or a temporary basis.[10]

This approach relegated the Constitution to the status of ordinary legislation; it has been described as 'clearly wrong'.[11] Article 2A, however, was unlike the PSA, 1927 in that, although it acted as an amendment of the Constitution, it did so expressly. The validity of Article 2A rested, partly at least, on whether or not the Constitution (Amendment No. 16) Act, 1929 had validly amended Article 50 to allow the Constitution to be amended by means of ordinary legislation for a further eight years. On this point the Supreme Court majority were correct to hold that the Oireachtas 'subject to the entrenched provisions safeguarded by the Treaty ... had a full power of amendment of the Constitution by ordinary legislation ... It followed that as Article 50 did not fall within these entrenched provision, it itself could also be amended.'[12] Since Article 50 had been validly amended, the Oireachtas was free to amend the Constitution by means of Article 2A. As FitzGibbon J stated in *Ryan,* 'the framers of our Constitution may have intended "to bind man down from mischief by the chains of the Constitution" but if they did, they defeated their object by handing him the key of the padlock in Article 50'.[13] The strength of the judgment of Kennedy CJ, may make it easy to sneer at the majority view as being weak, and what FitzGibbon J says is certainly not lacking in veracity,[14] but it is not fair to characterize the majority decision in *Ryan* as a sop to the executive. In *The State (O'Duffy) v. Bennett,* Hanna J described Article 2A as 'a kind of intermittent martial law under the harmless name of a constitutional amendment'.[15] In *Ryan,* Murnaghan J declared that Article 2A went 'far beyond anything having the semblance of legal procedure' and

case', p. 95. **10** Hogan, 'A desert island case', p. 81. See *R. (Cooney) v. Clinton* [1935] IR 245 (decided in 1924 but belatedly reported) and *Attorney General v. McBride* [1928] IR 451. **11** Hogan, 'A desert island case', p. 89–90. **12** Ibid., p. 90. **13** [1935] IR 170, 234. **14** Hogan, 'A desert island case', p. 100. **15** [1935] IR 70, 96.

furthermore, the 'judicial mind is staggered at the very complete departure from legal methods in use in these courts'.[16] Vitally, the courts were willing to prevent the attempts by the Oireachtas to rule out any right of appeal to the ordinary courts.[17] The only fair assessment is to say that the courts were willing to review the constitutionality of legislation and were unwilling to allow the executive 'have it all their own way' but that, Kennedy CJ aside, they were not willing to engage in extreme judicial activism. The judiciary were formalistic in their approach and acted correctly within the existing law.

2.10 Article 2A – the political challenges

The courts and Chief Justice Kennedy were not the only critics of Article 2A; a number of letters of condemnation were received from the United States. The Gaelic Athletic Association of Greater New York wrote to 'denounce the recent Coercion Act in Ireland [and] demand the release of all political prisoners in Irish and English prisons' and a Mr Kilroy of the Washington Street Improvement Corporation complained that

> seven hundred and fifty years of British tyranny and papal hypocrisy has taught you no lesson. It has now come to the time when we as Irishmen owe an apology for the slanderous propaganda we have circulated, the hatred and prejudice we have nurtured against the British; for in all their history they were never guilty of enacting laws as inhuman as that which you have sponsored.[18]

The number of such similar complaints necessitated the preparation of a draft response and on 11 January 1932 the president of the executive council agreed to this draft.[19]

Letters of complaint from the American diaspora are one thing, but the government and Article 2A were to face much more serious and sustained assault from a source closer to home. The Fianna Fáil Party and de Valera were also unhappy with the new legislation. This was predictable but nonetheless important. As long as de Valera and his colleagues remained

16 [1935] IR 170, 237/8. See Hogan, 'A desert island case', p. 95. **17** See *The State (O'Duffy) v. Bennett* [1935] IR 70, and *The State (Hughes) v. Lennon* [1935] IR 128. **18** It is interesting, though unsurprising, that Article 2A was immediately associated with the earlier British Coercion Acts. This was an undeniably naïve reaction to the legislation. The Department of An Taoiseach file S2267 contains a series of such letters. **19** Department of An Taoiseach file S2267, handwritten note to Mr Keane signed and dated 31/12/31 (that is 31 December 1931). The draft itself is numbered S4469/17 although it is included in file S2267. It refers to the inclusion of the President's Statement and the Joint Pastoral letter, both of which are included in file S2267, with all such replies. One can only wonder how Mr Kilroy, who criticised 'papal hypocrisy', must have reacted upon receiving the Joint Pastoral Statement.

outside the Dáil, the pro-Treaty parties could operate with a free rein without exposing the deficiencies of the Constitution. When Fianna Fáil did enter the Dáil, 'it was natural that they should want to exploit these weaknesses'.[20] The extraordinary measures contained in Article 2A allowed scope for such criticism. When introducing the bill to the Dáil, Cosgrave had made it clear that its provisions were 'not merely for this government, but for any government that may be in power if the will of the majority is to prevail'.[21] Despite such assurances, Fianna Fáil made their opposition clear. The argument from a Fianna Fáil perspective was obvious: citizens 'had a right to dispute the legitimacy of the 1922 Constitution and, consequently, to withhold their allegiance';[22] after all, Fianna Fáil, as a 'slightly constitutional party', objected to the Treaty and the Constitution, which had never been voted on directly by the people. Their stated policy was to 'govern without coercion and they proposed to remove the Oath, because, in their opinion, it involved government by coercion'.[23] For a party whose official position was to increase the legitimacy of the state and oppose rule by coercion, it was only to be expected that they should attack the new amendment.

Fianna Fáil also had less ideological reasons for opposing this measure. In terms of *Realpolitik* the establishment of a new military tribunal, so close to a general election, was invaluable propaganda for Fianna Fáil, because 'the IRA were of substantial benefit to de Valera in three ways: by actively campaigning for Fianna Fáil, by providing the occasion for an emotive "Release the Prisoners" agitation, and by furnishing an invaluable election plank in the shape of the land annuities issue'.[24] The land annuities issue was relevant to the election of 1932, but is not of interest here. The other two points impact directly on the Fianna Fáil policy of the time. To ensure IRA support, Fianna Fáil had to take a stance against the military tribunal, which was, at that time, largely aimed against that organization. Fianna Fáil thus adopted a policy of 'the enemy of my enemy is my friend'.[25] In other words, since the IRA opposed the Cosgrave government, Fianna Fáil were willing to align themselves, in private at least, with that group. Some leading members of the IRA were opposed to supporting Fianna Fáil. Michael Conway argued that, despite his present stance, de Valera would be as bad as Cosgrave when in government; he said, somewhat perceptively, 'he'll hang ye when he gets in'.[26] And, a 'Release the Prisoners' campaign was

20 Lyons, *Ireland since the Famine*, p. 473. 21 Coogan, *De Valera*, p. 410. 22 R. Fanning, 'Mr de Valera drafts a constitution' in B. Farrell (ed.), *De Valera's Constitution & ours* (1988), p. 42. 23 O'Sullivan, *The Irish Free State & its Senate*, p. 294. 24 Coogan, *De Valera*, p. 410. 25 Ibid., p. 413. 26 On 21 July 1936 Michael Conway was sentenced to death by the military tribunal, his sentence was commuted, by de Valera, to life imprisonment. However, as we will see later there was no such reprieve for the IRA. See Coogan, *De Valera*, p. 480.

bolstered by the involvement of a number of highly respected women with good political pedigrees. These women included

> the widow of the executed 1916 leader Major John MacBride, Maude Gonne, the woman Yeats loved; Helena Moloney, the trade unionist; Madame Despard, the socialist sister of Lord French, the former Lord Lieutenant; and Hannah Sheehy Skeffington, the widow of the pacifist who was murdered by a deranged British Officer in 1916.[27]

Such support was politically desirable during an election.

For all of these reasons Fianna Fáil opposed the introduction of Article 2A and the military tribunal. In the subsequent election the party was highly successful as table 2.1 illustrates.

Table 2.1[28]

Party	*1932 Dáil seats won*	*Increase/Decrease in party support*
Fianna Fáil	72	+16
Cumman na nGaedheal	57	−9
Independents	11	−2
Labour	7	−3
Farmers' Party	4	−2
Independent Labour	2	No change

This result meant that, with Labour Party support, Fianna Fáil could form a government. On 9 March 1932 de Valera was elected president of the executive council by a margin of 81 to 68.[29] The 'slightly constitutional party' was in power and sixteen years of de Valera rule were ushered in.

2.11 Fianna Fáil in government & Article 2A

Following his election de Valera began to implement his party policies. He moved quickly to appease the IRA and suspend the detested Article 2A. 'Within hours of being appointed Frank Aiken and James Geoghegan, the Ministers for Defence and Justice respectively, were dispatched from Leinster House to the military prison at Arbour Hill. Every IRA man was visited in his cell.'[30] The following day all IRA prisoners were released.[31] Extracts from the minutes of the executive council show that consideration was given to various categories of prisoner convicted by the Tribunal affecting some twenty-five individuals.[32] On 18 March the new government went a step further and suspended Article 2A. This had the effect of

27 Ibid., p. 411. **28** Ibid., p. 433. **29** Ibid., p. 437, two independent TDs also supported de Valera. **30** Ibid., p. 463. **31** Ibid. **32** Department of An Taoiseach file S2419, 'Sgeul, Constitution (special powers) Tribunal general release of prisoners' (March 1932).

dissolving the military tribunal, although de Valera did not accede to IRA demands that the Act be repealed.[33]

This process of suspending Article 2A went alongside a programme of constitutional reform. De Valera removed what he saw as the objectionable elements of the Constitution. This was designed, in Fianna Fáil eyes, to increase the legitimacy of the state. To this end he introduced a bill to remove the Oath of Allegiance to the British crown on 20 April 1932.[34] De Valera hoped that by removing the oath and other issues he could convince the IRA to disband and recognize the will of the majority. However, on 12 March 1932 Maurice Twomey, chief of staff of the IRA, wrote, 'Fianna Fáil declares its intention to chop off some imperial tentacles; every such achievement is of value and will be welcomed. Notwithstanding such concessions the Irish Republican Army must continue its work.'[35] This stance must have been a disappointment to de Valera, although it had been predictable. O'Sullivan notes that the IRA had 'made it clear ad nauseam that they had no intention of recognizing the Free State even if the Oath were removed'.[36] Despite these problems, the republican vote had been 'nursed' by the release of all ninety-seven IRA prisoners and the suspension of the 'Public Safety Act'.[37] Undoubtedly aware of this, de Valera took the decision to announce a 'snap' election on 2 January.[38] Fianna Fáil won an overall majority in that election; this allowed them to tackle the increasing problem of violence within the state.

Significantly, the contentious Article 2A had not been repealed. During the period after the 1932 election, violence again began to increase. De Valera and his government were closely linked with the IRA during the period and their 'leniency towards the IRA, coupled with the public's fear of the organization, made the courts increasingly ineffective'.[39] In 1932, for example, a jury returned a verdict of 'not guilty' in the case of Gerald Dempsey, an IRA officer charged with unlawful possession of firearms and ammunition; he had also failed to recognize the court. The Circuit Court judge in the case made clear his contempt for the verdict and sentenced Dempsey to three months for failure to recognize the court. The republican newspaper, *An Phoblacht,* demanded Dempsey's release and the Minister for Justice made such an order three days later.[40] In response to IRA activities, particularly their disruption of Cumman na nGaedheal political meetings, a new organization was formed, which began its history as the Army Comrades Association (ACA). By 1933 the ACA adopted a blue shirt as its uniform, and the organization became known as 'the Blueshirts';[41] it

33 O'Sullivan, *The Irish Free State & its Senate*, pp 19–20. 34 Coogan, *De Valera*, p. 446. 35 Ibid., p. 463. 36 O'Sullivan, *The Irish Free State & its Senate*, p. 294. 37 Lee, *Ireland, 1912–1985*, p. 177. 38 Coogan, *De Valera*, p. 455. 39 Ibid., p. 465. 40 Ibid. 41 O'Sullivan, *The Irish Free State & its Senate*, p. 329.

also adopted a straight arm 'Hitler salute'.[42] It is generally accepted that the ACA's 'fundamental raison d'être was the belief that de Valera was allowing the IRA run riot'.[43] This view was not without foundation.

In August 1932 the IRA had occupied Donamon Castle, Co. Roscommon, for use as a weekend training camp.[44] In May 1933 approximately sixty armed men occupied a house in Ballinacarriga, Co. Cork, and carried out military exercises.[45] Other examples of such behaviour also exist. Since one of the main activities of the IRA during the period was the disruption of public meetings, and since one of the main objectives of the Blueshirts was to protect those meetings, violence between the organizations was inevitable and frequent. The country was, once again, descending into anarchy. De Valera's response to this increase in violence was interesting. Having condemned the Cosgrave government for introducing Article 2A, he was quite willing to turn to that very same measure to tackle the situation. O'Duffy, the leader of the Blueshirts, had announced a march on Leinster House. De Valera cited the fascistic elements of the Blueshirt movement and 'elected to believe that O'Duffy's march would be along Mussolini lines[46] ... He banned the parade.'[47] More importantly de Valera took this opportunity to reintroduce Article 2A. 'At 12.45am on [12 August 1933] ... the government promulgated an Order bringing Article 2A of the Constitution into force, thus virtually putting the country under martial law.'[48] This could be described as a 'U-turn' in Fianna Fáil policy, but on 23 August 1933,[49] Ireland, once again, had a military tribunal with extensive powers. The tribunal established in 1931 had been suspended for a period in 1932/3 and was reintroduced for the period 1933 to 1937.[50]

2.12 Article 2A in practice

Following the 1933 election and Fianna Fáil's increased mandate, and the reintroduction of the military tribunal and Article 2A, the government began to move against illegal armies within the state. It is fair to say that de Valera began by moving forcefully against the Blueshirts and dealt with the IRA by stealth.[51] Reasons for this include the already noted links between the IRA and Fianna Fáil coupled with that party's sympathy for the IRA stance. 'The bulk of cases heard before the Military Tribunal in 1934 related to the Blueshirts.'[52] In late 1933, violence between the Blueshirts

42 Coogan, *De Valera*, p. 469. 43 Ibid., p. 466. 44 O'Sullivan, *The Irish Free State & its Senate*, p. 296. 45 Ibid., p. 328. 46 In Italy, 'the Fascists' seizure of power ... was preceded by the dramatic threat of a 'March on Rome.' D.S. Elazar, *The making of Fascism: class, state, and counter-revolution, Italy 1919–1922* (2001), p. 136. 47 Coogan, *De Valera*, pp 460–70. 48 O'Sullivan, *The Irish Free State & its Senate*, p. 333. 49 Department of An Taoiseach file S2438. 50 Hogan & Whyte, *Kelly*, para. 6.5.321. 51 Lee, *Ireland, 1912–1985*, p. 179. 52 Maurice Manning, *The Blueshirts* (1987), p. 130.

and the IRA worsened, and there was an increase in the tribunal's caseload.[53] The tribunal had convicted thirty-four members of the IRA by the end of 1933, and the number of arrests and convictions increased during 1934.[54] Table 2.2 shows the conviction patterns of the tribunal, broken down by year, and membership of the two relevant organizations.

Table 2.2[55]

	1934	1935	1936
IRA	102	112	129
Blueshirts	349	74	–

A bias against the Blueshirts is evident in 1934. By the end of 1934, however, the Blueshirts had essentially been defeated as a force and the government began to move, warily, against the IRA. 'De Valera long hesitated, however, to declare the IRA illegal, until two particularly callous murders, of a woman and an old man, gave him the opportunity to ban the organization in June 1936.'[56] On top of this, the fact that in 1936 the IRA began a bombing campaign in Britain and Northern Ireland allowed the Fianna Fáil administration to move against the organization.[57] Fianna Fáil must have been aware that a sizeable proportion of its electoral support in 1932 and 1933 had been derived from the support of the IRA and the party's stance on Article 2A. As a result of this, the early operations of the tribunal were largely directed against the Blueshirt movement, who were supporters of Cosgrave, and not the IRA. As IRA activities worsened and as the Blueshirt threat had abated, Fianna Fáil felt more confident in dealing with the threat from their own former comrades. Moreover, as has been noted, Fianna Fáil felt that by removing the Oath and other issues from the Constitution it had legitimated the state, and that they therefore had a right to protect this newly legitimated state from attack.

While the tribunal appears to have been used exclusively in the prosecution of those involved in violent disturbances, it is important to recognize that some lower level cases may also have been tried by the tribunal. On 25 May 1935, Deputy Fitzgerald Kenny raised the case of three Blueshirts in the Dáil; Clifford, Sullivan and Quirke, had been charged with conspiracy to fire into the dwelling house of a water bailiff. Deputy Fitzgerald Kenny argued that the Minister for Justice had incorrectly issued a certificate to have these men tried by the tribunal. Due to the level of executive control over the tribunal it is unsurprising that suggestions of political interference and bias were made. The attorney general pointed out that the men could

53 Lee, *Ireland, 1912–1985*, p. 179. 54 Manning, *The Blusehirts*, p. 129. 55 Coogan, *De Valera*, p. 479. 56 Lee, *Ireland, 1912–1985*, p. 180. 57 C. Fitzgibbon & G. Morrison, *The life and times of Eamon de Valera* (1973), pp 118–19.

have been charged before the tribunal without a certificate, on a charge of using of firearms; moreover, (he observed) because water bailiffs were appointed by the minister, interference with them was punishable in the same manner as interference with a police officer. He also noted that water bailiffs had been 'beaten up previously'.[58] The episode is instructive because it shows distrust of the political nature of the tribunal. Furthermore it displays a certain presumption in favour of using the tribunal where firearms were involved. Finally, the evidence of ongoing attacks on water bailiffs is interesting as is the view of water bailiffs as servants of the state, of equivalence to the police. An example of IRA activity is also instructive. The AG's files include a number of memoranda relating to an attack on a travelling cinema. On 18 September 1933, six armed men held up William Walsh's Travelling Cinema and made off with the film *Gallipoli.*[59] It was recommended that the individuals involved in the raid should be tried by military tribunal. This was, at least in part, due to the use of firearms;[60] however, other events also seem to have played a role in the decision. Following the arrest of the six men, the 'Battallion Commandant, IRA' led about fifty men to the local gaol demanding their release. The members of the procession were said to have carried banners with slogans such 'Why hesitate to join the IRA'; 'Boycott British Goods'; and 'Break Connections with England'.[61] This incident, similarly to the attack on the water bailiff, illustrates the point that something which may appear trivial (the theft of film reels) was in fact political; such incidents were calculated challenges to the authority of the state and could not be tolerated. Furthermore, the use of firearms in such incidents could be seen as indicative of the general level of gun violence within society. As such, the use of the military tribunal in such cases appears justified.

58 Attorney General's office, file 65/33, letter to Roinn An Uachtaráin, dated 26 May 1935, signed Priomh Aturnae. **59** Presumably the subject matter of the film was considered to be overly 'British' and offensive by the republicans. Although it might be somewhat disingenuous to describe such acts as part of Ireland's 'Cultural Revolution' when taken alongside incidents such as the murder of Vice-Admiral Henry Boyle, mentioned earlier, the symbolic significance of such an attack does become more apparent. **60** Attorney General's office, file 65/33, letter dated 22/9/33 (that is 22 September 1933), to Ch/Supt, Galway, signed Holland Fead Commissioner 'CS' This letter states that since Walsh, one member of the raid, carried a rifle every member of the party should be deemed to have been collectively in possession of a firearm, this is due to the fact that Walsh carried the rifle and the others kept their hands in the pockets to suggest that they too were armed. The case was referred to the tribunal on 18 October 1933 by Minister for Justice Patrick Rutledge. **61** Attorney General's office, file 65/33, letter dated 27/9/33 (that is 27 September 1933) to Commissioner 'CS' signed Sean O'Macain Supt (J Mackin) for C/Supt on Inspn.

2.13 Conclusions

It should now be obvious that the Irish Free State had considerable experience in the field of emergency powers and special courts. By 1937, de Valera was no longer satisfied with merely altering the Constitution of the Free State. A grander plan, involving a new, legitimate Constitution, was envisaged. To facilitate this process a constitutional review was to be conducted; and the Offences against the State Act, 1939 was one result of this process.

3

Constitutional review and the Offences against the State Act

3.1 The Constitution Review Group 1934

The policy of constitutional reform adopted by the Fianna Fáil government has been accurately described as one of 'piecemeal destruction'.[1] The removal of the Oath of Allegiance and all references to the British crown, as well a few miscellaneous amendments, often had knock-on effects. For example, the Constitution (Amendment No. 27) Act, 1936, which removed the governor general from the Constitution[2] had a significant impact upon Article 2A. Members of the Military Tribunal had been appointed by the governor general acting on the advice of the executive council.[3] This power was now transferred to the executive council.[4] The tribunal was already heavily controlled by the executive, but now had even this fig leaf of independence removed. Initially, reforms by the Fianna Fáil government seem to have been taken on a fairly *ad hoc* basis, with the aim of removing the features of the Free State Constitution considered objectionable by republicans. It was obvious that a more coherent approach was required. In 1934 a Constitution Review Group was established to consider the direction that future reforms might take. The committee was made up of four senior civil servants: Stephen Roche, secretary at the Department of Justice; Michael McDunphy, assistant secretary, Department of the President of the Executive Council; John Hearne, legal adviser to the Department of External Affairs; and Philip O'Donoghue, assistant to the attorney general.[5]

The review group was particularly interested in what provision should be made for emergency legislation. Although its Constitution had stated clearly in Article 70 that 'extraordinary courts shall not be established', the Free State had resorted to extraordinary courts, most notably the PSA, 1927, which was never implemented, and Article 2A, which was extensively utilized. It is, therefore, unsurprising that the old Article 70 approach was rejected. In fact the idea that any new constitutional arrangement should include provision for a special court seems to have been accepted from the

1 R. Fanning, 'Mr De Valera drafts a constitution', p. 35. 2 Coogan, *De Valera*, p. 488. 3 s. 4(2) Article 2A. 4 Department of An Taoiseach, file S2437, memorandum headed 'Rionn an Uachtarain, Sgeul Constitution (special powers) Tribunal. Appointments. Procedure File', dated 11.12.36 (that is 11 December 1936). 5 Hogan, 'The constitutional review group of 1934', p. 345.

start. The Department of An Taoiseach files show a few references to a statement made by the president of the executive council in which he said, 'it is necessary to ensure, in cases of real urgency and real public emergency, that an executive would not be prevented from taking the action that might be considered necessary to safeguard public interests'.[6] This statement and the implication that government will legitimately require special powers on occasion appear to have been generally agreed upon. Roche prepared an early note on Article 2A in which he made a series of interesting observations. McDunphy has annotated these notes with his own handwritten comments. The Department of Justice secretary believed in strong government; the assistant secretary at the Department of the Executive was more wary, noting that strong government could be a 'real danger' and stating that 'something more than strength is required'.[7] Roche maintained forcefully that

> with particular reference to Article 2A, I agree that, *in form,* that Article is grotesque as an Article of the Constitution. It must go. [McDunphy writes 'I agree' in the margin.] On the other hand, so long as we keep to the idea of a 'normal' written Constitution, with all sorts of snags and pit falls for the executive, we must have something, somewhere, on the lines of Article 2A.[8]

So, even Roche, with his belief in 'strong government', recognized that Article 2A was flawed. He was seeking to create a system more acceptable than Article 2A but still powerful enough to be of use to the executive. The 'snags and pitfalls' of a 'normal' Constitution are not specified but, given that Article 2A was intended not to be reviewed by the courts, it may be that Roche was referring to the requirement that emergency legislation be amenable to judicial review. Perhaps, he felt that such review would unduly hinder the executive. The group was to spend some time developing a suitable compromise between the need for constitutional legitimacy and the need to properly equip the government in dealing with extremism.

3.2 Proposals on jury trial

An examination of the files relating to the review group indicates that its work was thorough. The members appear to have taken their role seriously and it seems fair to say that they were willing to learn from the previous attempts at

6 Dáil Éireann, *Parliamentary Debates*, 26 April 1934, vol. 51 no. 6, cols 2479–80; Department of An Taoiseach file S2979 Extract from Dáil Debates; and Department of An Taoiseach file S8211, 'Extract from Constitution Committee Report, 1934', para. 7. 7 Department of An Taoiseach file S2979, 'Inter-departmental committee on the Constitution, note with special reference to Article 2A', by Mr Roche (Justice) signed and dated 16/6/34 (that is 16 June 1934). 8 Ibid.

similar such legislation. Along with considering Article 2A the group also made recommendations about Article 72 which stated that

> no person shall be tried on any criminal charges without a jury save in the case of charges in respect of minor offences triable before a court of summary jurisdiction and in the case of charges for offences against military law triable by court martial or other military tribunal.[9]

Combined with Article 70, this effectively prevented civilian non-jury trial for all but the least serious offences and those covered by the type of emergency envisaged by Article 70. The review group saw this as insufficient and did not recommend Article 72 for inclusion in any new Constitution. It argued that 'with an executive dependent on, and responsible to, a parliament elected on full adult suffrage, and with judges whose independence is guaranteed by the Constitution, which also forbid the setting up of 'extraordinary Courts' the right to trial by jury has lost its original importance'.[10] This appears to be a reasoned objection to a system of trial by jury and forms a theoretically sound basis for an alternative proposal. However, no alternative was proposed. It was noted that if Article 72 was included in any future Constitution,

> (a) that the Article does not bind us to the present English system of requiring a jury of twelve and a unanimous verdict
>
> and
>
> (b) that when the Oireachtas has designated any particular offence as a 'minor' offence, fit to be tried summarily, it shall not be open to a defendant to raise the point that the offence is so serious that it cannot reasonably be called a 'minor' offence and that the law declaring it to be triable summarily is therefore *ultra vires* Article 72 and invalid.[11]

It is clear, therefore, that the review group was not contemplating radical reform such as some type of inquisitorial trial process. It is undeniable that the group was dissatisfied with jury trials for some practical reason and as such were seeking 'loopholes'; thus the suggestion that 'jury trial' did not necessarily imply a jury of twelve with a unanimous verdict. It proposed justifications and practical suggestions to allow the government to limit trial by jury. This shows a clear lack of faith in the jury system. Although the group's

9 Article 72, Constitution of the Irish Free State. 10 Department of An Taoiseach, file S2979, 'Constitution Committee, 1934. Copy of Report on Part I of the Terms of Reference (as signed 3rd July, 1934). Appendix C. Article 72, Observations of the Committee'. 11 Ibid.

report does not explain the origin of this distrust, it must have arisen from the jury system's repeated failure to ensure justice. This distrust, coupled with the acceptance that an improved Article 2A was required, would become the foundation for a proposal which would itself form the basis of the Offences against the State Act, 1939.

3.3 The review group proposals

The proposal of the review group is included in Appendix 2 (see pages 197–200 below), a brief summary of the salient points shows an interesting, if at times convoluted, procedure. The proposal is broken down into Scheme A and Scheme B. Scheme A proposes that power should be provided in the Constitution allowing for the enactment of legislation to provide for trial by 'special courts' where it is certified by a judge or justice that such trial is 'in the interests of justice'. The special courts envisaged are to be similar to the Constitutional (Special Powers) Tribunal. Scheme B, a supplement to this, is a substitution for Article 2A and would involve an article of the Constitution specifically authorizing the Oireachtas to provide, by way of ordinary legislation, such measures as they saw fit 'to meet the requirements of any period during which the ordinary laws are not adequate'.[12] Importantly, Scheme B makes it clear that the legislation contemplated should 'state expressly that its object is to carry out the provisions of the said Article'.[13] Scheme A would be a permanent feature, while Scheme B would only be activated upon declaration of an emergency. Hogan explains that the 'Special Criminal Court would be the first step in curbing civil disorder and that the declaration of a state of emergency would be necessary in the final resort'.[14] The procedure for declaring a state of emergency is also explained.

Roche believed that the country required strong government which should not be 'hampered and humiliated' by the courts, and he felt that on occasion it was desirable to have a 'responsible executive to save the people from *irresponsible judges*'.[15] Despite, misgivings the proposal for the declaration of a state of emergency involved an interesting role for the judiciary. Under the proposals, initially suggested by Roche and accepted by McDunphy,[16]

12 Department of An Taoiseach file S8211, 'Extract from Constitution Committee Report, 1934, Appendix B, Emergency powers, Suggestions of the Committee', para.s 4–5. 13 Ibid. 14 Hogan, 'The constitutional review group of 1934', p. 347. 15 The words 'irresponsible judges' are underlined by hand and a '?' has been written in the margin, as such it appears that McDunphy was unsure about this argument. Department of An Taoiseach file S2979, 'Inter-departmental Committee on the Constitution, Note with Special Reference to Article 2A', by Mr Roche (Justice) signed and dated 16/6/34 (that is 16 June 1934). 16 McDunphy has written 'prima facie that seems sound' next to the proposal signed McD 16/6/34. For the original proposal see Department of An Taoiseach file S 2979, 'Inter-departmental committee on the Constitution, note with special reference to Article 2A', by Mr Roche (Justice) signed and dated 16/6/34 (that is 16 June 1934).

whenever the executive council was of the opinion that it is desirable to do so, the senior available judge of the High Court should be called upon to summon all judges or justices exercising criminal jurisdiction. This provision specifically excludes judges of the High and Supreme Courts and all temporary judges and justices. The purpose of this gathering would be to advise the executive council as to whether or not the state of the country is such that the ordinary laws are inadequate. If the assembled judges and justices affirm that the state is in such a condition then the executive council may by order declare all provisions of all emergency legislation to be in force.[17] Roche explained that the scheme was designed this way because de Valera was anxious for there to be some form of 'judicial, or at least non-political sanction for such a declaration'.[18] This is a considerable step forward, for the previous models had not allowed for any form of appeal and the Article 2A tribunal had been appointed by the executive council with no reference to any outside body.[19] Roche also justifies this rather complicated process by explaining that

> I have made the declaration of an 'emergency period' contingent on the consent of those judges and justices who travel the country and deal with crime locally … These judges and justices have a strong incentive to shift the burden of dealing with organized crime from their own shoulders, they see at close quarters the inadequacy of ordinary police and court methods in semi-revolutionary periods, they even run definite personal risks, and they are in the main sensible decent men, so that I have some hope that in any real emergency they will not be obstructive.[20]

Although the idea of some form of review is to be welcomed, a doubt about the judiciary persists. Those local judges and justices may be trusted because they operate at the coal face, and since they face a threat to their personal safety it is presumed they will be realistic when reaching their decision. Senior judges are specifically excluded from the process. It does not seem too great a leap to suggest that Roche was fearful that these senior members of the judiciary would 'hamper and humiliate' the executive.

The proposals of the committee are important. The influence of earlier

17 Department of An Taoiseach file S8211, 'Extract from Constitution Committee Report, 1934, Appendix B, Emergency powers, Suggestions of the Committee', para. 5(d)-(g). 18 Department of An Taoiseach file S2979, 'Inter-departmental committee on the Constitution, note with special reference to Article 2A', by Mr Roche (Justice) signed and dated 16/6/34 (that is 16 June 1934). 19 following the abolition of the Governor General. 20 Department of An Taoiseach file S2979, 'Inter-departmental committee on the Constitution, note with special reference to Article 2A', by Mr Roche (Justice) signed and dated 16/6/34 (that is 16 June 1934).

Free State experience can be seen; for example, the necessity of a non-jury court was immediately recognized. At the same time, the group recognized the failings of the Free State Constitution and went about rectifying them. The lack of a non-political body to keep a check on the executive was acknowledged as something to be redressed/ These proposals are a staging post between the provisions of the Irish Free State and the provisions of the new Constitution.

3.4 Bunreacht na hÉireann and the 'special courts'

The Dáil approved the draft Constitution on 14 June and it was put before the people in a plebiscite on 1 July 1937. The new Constitution, Bunreacht na hÉireann, was approved by a majority of the people, 685,105 in favour to 526,945 against.[21] If de Valera's previous reforms had been designed to increase the legitimacy of the state, he now felt that that mission had been completed. As soon as the people of Ireland 'had established a state in accordance with their own wishes, those who tried by violent means to overthrow that state should be held here, as in other countries, to be guilty of the most terrible crime'.[22] Therefore, since the people of Ireland had adopted this Constitution for themselves, it was legitimate for the state to protect itself using all available means. There was, however, one problem: the acceptance of the new Constitution meant that the 1922 Constitution was no longer active law; therefore, Article 2A was no longer operative. This fact 'prompted anxious consideration in the Department of Justice'.[23] Since the need for an emergency measure had been acknowledged by the review group in 1934, it is no surprise that the Department of Justice was anxious; yet despite all this advance consideration, between the introduction of the new Constitution at the end of 1937 and the enactment of the Offences against the State Act in June 1939, there was no statutory provision for any form of special court or military tribunal.[24]

The review group proposal of a two-pronged approach was discussed in the previous section. The new Constitution was influenced by these proposals and adopted a modified version. Two Articles of the 1937 Constitution are relevant to the issue of 'Special Courts'. Article 28.3.3° provides for a 'time of war or armed rebellion'. In such circumstances the Oireachtas is given broad freedom from constitutional restraint, as envisaged by the review group's Scheme B. The actual Article has abandoned the idea of a judicial assembly originally suggested and adopts the more efficient approach of allowing both Houses of the Oireachtas to determine if such a situation exists. The Article states that 'nothing in this Constitution shall be invoked to

21 Coogan, *De Valera*, p. 498. 22 Fanning, 'Mr De Valera drafts a constitution', p. 43, quoting de Valera. 23 Lee, *Ireland, 1912–1985*, p. 219. 24 G. Hogan & G. Whyte, *Kelly*, para. 6.5.324.

invalidate any law enacted by the Oireachtas which is expressed to be for the purpose of securing the public safety and the preservation of the state in time of war or armed rebellion'.[25] This Article could, therefore, be used to establish a special court during a time of armed rebellion. This construction covers the extension of military law to civilian populations during times of extreme emergency. It is, in that respect, similar to Article 70 of the Free State Constitution and the US case of *Ex parte Milligan,*[26] which allowed for the extension of military law to civilians during such times. It will be recalled that Article 70 provided that the jurisdiction of military courts could be extended to the civilian population during times of war or armed rebellion; however, it explicitly excluded areas 'in which all civil courts are capable of being held'.[27] Unlike Article 70, the new Constitution was more flexible and complemented this Scheme with a further provision.

In a variation upon the suggested Scheme A, the new Constitution provided that 'special courts may be established by law ... where it may be determined in accordance with such law that the ordinary courts are inadequate to secure the effective administration of justice'.[28] This is the polar opposite to Article 70 of the 1922 Constitution, which explicitly prohibited extraordinary courts. Under the 1937 regime a 'time of war or armed rebellion' need not exist for a special court to be established. 'Article 38.3 of the Constitution ... permits ... the establishment by law of special courts quite independently of any declaration of emergency under Article 28.3.3.'[29] Secondly, unlike the old Article 70, the 1937 Constitution does not necessitate military rule being applied to the civilian population. Furthermore, under the 1922 Constitution, in order to establish special courts the legislature had to amend that Constitution; this was not necessary under the 1937 Constitution because Article 38.3 provided for special courts to be established by law. By allowing the establishment of special courts in a wider variety of circumstances the new Constitution could be said to be less liberal than its predecessor. However, the liberalism of the 1922 Constitution hampered the Oireachtas in tackling the serious threat posed by dissident groups and, in part, led to the excesses of the 1927 and 1931 Acts; by granting the state the power to deal with subversive elements the 1937 Constitution ultimately provided a more stable political and constitutional environment.

The 1937 Constitution, therefore, differed in many respects from the 1922 model. Despite this, the impetus for the introduction of emergency legislation remained the same. It will be recalled that after the Public Safety Act of 1927 was repealed in 1928, there was a noticeable increase in crimes of violence and intimidation. Likewise, between 1937 and 1939 no legislation

25 Bunreacht na hEireann, Article 28.3.3(, also referred to as the 1937 Constitution. **26** 71 US (4 Wall) 2, 127. See Ten Broek et al., *Prejudice war,* p. 230. **27** Hogan & Whyte, *Kelly,* para. 6.5.317. **28** Article 38.3.1. **29** Hogan 'The constitutional review group of 1934', p. 352.

regarding special courts existed. During this period the IRA laid down a series of challenges to the authority of the state. On 17 December 1938 a body styling itself 'Dáil Éireann' declared that it was transferring its powers to the Army Council of the IRA.[30] Such a declaration may appear insignificant and indeed it appears to have been largely ignored by the public. However, 'the hand-over meant that Russell [an IRA leader] was now entitled, as de Valera himself had once done, to claim that the authority of the national parliament (the Dail) now lay outside that assembly'.[31] It was a symbolic challenge to the legitimacy of the Dáil and the state, and it was continued on 14 January 1939 when a formal letter signed Patrick Fleming 'on behalf of the government & Army Council of Óglaigh na hÉireann (Irish Republican Army)' demanded the immediate withdrawal of all British troops from Ireland. Rather boldly, the letter stated that 'a period of four days is sufficient notice for your government to signify its intentions in the matter of the military evacuation and for the issue of your Declaration of Abdication in respect of our country'.[32] The IRA was purporting to set the foreign policy of the state. At another time the government might have ignored such sabre-rattling; however, events were soon to take a far more serious turn. In 1939 the IRA began a bombing campaign on mainland Britain. One bomb claimed the lives of twelve people in Coventry and injured over fifty others on 23 August of that year.[33] This was a time of growing international friction with World War II looming large on the horizon. In its letter, the IRA had stated that 'the Irish people have no cause of hostility to any European nation, even those nations whose natural development may bring them into conflict with British interests'.[34] Under the circumstances, this could only be seen as a threat that the IRA might align itself with Britain's enemies. Roche advised de Valera that 'a small country cannot afford to invite attacks from without by a seeming inability to keep order within its own territory'.[35] To this end and with the powers available under the new Constitution, the Department of Justice set about preparing a piece of permanent legislation designed to tackle the situation. The result was the Offences against the State Act, 1939. 'In June 1939 the ... Act was passed, the IRA was declared an illegal organization and trial by military court replaced trial by jury.'[36] The new legislation drew heavily on the past models of 1927 and 1931 but there were some important differences.

30 Department of An Taoiseach, file S10454 'Annex, Extract From WOLFE TONE WEEKLY, Saturday, December 17, 1938. "IRA take over the government of the Republic."' 31 Coogan, *De Valera*, p. 523. 32 Department of An Taoiseach file S10454 'Annex, Copy/Oglaigh na hÉireann (Irish Republican Army), General headquarters Dublin, January 14 1939'. 33 Coogan, *De Valera*, p. 523. 34 Department of An Taoiseach file S10454 'Annex, Copy/Oglaigh na hÉireann (Irish Republican Army), General headquarters Dublin, January 14 1939'. 35 Lee, *Ireland, 1912–1985*, p. 220. 36 Fitzgibbon & Morrison, *Eamon de Valera*, pp 118–19.

3.5 The drafting of the Offences against the State Act, 1939

Article 38.3 provided for the establishment of Special Courts. It further stated that 'the constitution, powers, jurisdiction and procedure of such special courts shall be determined by law'.[37] The absence of any special court or tribunal had been a cause for concern in the Department of Justice, and from the time of the introduction of the new Constitution onward that Department appears to have been pushing for the preparation of the type of legislation envisaged by Article 38.3. Despite these concerns, the rest of Cabinet does not appear to have been interested in the issue. A document concerning 'special courts' was circulated to members of the executive council at the meeting of 21 December 1937, but the topic was postponed to the next meeting.[38] This is striking since the memorandum states that whether or not the executive decided to allow Article 2A lapse without a replacement in place, the Minister for Justice was of the opinion that it would be desirable to have a draft law for the establishment of a special criminal court ready. Despite the existence of a draft Special Criminal Court Act, 1937[39] and Department of Justice concerns about not having any special tribunal in place, no action was taken and the state operated without special courts from 1937 to 1939.

The early drafts of 1937 did allow appeal from the Special Criminal Court to the Court of Criminal Appeal[40] and could only impose such penalties as were provided for by the ordinary law;[41] these proposals were consdierable improvements on the Free State prototypes. The draft continued the practice of staffing the court with members of the Defence Forces and the panel was to be appointed by the President on the advice of the government.[42] The draft proposes unanimous verdicts[43] and a court consisting of nine members.[44] The parliamentary draftsman expressed some concern about these provisions, suggesting a court of five members for capital cases and three for ordinary cases. He also recommended that rather than having unanimous decisions it would be preferable to have the decisions of the court pronounced by the presiding member;[45] this would allow a majority of the court to reach a decision while ensuring that any dissent would not be revealed. This suggestion met with the approval of the AG and the Department of Justice.[46]

Throughout 1938, discussion continued about the need for special legislation. Various memoranda regarding the need for legislation providing for a

37 Article 38.3.2° 38 Department of An Taoiseach, file S10454, 'To each member of the executive council – establishment of a special criminal court', Department of Justice, 25 October 1937. 39 Department of An Taoiseach, file S10454, 'Suggested draft of an Act to provide for such special court as is mentioned in section 3 of Article 38 of the Constitution of Ireland'. See Appendix 3. 40 Ibid., s.13. 41 Ibid., s.12. 42 Ibid., ss. 6–7. 43 Ibid., s. 9 (1). 44 Ibid., s. 6 (2). 45 Department of An Taoiseach, file S10454, 'To each member of the executive council – establishment of a special criminal court', Department of Justice, 25 October 1937. 46 Ibid.

special criminal court exist, and there was an awareness that such legislation might 'become urgent at any time and complicated legislation which may meet with considerable opposition may be necessary'.[47] By 1939 the government began to seriously consider the issue again. The activities of the IRA, mentioned above, go some way toward explaining why special courts were once again on the agenda. Roche suggested that the choice was between two courses of action – to continually have strong powers available and thereby keep 'conspirators 'on the run' or to leave things as they were and deal with each crisis as it arose'. In a rather elaborate analogy he suggested that,

> it is as if we are dealing with an unruly lot of school-boys and had to choose between taking, and using, immediate and constant powers of supervision and correction or saying, 'Go on your own ways: meet in the dormitories after lights-out; and form secret societies ... get the school a bad name: we wont interfere until you actually set fire to the place or seriously hurt somebody; but then there will be floggings and expulsions'.[48]

This bizarre explanation does include some important points. Previous governments introduced legislation as a reaction to some outrage; Roche was proposing that it would be wiser to have the legislation in place before things went wrong.

It is important to note that during the early stages the proposal was for a specific piece of legislation to provide for special courts. Other related, but separate, legislation such as a Treason Bill and Anti-Social Organisations Bill were also proposed.[49] By January 1939, it was suggested that the Special Courts Bill should be combined with the Anti-Social Organisations Bill.[50] The desire to combine the bills stemmed from the view that 'it would be desirable to get as much of the controversial matter as possible into one bill' rather than spread it out.[51] A draft of the new Offences against the State Bill was presented to Cabinet on 10 February 1939.[52] It is interesting, that despite the clear relationship of this new legislation to Article 2A, the executive strongly wanted to avoid making any connection. Roche informed O'Muimhneachain that he was unsure whether an explanatory memorandum

47 Department of An Taoiseach, file S 10454, 'Copied from file S.10496, cabinet sub-committee general', signed P. O'Cinneide, 16.2.38 (that is 16 February 1938). 48 Department of An Taoiseach, file S10454 D, signed S.A. Roche, 8 March 1939. 49 Department of An Taoiseach, file S10454 A, 'Memorandum for government', Department of Justice, 19 January 1939. 50 Department of An Taoiseach, file S10454 B, letter to Roche, signed M O'M dated 25adh Eanair, 1939 (that is 25 January 1939). 51 Department of An Taoiseach, file S10454 B, 'Public safety legislation', signed S. Roche, 25 January 1939. 52 Department of An Taoiseach, file S10454, 'Extract from cabinet minutes, 10.2.39, draft Offences against the State Bill'.

should be issued with the text of the bill and was certain that if such a memorandum was attached 'such memorandum should not . . . go into details or refer at all to Article 2A of the old Constitution, but should be short and dedicated mainly to emphasizing the fact that two parts of the bill may never come into operation'.[53] This statement corroborates the view that the government were anxious not to appear as though they were re-enacting Cosgrave's legislation. As Joe Lee observes,

> Roche was authorized to include as many of the Cosgrave provisions as he felt necessary. But he should adopt the device of actually repealing the relevant legislation, and only then should he re-enact the substance of it, as far as required, while taking care to change the phraseology as far as possible.[54]

The use of this parliamentary sleight of hand has resulted in a cross-over between parts of the relevant legislation. The three Acts allowed the government to decide when such special provisions should be in force – s.20(1) of the PSA 1927; s.1 of Article 2A; and s.35(1) of the OAS Act, 1939. Differences of language do occur, which may substantiate Lee's argument. In s.20(1) the executive council may make an order establishing non-jury courts when it 'is of opinion that it is necessary in order to secure the due administration of justice'. Article 2A uses similar language and empowers the executive to make such an order when it 'is of opinion that circumstances exist which render it expedient' that the relevant Parts be introduced. The 1939 Act uses an alternative formula. It essentially restates Article 38.3 of the Constitution. The government, again, has the power to make an order when it 'is satisfied that the ordinary courts are inadequate to secure the effective administration of justice'.[55] It would be difficult to assess which one of these formulae is the more stringent, but they all have similar effect and, bar linguistic juggling, amount to the same thing.

Other sections are also of interest. It will be remembered that Article 2A attempted to prevent any appeal from the tribunal to the ordinary courts of law.[56] The courts rejected this limitation and the decisions of the tribunal were said to be open to review.[57] The drafters of the 1939 Act were aware of this, and s.44(1) specifically allows for an appeal from the Special Criminal Court in two circumstances: firstly, if the defendant obtains a certificate from the Special Criminal Court allowing him to appeal; and secondly, if the Special Criminal Court refuses such a certificate, the Court of Criminal

53 Department of An Taoiseach, file S10454, 'Copy for M O'Muimhneachain', signed S.A.R. 24/2/1939 (that is 24 February 1939). 54 Lee, *Ireland, 1912–1985*, p. 221. 55 s.35(1) The Offences against the State Act, 1939. 56 s.6(5) Constitution (Amendment No 17) Act, 1931. 57 *The State (O'Duffy) v. Bennett* [1935] IR 70 and *The State (Hughes) v. Lennon* [1935] IR 128.

Appeal may still grant him that right. Ultimately, therefore, an appeal was available from both the Article 2A tribunal and the 1939 court. The desirability of a route of appeal was noted by the AG in January, 1939. He argued that

> the provision of an appeal will tend to increase confidence in the findings of the Court. The view has been largely shared in this office that few, if any, of the late Tribunal's decisions on questions of fact would have been reversed by the Court of Criminal Appeal. The absence, however, of such appeal was frequently urged as a criticism of the late system.[58]

Although both models were ultimately subject to judicial review, the fact that the OAS Act, 1939 provided for such a review at the outset and unlike Article 2A did not attempt any interference with the right to a judicial hearing, must be seen as a sign of positive development. This provision significantly adds to the legitimacy of the court.

A further point of interest is the composition of the courts. The Article 2A tribunal consisted entirely of members of the Defence Forces,[59] whereas the 1927 Act provided that the tribunal should consist of three or more members, 'of whom at least one (who may be or may not be an officer of the Defence Forces)' shall be certified as legally knowledgeable.[60] The Offences against the State Act was more liberal. It provided for the appointment of members of the judiciary, barristers and solicitors of not less than seven years' standing, or members of the Defence Forces.[61] Despite this provision allowing members of the judiciary to sit in the court in its early years, its staff were in fact drawn entirely from the ranks of the military.[62] Cosgrave's difficulties with the judiciary during the drafting of the PSA, 1927 may have been influential in this regard. It will be recalled that he stated in 1931 that members of the Supreme Court had made clear their willingness to resign if they were asked to sit as a court under the 1927 Act.[63] This principled decision not to allow the political nature of the PSA, 1927 tarnish their judicial independence may have, in fact, discouraged the executive from considering the appointment of judges to the Article 2A tribunal. By the time the OSA, 1939 was drafted, the appointment of members of the Defence Forces to such bodies had become the established practice. So, it is in fact commendable that provision was now being made for the appointment of members of the judiciary.

58 Department of An Taoiseach, file S10454 B, 'Draft of Special Criminal Court Bill, observations of the Attorney General's office'. 59 s.4(2) Constitution (Amendment No 17) Act, 1931. 60 s.22(1) The Public Safety Act, 1927. 61 s.39(3) The Offences against the State Act, 1939. 62 Hogan & Whyte, *Kelly*, para. 6.5.335. 63 O'Sullivan, *The Irish Free State & its Senate*, p. 261.

3.6 The legislation in brief

The OAS Act, 1939 clearly was a considerable improvement over the PSA, 1927 and Article 2A, yet the Act still provided for a considerable restriction upon the right to trial by jury. As such, the legitimacy of the Special Criminal Court depends upon the legitimacy of this restriction. As we have seen, Lord Devlin famously proclaimed:

> The first object of any tyrant in Whitehall would be to make parliament utterly subservient to his will; and the next to overthrow or diminish trial by jury, for no tyrant could afford to leave a subject's freedom in the hands of twelve of his countrymen. So that trial by jury is more than an instrument of justice and more than one wheel of the constitution: it is the lamp that shows that freedom lives.[64]

The OAS, 1939 combined with Article 38.3 of Bunreacht na hÉireann provides for the interference with the right to trial by jury and as such, in the view of Lord Devlin at least, paves the way for any would-be tyrant. As should be clear from Chapter 1, I am of the opinion that the importance of trial by jury to have been grossly overstated and, therefore, I reject this argument.

As has been noted, the government must issue a proclamation bringing Part V of the OAS, 1939 into force before the Special Criminal Court can be created. The jurisdiction of the court is set down in s.43 of the Act where it is stated that 'a Special Criminal Court shall have jurisdiction to try and to convict or acquit any person lawfully brought before that Court for trial under this Act'. Although the creation of the Special Criminal Court is anticipated by Article 38 of the Constitution, the court itself 'is a creature of statute and has no inherent jurisdiction of its own'.[65] The means of invoking the jurisdiction of the court will be discussed in more detail in Chapter 8.1, but here it is only necessary to point out that there are three means of invoking the jurisdiction of the court: an accused can be charged directly before it; the accused may be returned for trial before the Special Criminal Court by the District Court; or the High Court may order that a case awaiting trial before the Central Criminal Court or Circuit Court should be transferred to the Special Criminal Court.[66] Although the Special Criminal Court is bound by the rules of evidence, practice and procedure of the Central Criminal Court,[67] it does not possess the same jurisdiction as that court. Its jurisdiction is regulated solely by statute; therefore, 'in the absence of appropriate statutory provisions, the Special Criminal Court is under no obligation to deliver a reasoned verdict,[68] has no power to return alternative verdicts and

64 Devlin, *Trial by jury*, p. 164. 65 Dermot Walsh, *Criminal procedure* (Dublin, 2002), p. 981. 66 ss. 45–48 Offences against the State Act, 1939. See Walsh, *Criminal procedure*, p. 981. 67 S.41(4) Offences against the State A, 1939. 68 For a more detailed discussion of this point

has no power to accept amendments rectifying errors in an indictment'.[69] There exists, therefore, a legislative lacuna between the practice and procedure of the Special Criminal Court and its jurisdiction.[70]

Before moving on to consider some of the other provisions of Part V of the OAS, 1939, it is worth noting that the Act provides for the creation of multiple Special Criminal Courts.[71] This point was of mere academic interest until early 2005, when as a result of the creation of a extra Special Criminal Courts it became necessary to amend the OAS, 1939. The Criminal Justice (Terrorist Offences) Act[72] 2005, s.53, amends s.49 of the OAS, 1939 by inserting ss.49(2) to 49(7), the purpose of these new sections being to facilitate the transfer of a case from one Special Criminal Court to another. A further interesting feature of the CJTOA, 2005 is that s.49 amends s.21 of the OAS, 1939 in order to create the new offence of rendering assistance, financial or otherwise, directly or indirectly, to an unlawful organization.[73]

A few miscellaneous points of interest about the court include the fact that it has considerable discretion over its day-to-day functions. For example, under the provisions of the OAS, 1939, the court itself determines the time and place of its sitting.[74] According to the Special Criminal Court Rules, the Registrar must give notice to all relevant parties of these details.[75] While the members of the court are appointed, the court itself decides which of its members shall preside.[76] On a more important point, Article 34.1 of the Constitution, which states that justice shall be administered in public, does not apply to the Special Criminal Court. However, Walsh notes that despite this the court rarely sits *in camera*.[77] Finally, standing mute before the court can result in one being found in contempt of court.[78] This situation is likely to arise where an accused refuses to recognize the authority or legitimacy of the court. Given that the IRA purported to set the foreign policy of the state and refused to recognize its legitimacy, this provision was almost certainly directed against that organization. Other provisions of the OAS, 1939 will be discussed in more detail where relevant, this section has merely outlined some of the provisions.

3.7 Conclusions

The establishment of special courts under the constitutional regime of Bunreacht na hÉireann was the result of much drafting and deliberation. Numerous drafts, two Articles of the Constitution and four bills were all

see Chapter 9.1 **69** Walsh, *Criminal procedure,* pp 1000–1. **70** Ibid. **71** s. 38(2) Offences against the State Act, 1939. **72** Hereinafter the CJTOA, 2005. **73** S. 49 Criminal Justice (Terrorist Offences) Act, 2005. **74** s. 41(1) Offences against the State Act, 1939. **75** The Offences against the State Act, 1939–1972 Special Criminal Court Rules, 1975, Rule 5. See Walsh, *Criminal procedure,* p. 1002. **76** The Offences against the State Act, 1939–1972 Special Criminal Court Rules, 1975, Rule 6(1). See Walsh, *Criminal procedure,* p. 1002. **77** Walsh, *Criminal procedure,* p. 1002. **78** s. 51(3) Offences against the State Act, 1939

filtered down into one Act. However, the heritage of that Act is clear. The title 'Special Criminal Court' was used in a draft of the PSA, 1927. The composition of the court and many of the procedures and technicalities relating to it are derived from earlier models. The very development of two Articles of the Constitution was a response to the failure of Article 70 and 72 of the old Constitution. While its genealogy is obvious, the OAS Act, 1939 does differ considerably from its forerunners. It is, at times, all too easy to conceive of the OAS, Act 1939 as a continuation of the draconian powers encapsulated in the PSA, 1927 and Article 2A; that would be a mistake. The OAS Act, 1939 provided for a right of appeal to the ordinary courts. Admittedly the inclusion of such a right may have been due to the decisions of the courts in *O'Duffy* and *Hughes*, but it was nonetheless a tremendous improvement upon the earlier experiments. The provision for ordinary members of the judiciary as members of the Special Criminal Court, although not immediately utilized, is also a welcome feature. Significantly, the 1939 legislation states clearly that

> the practice and procedure applicable to the trial of a person on indictment in the Central Criminal Court shall, so far as practicable, apply to the trial of a person by a Special Criminal Court, and the rules of evidence applicable upon such trial in the Central Criminal Court shall apply to every trial by a Special Criminal Court.[79]

The practicalities of this measure will be considered in subsequent chapters. When considered in tandem with s.43(1)(a), which limits the jurisdiction of the court to impose those sentences as are provided for by law, it becomes clear that the Court is a far more regularized than its predecessors. It is, in essence, as 'ordinary' a court as is possible and is, therefore, considerably less draconian than either the PSA, 1927 or Article 2A. (Contrary to the views of Blackstone and Lord Devlin, the right to jury trial is no guarantee of justice, and interferences with that right is no not necessarily evidence of tyranny.)

Despite the considerable improvements, outlined above, the OAS Act, 1939 was greeted by a howl of protests. A number of local authorities passed motions objecting to it: Tipperary, Ballyhaunis and Cork branches of 'the Old IRA' wrote to complain; the ICTU and Labour requested meetings to discuss the legislation; and bizarrely, the Committee of Managements of Co. Clare Mental Hospital and the Joint Committee of Management of Sligo Mental Hospital wrote letters of protest.[80] In 1931, those who had written to protest against Article 2A were rewarded with a copy of a joint pastoral letter.[81] No such action appears to have been taken in 1939. As in 1931, the protests were unsuccessful and the legislation was introduced.

79 s. 41(4) The Offences against the State Act, 1939. 80 Department of An Taoiseach, file S11129. 81 Department of An Taoiseach file S2267, 'Joint Pastoral issued by His Eminence, Cardinal MacRory, and the Archbishops and Bishops of Ireland' (October 1931).

4

The Emergency, 1939–1946

4.1 Neutrality, the IRA and the threat from abroad

The Irish government declared a policy of neutrality at the outset of World War II based on the belief that 'maintaining neutrality would both spare the twenty-six counties the horrors of war and demonstrate the state's sovereignty'.[1] This policy gained almost universal acceptance as the war progressed.[2] A successful policy of neutrality was not easy to maintain since 'any apparent division within the country, and especially possible IRA support for the Nazis, might encourage German designs on Ireland or provoke a pre-emptive British strike'.[3] (Nazi interest is evident by the fact that throughout the war Germany broadcast propaganda in English and Irish, to Ireland, employing a combination of Irish ex-patriots and Germans with knowledge of Ireland and its culture.)[4] To maintain neutrality it was vital that the government neutralize any and all internal threats. The IRA, with their anti-British sentiment, was an obvious cause for concern but they were not alone; any remaining Blueshirt elements, due to their fascist tendencies, might prove problematic, and the 'tiny communist movement, whose contacts with Moscow had apparently been revitalized through the participation of its leading lights in the Spanish civil war', could again be viewed with suspicion.[5] Although the fear of communist elements in Ireland had been exaggerated in the past,[6] in the context of the Emergency it appears more believable. Ireland may not have been on the verge of a 'Workers' Revolution', but German efforts to train and return Ryan and Russell to Ireland[7] lends credence to the view that this was more than the usual 'red scare'. Interesting and all as the existence of other groups may have been the IRA clearly posed the greatest risk.

As we have seen, a significant feature of the IRA was that it portrayed itself

1 Coogan, *De Valera*, p. 521. 2 Ibid., 521. 3 Lee, *Ireland, 1912–1985*, p. 221. 4 Most notably Francis Stuart. For a detailed account of German propaganda radio broadcasts to Ireland see D. O'Donoghue, *Hitler's Irish voices, the story of German radio's wartime Irish service*, (1998). 5 O'Halpin, *Defending Ireland: the Irish state & its enemies since 1922*, (1999), pp 200–1. 6 For example when President Cosgrave introduced Article 2A he referred to the threat of Communism. See President W.T. Cosgrave, 'Consitituion (Amend No. 17) Act, 1931. Summary of Opening Statement Made by the president in Dáil Éireann, on 14th October, 1931'. Department of An Taoiseach file S2267. 7 Russell was trained in Berlin and Ryan was freed from a Spanish jail where he had been since the Spanish Civil War, upon his release he was brought to Berlin and reunited with Russell. An attempt to return them to Ireland known as 'Operation Dove' was aborted when Russell died. Carroll, *Ireland in the war years* (1975), p. 65.

as representing the people of Ireland. Thus on 8 December 1938 the seven remaining members of the Second Dáil, describing themselves as 'the executive council of Dail Eireann [sic], government of the Republic', purported to 'delegate the authority reposed in [them] ... to the Army Council'.[8] Following this, in January 1939, the newly 'empowered' IRA declared war on Britain.[9] This was a serious threat to the sovereignty of a neutral nation. The Taoiseach made his position clear when he stated that

> the people who are assuming to act in the name of our people have not ever been elected by the Irish people in any election which they were free to go up for, if they chose to go up. They are usurping authority here, and they cannot be permitted to do so. The state must be in a position to defend itself against them.[10]

The battle lines were drawn, and clearly Fianna Fáil had moved on since the days when Seán Lemass had described them as a 'slightly constitutional party'.[11] The threat posed by the IRA became all the more real when they embarked upon a bombing campaign in Britain from January 1939, causing explosions in British factories, power stations and telephone exchanges. In July alone Britain suffered over one hundred explosions. 'The campaign reached its moral nadir back home with a bombing in the Irish country hotel where Prime Minister Neville Chamberlain's son Francis was spending a hunting holiday.'[12] Britain could not tolerate such outrages; as was previously noted, Roche had advised de Valera that 'a small country cannot afford to invite attacks from without by a seeming inability to keep order within its own territory'.[13] If Ireland wanted to avoid a British attack it would have to ensure that it controlled its own subversive elements. So, 'having declared Irish neutrality, de Valera's major preoccupation was to neutralize the IRA who would naturally see in England's difficulty Ireland's opportunity'.[14]

The threat to Irish neutrality was even greater because the potential for unwanted German attention also existed:

> Abwehr II[15] ... specialised in sabotage operations against the enemy and so was especially interested in the potential offered by IRA

8 Department of An Taoiseach, file S10454 'Annex, Extract From WOLFE TONE WEEKLY, Saturday, December 17 1938. "IRA take over the government of the Republic."' 9 Department of An Taoiseach file S10454 'Annex, Copy/Oglaigh na hÉireann (Irish Republican Army), General headquarters Dublin, January 14, 1939'. 10 Dáil Éireann, *Parliamentary Debates*, 3 January 1940, vol. 78, col. 1358. 11 Dáil Éireann, *Parliamentary Debates*, 21 March 1928; vol. 22, col. 1615, see McLoughlin (ed.), *Great Irish speeches*, pp 144–5. 12 Packard, *Neither friend nor foe: the European neutrals in World War II* (1992), p. 114. 13 Lee, *Ireland, 1912–1985*, p. 220. 14 Carroll, *Ireland in the war years*, p. 14. 15 The German military secret service, see Carroll, *Ireland in the war years*, p. 15.

> saboteurs for operations in Northern Ireland and to a lesser extent in Britain.[16]

Aware of this threat, de Valera warned that 'any attempt to co-opt "anti-British radical nationalist groups"' [the IRA] to carry out espionage against Britain anywhere on the island – including Ulster – would inevitably lead Éire into closer cooperation with Britain'.[17] Such warnings did not go unnoticed. Hempel, the German minister plenipotentiary in Dublin, is said to have 'distrusted the organization, convinced it presented a potential threat to de Valera's government and thus to Ireland's neutrality'.[18] Despite such reservations Germany did, in fact, conduct a number of operations in Ireland. These included the parachuting of Capt. Goertz into Ireland for the purpose of using the IRA in sabotage operations,[19] and the plan to train and return Russell and Ryan.[20] Arguably the most alarming example was 'a crude plan for a German sea landing near Derry in Northern Ireland to be supported by an IRA force crossing the border from Co. Leitrim', which was unearthed by the Gárdaí in 1940.[21]

4.2 The government moves against the IRA

It was noted in a previous chapter that the Fianna Fáil government's initial response to the IRA was somewhat lenient. As Minister for Justice, Ruttledge, stated in the Dáil,

> in 1932, when this government was first elected, an amnesty was declared. In 1937, when the Constitution was passed, there was a similar position, a similar jail clearance. Then, over a technical case in the courts, on another occasion, I think some thirty-four prisoners were released.[22] We have tried to do everything possible to carry on as a government with the least possible force.[23]

Although, in 1937 Seán MacBride, chief of staff of the IRA, had accepted the new Constitution and declared that the IRA had no further role,[24] the organization continued its violent campaign. Just as signs of government leniency were not rewarded in 1932, examples of mercy during the early stages of the Emergency were also ignored. For example, when Patrick McGrath, a disabled veteran, went on hunger strike, de Valera relented and had him released.[25] McGrath was to survive, but

16 Ibid., p. 61. **17** Packard, *Neither friend nor foe*, p. 111. **18** Ibid., pp 107–8. **19** Carroll, *Ireland in the war years*, p. 61. **20** 'The ultimately aborted episode became the stuff of IRA legend with Russell teaming up with … Ryan, to sail a U-boat to Ireland'. See O'Donoghue, *Hitler's Irish voices*, p. 51. **21** Carroll, *Ireland in the war years*, p. 61. **22** This appears to be a reference to *the State (Hughes) v. Lennon,* referred to in chapter 2. **23** Dáil Éireann, *Parliamentary Debates,* 2 March 1939, vol. 74, cols. 1291–2. **24** Patterson, *The politics of illusion: a political history of the IRA* (1997), p. 81. **25** Lee, *Ireland, 1912–1985*, p. 222.

> the sequel was to be tragic and worse than de Valera feared ... A second hunger strike began some months later and two young men ... died in consequence in April, 1940 ... In the following August two detective officers were shot dead in arresting Patrick McGrath and Francis Harte. Both ... were [later] executed. De Valera felt that six lives were lost because of his giving in when faced with McGrath's hunger-strike.[26]

The government employed a variety of tactics against the IRA during the period. These included internment, military tribunal, trial by Special Criminal Court and execution, all of which will be outlined below.

> In its resolve to defend the state, the cabinet had six IRA men executed during the war for the murder of servants of the state whose legitimacy they denied, allowed three to die on hunger strike, had more than 500 interned without trial, and had another 600 committed under the Offences against the State Act.[27]

The popularity of the policy of neutrality assisted the government at this stage. As Lyons notes, 'it is doubtful whether the IRA, even if they had been more efficient or the Germans had paid them more attention could have achieved very much. The mood of the country was set on neutrality'.[28] By 1943 the IRA had been 'paralysed'.[29] The success of the Irish government in neutralizing the IRA undoubtedly contributed to the Allied acceptance of the state's neutrality.[30]

4.3 Internment, *The State (Burke) v. Lennon*[31] and the Magazine Fort raid

On 3 September 1939 a comprehensive Emergency Powers Act (EPA) was passed. Initially this Act excluded the internment of natural-born Irish citizens, though this was later amended.[32] A further internment provision, in Part VI of the OAS, 1939, provided that a Minister of State who was satisfied that 'any particular person is engaged in activities calculated to prejudice the preservation of the peace, order, or security of the state' could issue a warrant for the arrest and detention of that person.[33] During the course of the war, internment became a vital part of government strategy. 'Upwards of 1,500 may have passed through [the Curragh internment camp] ... although the peak number held behind five rows of barbed wire, a deep trench and armed

26 The earl of Longford & T.P. O'Neill, *Eamon de Valera* (1970), p. 357. 27 Lee, *Ireland, 1912–1985*, p. 223. 28 Lyons, *Ireland since the famine*, p. 556. 29 Packard, *Neither friend nor foe*, p. 329. 30 O'Halpin, *Defending Ireland*, p. 200. 31 [1940] IR 136. 32 Hogan & Whyte, *Kelly*, para. 7.4.182, footnote 375. 33 The Offence against the State Act, 1939, s.55. 34 MacEoin, *The IRA in the twilight years: 1923–1948* (1997), v.

sentries, reached only 547 in March 1943.'[34] Given the importance of internment to government policy, any potential challenge to the legislation would be a matter of concern. The internment provisions were challenged in the celebrated case of the *The State (Burke) v. Lennon.*

As with *Childers* and *Hughes* before, the case of *Burke* was an application for *habeas corpus.* It is important for a number of reasons. Firstly, it was the first significant challenge to the constitutionality of legislation brought under the new Constitution.[35] Secondly, the case involved an unusual twist at the outset. It was initially scheduled to be heard by Maguire P and O'Byrne and Gavan Dufyy JJ; however, counsel for the applicant objected, arguing that it was 'a fundamental right of a citizen bringing a *habeas corpus* application to select the judge before whom he would move his application'.[36] Counsel may have objected because they believed that the best chance of securing the release of their client was to make their application to Gavan Duffy J alone, since they believed that Maguire P and O'Byrne J would have outvoted him.[37] The case was eventually heard by Gavan Duffy J sitting alone. In light of the domestic and international circumstances and the fact that this was the first major constitutional challenge, Mr Justice Gavan Duffy's judgment can be regarded as a *tour de force.*[38]

The decision in *Burke* was largely based on the view that in *satisfying* himself that a person was 'engaged in activities calculated to prejudice the preservation of the peace, order, or security of the state' and in thereby ordering the arrest and detention of such a person, a minister was acting in a judicial manner and was, therefore, *ultra vires* the Constitution. Importantly Justice Gavan Duffy accepted that the

> legal position would be different were I concerned with a war measure, a law 'expressed to be for securing the public safety and the preservation of the state in time of war' under Article 28; but I am not, for the Offences against the State Act, 1939, is not such a law.[39]

It will be remembered that the Constitution Review Group of 1934 suggested a two-pronged approach to the provision of emergency legislation. At first glance it may appear that the judgment of Gavan Duffy J is a criticism of that approach. After all, the learned judge of the High Court states that had the legislation been emergency legislation under Article 28 he would not have found it to be unconstitutional. (Despite this, I do not consider the approach of the Review Group and indeed Bunreacht na hÉireann to be fatally flawed. Rather, it is the drafting of Part VI of the OAS, 1939 which causes the

35 as was noted by Gavan Duffy J in his judgment. *The State (Burke) v. Lennon* [1940] IR 136, 143. 36 Hogan, 'Offences against the State (Amendment) Bill, 1940' (2000) 35, *Irish Jurist,* 238, 241. This article includes a detailed account of the proceedings and the case as a whole. 37 Ibid., 243. 38 Ibid., 244. 39 (1940) 74 *ILTR*, 36, 45.

minister to behave in a judicial manner.) As a result of the wording of s.55 the detentions was declared unlawful and the release of Burke was ordered. These decisions were not taken lightly. Justice Gavan Duffy stated that

> any judge of the High Court must regret interfering with executive action at this time, when in fact the government, with its special knowledge, has officially declared that the ordinary courts are inadequate … but any such consideration is subsidiary to the right of the citizen under the Constitution to an order of habeas corpus.[40]

Burke and fifty-three other prisoners interned under the same provision were released.[41]

There were three main consequences arising from the decision in *Burke.* Firstly, as we have seen, the internees were released. Secondly, on 23 December 1939 the IRA raided the Magazine Fort in the Phoenix Park,[42] seizing 1,084,000 rounds of ammunition.[43] This was a considerable blow to the state at such a time, although much of the ammunition was later recovered.[44] The importance of the event was twofold: it depleted the reserves of the Defence Forces in a time of war when munitions were already in short supply; and it gave the IRA a considerable propaganda boost.[45] Unsurprisingly, 'some of the persons just released were believed to be implicated'.[46] The link between the decision in *Burke* and the raid on the Magazine Fort was asserted and led to an extraordinary verbal assault on the judiciary by the Minister for Justice. Speaking in the Dáil, he stated, 'I am satisfied that had it not been for the decision of the courts – I do not want to comment on the decision of the judge – that raid would not have occurred.'[47] This was a severe criticism of a court judgment by a member of the executive and further illustrates the sensitivity surrounding the issue at the time.

In light of the decision in *Burke,* the release of the internees and the raid on the Magazine Fort, it is hardly surprising that the final outcome of the judgment was a tightening of existing legislation and the enacting of new provisions to cover the internment of Irish citizens. The Constitution Review Group of 1934 had attempted to establish a legislative and constitutional framework which put emergency provisions in place before any emergency arose; but now Ireland was once again introducing emergency provisions as a response to an outrage. The *Irish Times* made its position clear when it argued that 'it is obvious that the government must have new powers to replace those of which it has been deprived by the courts … The position is far too grave

40 Ibid., 38. 41 Carroll, *Ireland in the war years*, p. 39. 42 Ibid., 39. 43 Dáil Éireann, *Parliamentary Debates,* 3 January 1940, vol. 78, col. 1322. 44 Ibid. 45 Hogan, 'Offences against the State (Amendment) Bill, 1940', 253. 46 Kelly, *Fundamental rights*, p. 83. 47 Dáil Éireann, *Parliamentary Debates,* 3 January 1940, vol. 78, col. 1323.

for constitutional or juridical niceties ... there must be an end to all forms of playacting'.[48] The government clearly agreed. In a strongly worded statement the Taoiseach announced that 'we want the powers we believed we had in the Act which was declared unconstitutional. We believe they are the powers best fitted to deal with the situation.'[49] The government was, in fact, given these powers.

4.4 In re Article 26 and the Offences against the State (Amendment) Bill, 1940[50]

The Offences against the State (Amendment) Act, 1940 was enacted. In a rather literal interpretation of Gavan Duffy J's judgment, the provisions were amended so that a minister no longer had to be 'satisfied'; he merely had to be 'of opinion' that 'any particular person is engaged in activities which, in his opinion, are prejudicial to the preservation of public peace and order or to the security of the state'.[51] This alteration was, in many respects, irrelevant since the rationale of the judgment of the High Court was based on the effect of the warrant and not on the state of mind of the minister. Having been passed by both Houses of the Oireachtas, the bill was sent to the President for signing; the President exercised his powers under Article 26 and referred the bill to the Supreme Court for a determination on its Constitutionality. On the same day as the bill was passed, the *Irish Press* had reported that the President might refer the bill to the Supreme Court.[52] 'This suggests that the Article 26 reference was part of a pre-arranged plan on the part of the government whereby the Article 26 procedure would operate as a substitute form of an appeal from Gavan Duffy J's decision.'[53]

If the Supreme Court declares a bill to be valid by means of an Article 26 reference, its constitutionality is permanently established and cannot be challenged later;[54] however, this is the result of the final Constitutional Amendment passed by means of ordinary legislation.[55] The Supreme Court pronounced judgment in *In re Article 26 and the Offences against the State (Amendment) Bill, 1940* on 8 February 1940 while the Constitutional Amendment of Article 26 was not signed into law until 31 May 1941.[56] The

48 *Irish Times*, December 30, 1939, cited in Hogan, 'Offences against the State (Amendment) Bill, 1940', 253–54. 49 Dáil Éireann, *Parliamentary Debates*, 3 January 1940, vol. 78, col. 1358. 50 [1940] IR 470. 51 Offences against the State (Amendment) Act, 1940, s.4(1). 52 Hogan, 'Offences against the State (Amendment) Bill, 1940', 254. Much of the information contained within this section has been gathered from the pages of this article. In it Dr Hogan provides a wide-ranging and thorough review of the Court's proceedings, the historical context and the attitude of later Supreme Courts towards the judgment. It has been an invaluable resource. 53 Ibid., 255. 54 Morgan, *Constitutional law of Ireland* (Dublin, 1985), 106. 55 B. Doolan, *Lawless v. Ireland (1957–1961): the first case before the European Court of Human Rights, an international miscarriage of justice?* (2001), p. 21. 56 Ibid., 22.

OAS (Amendment) Act, 1940 was not challenged during this potential lacuna since the statute was not in force and therefore no one with adequate standing existed.[57] From an academic viewpoint, a question surrounding the amendment exists: Does the amendment have retrospective effect? If so, the OAS (Amendment) Act, 1940 is immune from all future constitutional challenge; if not, it is still capable of being overturned. There does not appear to be any clear-cut answer to this question, though Doolan posits a series of arguments against the retrospective effect of the Amendment.[58]

Whether the decision of the Supreme Court was to be eternally binding or not the situation was definitely grave. The government, however, had reason to be confident.

> Given that the Supreme Court had never previously held any legislative measure to be unconstitutional, the government must surely have expected that the bill would have had a relatively easy passage. This belief was probably reinforced by the fact that this was a war time measure and where the security implications of a finding against the bill were plain to behold as witnessed by the calamitous aftermath of Gavan Duffy J's original ruling in the High Court.[59]

As if to fuel conspiracy theories, the government was in a position to make an appointment to the Supreme Court before the hearing of this most important of cases. Ultimately, Byrne J was nominated to succeed the retiring Judge Johnston. Hogan considers the possible interpretations of this appointment and concludes that 'Mr de Valera appears to have been completely fair-minded regarding judicial appointments', so, it would be unreasonable to suggest that there was any attempt to load the court.[60] Further solace can be gleaned from the fact that the measure did not receive the easy passage that was expected but; importantly, it was found to be constitutional.

Article 26 demanded that the court issue a single judgment in cases of this sort, and that judgment was delivered by Sullivan CJ; however, the chief justice made it clear that the decision of the court was a majority decision.[61] The judgment can be fairly described as positivist. The court drew attention to the fact that, although internment measures had been employed by the Irish Free State, the 1937 Constitution did not explicitly prohibit internment without trial.[62] The tenor of this approach is that if the drafters of the

57 Ibid. 58 Ibid., 21–4. 59 Hogan, 'Offences against the State (Amendment) Bill, 1940', 279. 60 Ibid., 260, see Hogan, 'Offences against the State (Amendment) Bill, 1940', 258–260 for a detailed analysis of this point. 61 This provision was later amended by the Second Amendment of the Constitution Act, 1941. See Hogan, 'Offences against the State (Amendment) Bill, 1940', 271. 62 *In re Article 26 and the Offences against the State (Amendment) Bill, 1940* [1940] IR 470, 478.

Constitution intended to prevent internment without trial they would have done so expressly. On a separate point, the court adopted an extremely worrying interpretation of personal liberty provisions of Article 40.3 1°. It was stated that

> this clause is not in respect of any particular citizen, or class of citizen, but extends to all of the citizens of the state and the duty of determining the extent to which the rights of any particular citizen, or class of citizens, can properly be harmonized with the rights of the citizens as a whole seems to us to be a matter peculiarly within the province of the Oireachtas.[63]

This deferential attitude toward parliament was augmented by the court's interpretation of Article 40.4.1°. Remarkably the Supreme Court was of the opinion that

> the phrase 'in accordance with law' ... means in accordance with the law as it exists at the time when the particular Article is invoked ... Accordingly, in our opinion, this Article cannot be relied on for the purposes of establishing the proposition that the bill is repugnant to the Constitution – such repugnance must be established by reference to some other provision of the Constitution.[64]

This approach, which could have completely undermined the utility of the personal liberty provisions of the Constitution, has been described as an emphatic denial of any natural law element within the provisions.[65] Fortunately, later Supreme Courts did not adopt this reasoning.[66]

It will be remembered that Gavan Duffy J had placed much emphasis on the point that, in satisfying himself that an individual was engaged in activities prejudicial to the security of the state, a minister was usurping the judicial role. The Supreme Court was less impressed with such reasoning. Sullivan CJ differentiated between a measure designed to punish, and a precautionary measure. Significantly, the court concluded that the OAS (Amendment) Bill, 1940 did not purport to create a criminal offence and a system of punishment, but rather established a system of precautionary detention.[67] The UK House of Lords decision in *R. (Zadig) v. Halliday*,[68] which had created a similar differentiation, was cited approvingly. Moreover,

63 [1940] IR 470, 481. **64** [1940] IR 475, 482. **65** Kelly, *Fundamental rights*, p. 814. **66** Hogan, 'Offences against the State (Amendment) Bill, 1940', 267. This article provides a thorough and in-depth analysis of these points and provides an interesting review of the judgements of later Supreme Courts. **67** [1940] IR 470, 479. **68** [1917] AC 260. **69** [1924] 2 IR 104.

the court cited the Irish Free State case of *R. (O'Connell) v. Military Governor of Hare Park Camp*,[69] noting the similarity of the provisions under the Free State Constitution, and it cited the fact that internment provisions were upheld under that Constitution. Hogan notes that, although the analysis of *O'Connell* is largely accurate, the strength of the authority may be questioned. (The decision in *O'Connell* concerned a temporary item of legislation, and two of three judges appeared to doubt the constitutionality of any permanent internment legislation. Furthermore, the Court of Appeal had held that it had no jurisdiction to question the validity of Irish Free State legislation while the transitory eight-year period was in operation.)[70] In the final event the Supreme Court upheld the constitutionality of the OAS (Amendment) Bill, 1940.

4.5 Placing the Supreme Court judgment in context

The judgment of the Supreme Court was by no means the judicial *tour de force* of Gavan Duffy J in *Burke*, but the historical context must be recognized. The courts of the US were to adopt a similarly accommodating view in the Japanese American Internment cases with less justification.[71] The Fifth Amendment of the US Constitution enshrines the principle that no person shall be deprived of his liberty without due process. However, following Pearl Harbor restrictions were imposed on the liberty of citizens of Germany, Italy and Japan resident in the USA. During the months after Pearl Harbor those controls were used increasingly against Japanese nationals and Americans of Japanese extraction but were relaxed for Germans and Italians.[72] President Roosevelt signed Executive Order 9906 on 19 February 1942 whose aim was to facilitate the war effort by providing protection against espionage and sabotage. The Secretary of War, or any military commander he might choose, was authorized to 'prescribe military areas in such places and of such extent as he ... may determine, from which any or all persons may be excluded'.[73] The Order was supplemented by Public Law 503 which provided an enforcement mechanism.[74] Together, these laws provided the basis for relocation from the West Coast and the subsequent internment of Japanese Americans.[75]

Gen. DeWitt, head of the Western Defence Command, was ordered to

70 Hogan, 'Offences against the State (Amendment) Bill, 1940', 265–6. 71 In Ireland the Oireachtas sought the power to intern those believed to be associated with a terrorist organization which was placing the Government policy of neutrality at risk. Executive Order 9906 allowed for the internment of an entire group based solely on racial lines. See Rostow, 'The Japanese American cases', 489. 72 Ten Broek et al., *Prejudice war*, p. 99. 73 Ibid., 112, cit.ing Executive Order 9906. 74 Peter Irons, *Justice at war*, (1983), p. 7. 75 Rostow, 'The Japanese American cases', 489. This article provides an in-depth review of the Japanese American cases and the issues surrounding the relocation and internment of Japanese Americans. It has proven to be an invaluable resource and is all the more remarkable given that it was published in 1945.

implement the policy of Executive Order 9906, and he did so. In March 1942 a policy of encouraging Japanese Americans to relocate away from the West Coast was introduced. By early April exclusion orders were being issued which applied only to Japanese Americans and Japanese aliens. Named individuals were excluded from the West Coast area and ordered to report to control stations. From here they were detained in camps organized by the War Relocation Authority (WRA).[76] Initially these camps were to provide temporary accommodation for those who were unable to secure an alternative. However, that policy soon changed, and detention in the camps was compulsory to facilitate 'loyalty examinations'. Surprisingly, a determination of loyalty, did not guarantee freedom: 'officials were required to ascertain that community sentiment was not unfavourable to the presence of such citizens before they were permitted to enter the community'.[77] Therefore, those individuals who had established their loyalty found that their release was dependent on public opinion.

The internment procedure was challenged, unsuccessfully, in a number of cases. If the courts had held that the detentions were not validated by military necessity the measure would have been unconstitutional. As has been noted earlier, the US courts were not without precedent in determining this issue; in *Ex parte Milligan* Davis J had established the principle that martial law could not exist in any area where the courts are open and carrying out their business in an unobstructed manner.[78] As a matter of fact, the ordinary courts were open and operating along the West Coast, and although the nation was at war it was not a time of insurrection or invasion.[79] During the cases in question, 'the strategy devised by the WRA lawyers depended on the argument that the 'racial characteristics' of Japanese Americans predisposed them to the commission of subversive acts'.[80] This argument appears to have won favour with some of the judiciary. In the Seattle District Federal Court, Black J 'raised the spectre of 'fifth columnists ... pretending loyalty to the land where they were born' but who might 'become enemy soldiers overnight''.[81] In *Hirabayashi*[82] the court considered two counts for which concurrent sentences had been imposed. The first count raised the legality of forced transportation and detention in a WRA camp; the second concerned the legality of a breach of curfew. 'The Court considered the violation of the second count first, upheld the curfew order and the sentence imposed for

76 Ibid., 498. 77 Ibid., 500. 78 71 US (4 Wall) 2, 127, see TenBroek et al., *Prejudice war*, p. 230. 79 'No Japanese submarines had been seen off the West Coast for many months. Midway was won; Libya, Tripolotania and Tunisia had been conquered ... We had suffered no defeats since the fall of Tobruk in July 1942, and we had won a long series of preliminary victories.' Rostow, 'The Japanese American cases', 502–3. 80 Irons, *Justice at war*, p. 132. 81 Ibid., 113. 82 *Hirabayashi v. United States*, (1943) 320 U.S. 81. 83 Rostow, 'The Japanese American cases', 504.

violating it. Since the two sentences were concurrent, it said, there was no need to consider the conviction on the first count.'[83] In doing so, the court avoided the issue. The unwillingness of the judiciary to intervene ensured that 'not until the middle of 1946 – almost a year after the surrender of Japan in the wake of the Hiroshima and Nagasaki bombings that ushered in the atomic age – did the last residents of these dusty, barren camps return to their West Coast homes'.[84]

The internment of the Japanese American population of the West Coast has been described as the climax of a long history of anti-Asian racism.[85] On 10 August 1936, three years before the outbreak of war in Europe and five years before American involvement in hostilities, President Roosevelt had suggested that the Japanese American community should be singled out for observation with a view to placing them in 'a concentration camp in the event of trouble'.[86] Long before hostilities had erupted, those of Japanese ancestry were viewed with suspicion at the highest levels of the US administration.

Following the events at Pearl Harbor the situation of Japanese Americans deteriorated rapidly. Gen. DeWitt, argued that,

> The Japanese race is an enemy race and while many second and third generation Japanese born on United States soil, possessed of United States citizenship, have become 'Americanized', the racial strains are undiluted ... It therefore follows that along the vital Pacific Coast over 112,000 potential enemies of Japanese extraction are at large.[87]

This passage is quoted at length since it provides a clear statement of the motive behind the removal of Japanese Americans from the West Coast by the general authorized to implement the policy. Like the WRA arguments before the courts, this view is based upon an assumption about racial characteristics inherent in the Japanese race. Some factors influencing this opinion seem to have been that: Japanese Americans tended to live near strategic sites such as harbours; they had been discriminated against in the past and (it was suggested that) this might have given rise to some resentment; and the government of Japan operated a system of nationality which was seen as giving rise to 'dual citizenship'; all this was used to cast doubt on the loyalty

84 Irons, *Justice at war*, p. 492. 85 Robert Schaffer, 'Opposition to internment: defending Japanese American rights during World War II', Historian (Spring, 1999) http://www.findarticles.com/p/articles/mi_m2082/ is_3_61/ai_55426755 accessed on 16 August 2004. 86 He stated that, 'One obvious thought occurs to me – that every Japanese citizen or non citizen on the island of Oahu who meets these Japanese ships or has any connection with their officers or men should be secretly but definitely identified and his or her name placed on a special list of those who would be the first to be placed in a concentration camp in the event of trouble'. Irons, *Justice at war*, p. 7. 87 TenBroek et al., *Prejudice war*, p. 110. 88 Rostow, 'The Japanese American cases', 521.

of these individuals.[88] Some of these factors are more valid than others (for example, the residence of Japanese Americans near strategic sites), but this hardly justified the wholesale internment of an entire racial group. Furthermore, Italian and German Americans were treated differently. Here again the words of Gen. DeWitt are instructive:

> you needn't worry about the Italians at all except in certain cases. Also, the same for the Germans except in individual cases. But we must worry about the Japanese all the time until he is wiped off the map. Sabotage and espionage will make problems as long as he is allowed in this area – problems I don't want to have to worry about.[89]

This can only be described as racial prejudice.

The threat of Japanese sabotage was grossly overestimated. The best point of comparison is the period between Pearl Harbor and the introduction of restrictions on the Japanese community. Immediately following Pearl Harbor, known enemy sympathizers of Japanese and non-Japanese extraction were arrested. There were no reported incidents of sabotage by individuals of Japanese extraction in Hawaii or on the West Coast. By 1946 no resident of Japanese extraction had been convicted of sabotage or espionage.[90] One reason for this may have been that the authorities were capable of neutralizing any such threat due to their excellent intelligence. In March 1941, nine months before Pearl Harbor, US agents had seized a list of Japanese agents and sympathizers during a break-in at the Japanese consulate in Los Angeles.[91] As a result, the intelligence agencies had broken the Japanese espionage ring before President Roosevelt signed Executive Order 9906.[92] Despite this, a programme of mass internment was introduced.[93]

The authorities chose to intern an entire population rather than attempt to identify those who posed an actual risk. Therefore the action was racist and disproportionate. The control exercised over the Italian and German populations, coupled with the absence of an internment mechanism for Japanese Americans in Hawaii, illustrates that mass relocation and internment was not required. If the precedent of *Ex parte Milligan* had been applied, this outcome could have been avoided. The Civil Liberties Act, 1988, signed into law on 10 August 1988 by President Reagan, acknowledges the injustice of that relocation and internment and provides for restitution;[94] the compen-

89 Ibid., 532. 90 Ibid., 496/497. 91 Irons, *Justice at war*, p. 22. 92 Ibid., p. 23. 93 It seems likely that pubic opinion played a role in this. On 15 February 1942, for example, the *Washington Post* declared that, 'the Japanese in California should be under armed guard to the last man and woman right now – and to hell with *habeas corpus* until the danger is over'. Ibid., p. 61. 94 Department of Justice, 'Memorandum for Deval Patrick, Asst. Attorney General Civil Rights Division' (10 May, 1994), http://www.usdoj.gov/olc/14815mem.htm accessed on 16 August 2004. 95 Department of Justice 'Ten year program to compensate Japanese Americans interned

sation programme concluded in 1999 following the payment of $1.6 billion to more than 82,250 persons of Japanese ancestry.[95]

The story of American internment is recounted since it provides an interesting contemporaneous comparative. Despite the fact that the American model of internment was racist and illegitimate, the courts of the USA were unwilling to interfere with an executive involved in the prosecution of a war. The lack of judicial activism on behalf of the Irish Supreme Court was similarly accommodating toward the executive, but the result was less objectionable. In order to cement its position the Irish government introduced an emergency piece of legislation, covered by Article 28.3.3°, providing for the internment of Irish citizens,[96] a category that had been excluded from the jurisdiction of the Emergency Powers Act, 1939.[97] As emergency legislation, that Act was immune from judicial review under Article 28.3.3°. The government was now armed with two comprehensive internment powers.

4.6 The military tribunal

The last chapter detailed the circumstances in which special courts could be established. Article 38.3.1° of the Constitution allows for the establishment of Special Criminal Courts 'where it may be determined in accordance with law that the ordinary courts are inadequate to secure the effective administration of justice'. The Offences against the State Act, 1939 provides the legislative framework for this. However, as was noted in Chapter 2, Article 28.3.3° gives the government broad powers in 'time of war or armed rebellion'; it states that 'nothing in this Constitution shall be invoked to invalidate any law enacted by the Oireachtas which is expressed to be for the purposes of securing the public safety and the preservation of the state in time of war or armed rebellion'; so, this Article was available to the government if it wished to extend military rule to the civilian population during such a crisis. If it considered that the ordinary courts and the Special Criminal Court were not sufficient to cope with an emergency, it had the authority to establish a further 'emergency' court. This is precisely what it did. De Valera explained its position when he stated that the IRA

> will not be allowed to continue their policy of sabotage ... The law will be enforced against them. If the present law is not sufficient, it will be strengthened; and in the last resort, if no other law will suffice, then the government will invoke the ultimate law – the safety of the people.[98]

during World War II closes its doors' (19 February, 1999), http://www.usdoj.gov/opa/pr/1998/June/276.htm.html accessed on 16 August 2004. **96** The Emergency Powers (Amendment) Act, 1940. **97** The Emergency Powers Act, 1939, s.2(k). **98** Fanning, '"The rule of order": Eamon de Valera & the IRA 1923–1940', in O'Carroll & Murphy (eds), *De Valera & his times*, (1983), pp 160–72 at p. 170. **99** Ibid., p. 169.

In the circumstances, the OSA, 1939 'was deemed to be inadequate to meet the menace of war in Europe in which the Irish government was determined to keep Ireland neutral'.[99] Therefore, a military tribunal was introduced.

It is, at first, difficult to identify the inadequacies of the Special Criminal Court that necessitated such a development. The members of the court were, at the time, all officers of the Defence Forces,[1] and when the Military Tribunal was established it consisted of 'senior officers who were already members of the Special Criminal Court'.[2] Indeed, looking at its membership, it is impossible to differentiate between the Constitution (Special Powers) Tribunal, established under Article 2A of the old Constitution, the Special Criminal Court and the Military Tribunal.[3] The advantage, from a government standpoint, of the Military Tribunal was that it was not susceptible to judicial review. Article 28.3.3° ensured that the tribunal could act free from constitutional restraint. Unlike the Special Criminal Court, and earlier models, such as Article 2A,[4] discussed in the preceding chapters, there was no appeal from the decisions of this tribunal.[5] It would not be 'hampered and humiliated' by the courts.[6] The establishment of the tribunal was provided for by the Emergency Powers (Amendment) (No. 2) Act, 1940. S.2(5) of the parent act, the Emergency Powers Act, 1939, had expressly prohibited 'the making of provision for the trial by court martial of persons not being subject to military law'. However, the 1940 Act amended this and s.3 stated that 'the government may by an order under s.2 of the principle Act make provision for the trial, in summary manner, by commissioned officers of the Defence Forces'.[7] The Military Court was established by the Emergency Powers (No. 41) Order, 1940.

The EPA and the Military Court established by it have attracted more than their fair share of comment and criticism. The trial and punishment of offenders provided for were more stringent than those in the British equivalent upon which it was modelled,[8] and the court itself has been described as 'curious and sinister';[9] when a brief examination of its operations are conducted it is not entirely difficult to understand why. A striking example can be found in the form of the Emergency Powers Orders (Nos. 41F and 139), 1941 which,

1 Department of An Taoiseach, file S11387B, Memoranum for government – Department of Defence, dated 3 November 1951. 2 Hogan & Whyte, *Kelly*, para. 6.5.351. 3 Department of An Taoiseach, file S11387B, para. 11(4). 4 It will be recalled that initially there was an attempt to prevent appeal from the Constitution (Special Powers) Tribunal to the ordinary courts. However, in *The State (Hughes) v. Lennon* [1940] IR, 128, 142, the court reaffirmed that that tribunal was an inferior court subject to review. 5 O'Halpin, *Defending Ireland*, p. 202. 6 Department of An Taoiseach file S2979, 'Inter-departmental committee on the Constitution, note with special reference to Article 2A', by Mr Roche (Justice) signed and dated 16/6/34 (that is 16 June 1934). 7 Hogan & Whyte, *Kelly*, para. 6.5.351. 8 Fanning, '"The rule of order"', p. 168.

made huge inroads on the ordinary laws of evidence; unsigned statements, by persons who were not called to give evidence in Court, were admissible, and the Court, if it considered it 'proper that it should not be bound by any rule of evidence, whether statutory or at common law', was not to be bound by any such rule.[10]

These are considerable deviations from the established laws of evidence and give a worrying amount of discretion to a court staffed entirely by members of the Defence Forces. It is important to consider that the law has long distrusted *accomplice* evidence due to their perceived lack of credibility.[11] These Orders go even further and allow for *anonymous statements* with no requirement that the author of such statements stand over them in court. Two key cases will illustrate the workings of this 'curious and sinister' beast.

4.7 In *re McGrath & Harte*[12] and *The State (Walsh) v. Lennon*[13]

Patrick McGrath must have seemed like a source of unending trouble to Eamon de Valera. His hunger strike and release were commented upon earlier. McGrath was then involved in the murder of two Gardaí and was sentenced, by the Military Court, to death by shooting. The subsequent court case, In *re McGrath & Harte*, was the first case arising from a conviction before the Military Tribunal. Furthermore, it was Gavan Duffy J, of *Burke*, who granted a conditional stay of execution; however, he did so only because of the imminence of the sentence. He stated that he could not 'in a capital case, without seeing the text of the two vital Orders, make the grave assumptions against the condemned men involved in blindly taking for granted the contents of the two Orders as justifying the departure from the ordinary law'.[14] In *Burke,* Justice Gavan Duffy had displayed a degree of sympathy and a willingness to make unpopular decisions; in *McGrath & Harte,* however, he showed no such leniency. The court rejected a series of technical arguments. Initially it was argued that the President had signed the first amendment to the Constitution contrary to Article 25 which provides that the President shall sign an amendment 'not earlier than the fifth and not later than the seventh day after the date on which the bill shall have been presented to him'.[15] This argument was rejected, as was the contention that the President had an obligation to consult the Council of State.[16] The court, similarly, dismissed an argument based on the logic that the Emergency Powers (No. 41) Order, 1940 'could not operate in respect of offences alleged to have been

9 Kelly, *Fundamental rights*, p. 274. 10 Hogan & Whyte, *Kelly*, para. 6.5.352. 11 Wigmore, *A treatise on the Anglo-American system of evidence in trials at common law* (1940), vol. 17, p. 2056. 12 [1941] IR, 68. 13 [1942] IR, 112. 14 [1941] IR, 68, 70. 15 Bunreacht na hÉireann, Article 25.2.1°. 16 [1941] IR, 68, 72. 17 Kelly, *Fundamental rights*, p. 276, see also, Sullivan CJ [1941] IR, 68, 77. 18 [1941] IR, 68, 73.

committed before the making of the Order'.[17] The learned High Court judge stated categorically that Article 28 made it 'impossible for this Court to invalidate either the committal order or orders 41 and 41A'.[18] This position was not surprising since, in *Burke*, he had noted that 'the legal position would be different were I concerned with a war measure ... under Article 28'.[19] When faced with such a situation Gavan Duffy J was true to his word. McGrath and Harte were shot in Dublin, by firing squad, on 6 September 1940.[20]

The Emergency Powers Orders (Nos. 41F and 139), 1941, were also central to the case of *Walsh*. The detail provides the real points of interest in this case. The trial of the accused had begun in the Special Criminal Court when the prosecution entered a *nolle prosequi* against each of the accused.[21] At this point the government made two Orders, namely Emergency Powers Orders (No. s 41F and 139), 1941. Following this the trial of Walsh proceeded before the Military Court. As counsel for the prisoners noted, 'the procedure followed meant that if a criminal case in which the state was interested was at trial "the trial might be stopped and the law changed and the accused brought to trial under the altered law"'.[22] Such a procedure is undoubtedly a cause for concern. Although the case established no new law as to the effect of entering a *nolle prosequi*, it is remarkable in that it was the first case where having entered a *nolle prosequi* after the case had begun, the attorney general then attempted to prosecute the same individuals on the same charge.[23]

The court recognized that the Orders in question were 'a radical departure from the recognized rules of procedure'.[24] However, it felt it had no option but to uphold the convictions. The executive was granted a wide discretion and Gavan Duffy J, who had been so strong-willed in *Burke*, meekly stated that

> in time of war or armed rebellion apprehension of judicial intervention may at some delicate moment hamper the legislative or executive authority when government needs all the possible strength and freedom to steer the ship of state through the crisis, consequently the Constitution has placed in the hands of the Oireachtas, as law-giver, special authority to suspend judicial control over the other organs of government during any emergency.[25]

Given his earlier heroics, this judgment may be a disappointment. However, as we have seen, such a position was, in fact, consistent with his approach in *Burke* and *In re McGrath & Harte*.

19 (1940) 74 *ILTR*, 36,45. **20** Kelly, *Fundamental* rights, p. 276. **21** [1942] IR, 112, 112. **22** Kelly, *Fundamental rights*, p. 277. **23** 'Prosecution on the same charge after entering a nolle prosequi, *The State (Walsh) v. Lennon*' (1942) 6 *Journal of Criminal Law*, 205. **24** [1942] IR, 112, 118. **25** Ibid., 118.

4.8 In time of war or armed rebellion

'Both the High Court and Supreme Court had no difficulty in holding that by virtue of Article 28.3.3° their jurisdiction to interfere with acts of government or of the military court appointed by the government under emergency legislation was completely ousted.'[26] Thus, the government and its Military Court were free from judicial control and there was no possibility of another embarrassing *Burke* case. As we have seen, the unwillingness to interfere with the executive during a time of war was by no means limited to the Irish judiciary. It could be argued that, although the Irish judiciary was unwilling to interfere it was at least willing to openly consider the issues.

Unlike the Special Criminal Court, which was bound by the criminal law,[27] the Military Court was free to act as it saw fit. Given this freedom from appeal and its exceptional powers, it is unsurprising that it achieved an impressive conviction rate as table 4.1 illustrates

Table 4.1
Acquittals before the Military Court, 1940–1943[28]

Year	*Number of persons tried*	*Number of persons found* not *guilty*
1940	3	-
1941	4	2
1942	5	1
1943	1	1
Total	13	4

The relatively small numbers involved are noteworthy for two reasons: firstly they ensure that no firm statistical conclusions can be drawn; and secondly, they illustrate that, despite its considerable powers, the Military Court was not being widely utilized; in fact the court sat for last time in 1943.[29] Despite being subject to the minor irritation of judicial review and an appeals mechanism, the Special Criminal Court was just as capable of coping with the emergency as the Military Court was. In 1943, for example, 106 people were tried before the Special Criminal Court with only nine acquittals.[30]

26 Kelly, *Fundamental rights*, p. 277. 27 *The State (Walsh) v. Lennon*, [1942] IR, 112, 121. 28 Dáil Éireann, *Parliamentary Debates*, 11 July 1946, vol. 102, col. 610. 29 *Committee to Review the Offences against the State Acts, 1939–1998*, para. 4.26. 30 Dáil Éireann, *Parliamentary Debates*, 11 July 1946, vol. 102, col. 609.

4.9 The Special Criminal Court, 1939–46

When the then Minister for Justice, Patrick J. Ruttledge, introduced the OAS Bill, 1939, he made it clear that the measure was being sought in response to a subversive threat. Speaking in the Dáil he stated that

> as to the necessity for the bill I do not think there is anybody in the House who is not conversant with things which have arisen in the recent past which showed the necessity for dealing with a situation such as we recognize has now arisen … As Deputies are aware, a proclamation was issued, on 8 December last, by a certain body which purported to hand over what it maintained it held, that is, certain government functions. It described itself as a government and it purports, under that proclamation, to hand over to the Irish Republican Army, as they call it, those functions of government. That is a position which the government is not going to tolerate.[31]

This passage provides an insight into the role envisaged for the Special Criminal Court. The OAS, 1939 is clearly portrayed as being a response to the threat to national security posed by the IRA proclamation. It is, therefore, reasonable to assume that its provisions would be directed against subversives. Indeed, the Minister made it clear that the cases to be dealt with by the Special Criminal Court were 'offences that relate to armed intimidation and to violent means'.[32] The court was not, however, directed solely against subversives.

Between 1939 and 1946 the court handled a range of offences, from black marketeering to murder.[33] It is important to recall that the 'jurisdiction of the Special Criminal Court is restricted to the offences in relation to which the government is satisfied that the ordinary courts are inadequate to secure the effective administration of justice'.[34] In December 1942 the Taoiseach, Minister for Justice and Supplies and the attorney general,

> agreed in principle that grave breaches of the Emergency Powers Orders in black market cases or where such cases disclosed a deep seated conspiracy, the proceedings should be taken before the Special Criminal Court. As far as possible all other similar breaches of a less serious kind should be prosecuted in the District Court. The unsuitability of the Circuit Court for this type of case was appreciated.[35]

31 Dáil Éireann, *Parliamentary Debates*, 8 February 1939, vol. 74, col. 90. 32 Dáil Éireann, *Parliamentary Debates*, 2 March 1939, vol. 74, col. 1290. 33 Kelly, *Fundamental rights*, p. 278. 34 *The People (DPP) v. Quilligan* [1986] IR 495, 506, *per* Walsh J. 35 Department of An Taoiseach, file S13069, Attorney General's Office, memorandum to Mr M Moynihan, dated 22 December, 1942, signed P.P. O'Donoghue.

This raises a number of important points. Firstly, it is clear that following this meeting official policy was that the Special Criminal Court was a suitable venue for trials of a non-subversive nature, yet the Dáil was never informed of this important shift in policy. True, the focus is on serious black market cases, but there is, nonetheless, a shift from the original position as outlined by Ruttledge. Secondly, the venues identified as suitable for black market cases are the Special Criminal Court and District Court, the Circuit Court being specifically recognized as unsuitable; the only explanation for this is a desire to avoid trial by jury.

Black market cases were to form the core of the court's business. I have identified six cases tried before the court during the period which were later appealed to the Court of Criminal Appeal;[36] five of these relate to black market trading. The offences range from the export of watches without a licence, in *The People (AG) v. Shribman & Samuels*,[37] to the sale and distribution of tea, flour and other commodities in *The People (AG) v. O'Conor & O'Reilly*.[38] In 1946, Minister for Justice, G Boland, provided a more detailed account of the offences tried before the Special Criminal Court – these figures are set out in table 4.2:

Table 4.2
Number of persons proceeded against & classification of offences, 1939 – 23 October 1946[39]

Classification of offence	*No. of Persons*	
	Proceeded against	*Convicted*
A	42	34
B	158	141
C	42	39
Total	242	214

As the minister explained, Class A consisted of 'security offences', including 'unlawful possession of a wireless transmitting apparatus, landing or disembarking at a place other than an approved seaport or airport, interference with the military or police, unauthorized possession of military information, etc.' The largest categories, Class B and Class C offences, could be described as black market cases. Class B covered the breach of 'various Orders concerned with the maintenance of essential supplies and services'; particular reference is made to rationing offences. Class C offences consist of

36 This review involved an examination of Frewen, *Judgments of the Court of Criminal Appeal 1924–1978*, (1983). 37 [1946] IR 431. 38 Unreported judgment, 26 July 1943, see also Frewen, *Judgments of the Court of Criminal Appeal*, p. 42. 39 Dáil Éireann, *Parliamentary Debates*, 23 October 1946, vol. 103, Table 1, cols. 163–64.

cases involving the unlawful trade of gold, currency, watches and similar items.[40]

Although the court was established to tackle a subversive threat, it soon evolved into a suitable venue for the prosecution of economic offences. To understand this it is important to remember that 'rationing was the essential method of alleviating the worst consequences of scarcity'.[41] In times of crisis, the equitable distribution of scarce resources can be an important element in the maintenance of public order. Furthermore, although the files do not explicitly refer to this difficulty, the accepted unsuitability of the Circuit Court, and thereby of trial by jury, may have been due to difficulty in persuading juries to convict in such cases. In 1974 Robinson commented that the possibility that individuals not associated with unlawful organizations could be tried by this extraordinary court was a 'serious allegation, in that it amounts to an erosion of the right to trial by jury'.[42] Serious and all as the allegation may be, it has happened, and the possibility of such trials were contemplated and approved by the Taoiseach, Minister for Justice and Supplies and the AG. The importance of tea and flour may not be apparent at this remove, but, arguably, it was necessary to try such cases before the Special Criminal Court in order to 'secure the effective administration of justice'.[43]

4.10 The procedures of the Special Criminal Court

A significant factor in the early development of the Special Criminal Court was its departure from the standard rules, and the willingness of the ordinary courts to accommodate it. It has already been noted that the ordinary courts offered little resistance to the Military Court (Article 28.3.3° prevented such interference). The Special Criminal Court, on the other hand, was said to be 'bound by the criminal law'.[44] Notwithstanding this, the ordinary courts were very accommodating towards it, as is apparent from a number of cases where the uncorroborated evidence of an accomplice was admitted, such as in *The People (AG) v. Shribman & Samuels*[45] and in *The People (AG) v. Mazure.*[46] In the past 'judges have uniformly told juries that they ought not to pay any respect to the testimony of an accomplice unless the accomplice is corroborated in some material particular'.[47] Although juries did have the power to convict on the basis of uncorroborated accomplice evidence there exists a 'very strong, indeed, imperative, rule of practice that the judge should warn

40 Ibid., 163. 41 Murphy, *Ireland in the twentieth century*, p. 104. 42 Robinson, *The Special Criminal Court*, (1974), p. 35. 43 Later chapters will return to the theme of the court's use in non-subversive cases. For now it should be noted that this has been a point of controversy over the years and it is interesting that the issue first arose so early in the court's development. 44 *The State (Walsh) v. Lennon* [1942] IR 112, 121. 45 [1946] IR 431. 46 [1946] IR 448. 47 Wigmore, *A treatise on the Anglo-American system*, p. 2056.

the jury of the danger'.[48] In the Special Criminal Court, the judge (a member of the Defence Forces without legal qualifications) would presumably warn himself and his colleagues. Despite these difficulties, the use of this evidence was sanctioned by the ordinary courts. . In *Shribman* the appeal court argued that 'it was not too much to assume that [the Special Criminal Court] . . . has a correct understanding of the legal position on this troublesome point',[49] and in doing so completely ignored the lack of legal expertise on the bench.

The case law displays another even more worrying fact. In *Mazure,* 'the only witness, Philip Kay, who gave evidence . . . not only was not corroborated, but was himself *awaiting sentence* for a similar offence to that with which the applicant was charged'.[50] The Court of Criminal Appeal recognized the importance of this extra factor; it was said to render 'it *more than usually dangerous* to act on this evidence'.[51] It has been argued that 'an accomplice against whom proceedings are pending must not, as a matter of practice, be called on behalf of the prosecution unless it is made plain that the proceedings will be discontinued'.[52] In *Mazure* the evidence of a convicted person who was awaiting sentence *was* called; and despite the dangers of such evidence, which was apparent to the appeal court, the conviction was allowed to stand. The Court of Criminal Appeal stated that 'it would have been wiser for the Special Criminal Court to have sentenced Kay before he gave his evidence in this case. No authority, however, has been cited to us to support the view that his evidence was inadmissible.'[53] In 2003 the evidence of David Rupert was central to the conviction of Michael McKevitt. Rupert's evidence was controversial because he 'was paid $1.25 million (£773,000) by the FBI'.[54] The issues are largely similar, the concern being that the evidence was unreliable because an incentive had been given. In Rupert's case he had been paid; in *Mazure,* the possibility of a reduced sentence in return for 'good' evidence existed. It is unsettling that such evidence was accepted by the Special Criminal Court and that the ordinary courts were willing to allow the conviction stand.[55]

Other procedural irregularities can also be identified. In *The People (AG) v. Kerins,*[56] the initial transcript to the proceedings provided to the Court of Criminal Appeal was incomplete. The missing sections concerned an address by the prosecution to the court; this address was the subject of one of the defence grounds for appeal; the situation was later rectified. On the

48 *The People (AG) v. Duffy* [1931] IR 144, 149. 49 [1946] IR 431, 444. 50 [1946] IR 448, 449. 51 Ibid. 52 Tapper, *Cross & Tapper on evidence* (1995), p. 245. 53 [1946] IR 448, 449. 54 Harding, 'The butcher of Omagh faces life: families hail Real IRA conviction', *Daily Telegraph,* 7 August, 2003. This amount corresponds to approximately €1,035,000. 55 In McKevitt's case the payment had already been received which is somewhat preferable to the circumstances in *Mazure*. Further consideration will be given to the McKevitt trial in later chapters. It was merely raised here for the purpose of comparison. 56 [1945] IR 339, 343–44.

substantive issue of the address, the appeal court appears to have been quite obliging; it held that 'an address, delivered in such circumstances, was addressed to the Court as a tribunal of law' not a tribunal of fact, and as such the address was acceptable.[57] The difficulty here is that the three judges constitute both the tribunal of fact and the tribunal of law; therefore applying rules designed for trial by jury to such circumstances can at times appear somewhat incongruous.

A series of cases called the military nature of the court into question but to little avail. In *In re MacCurtain* it was pointed out that the court 'sat in a military barracks and was composed solely of officers of the Defence Forces'.[58] The argument was rejected. Gavan Duffy J declared that 'the fact that provisions is made for the setting up of military tribunals in another section of the Constitution ... cannot fairly be used to cut down the express power which the Constitution gives to the Oireachtas to create special courts and prescribe their constitution by law'.[59] Sullivan CJ went so far as to claim that, despite the similarity in personnel, the Special Criminal Court was 'a tribunal quite distinct from the Military Tribunal'.[60] A variation on this theme also failed in *Kerins*, where it was argued that the lack of legal training on the part of the officers who constituted the Special Criminal Court meant that they might be swayed by the prosecutor's address in a way that lawyers would not. The Court of Criminal Appeal was unimpressed. It stated:

> we would like to point out that the fact that the Court in this particular case was so composed is an accidental circumstance which cannot govern the matter. Under the Act, a Special Criminal Court may consist entirely of High Court judges and the same ruling must apply to all Special Criminal Courts, however constituted.[61]

It is difficult to argue with the Court of Appeal in terms of the law. The OAS, 1939 does allow the Special Criminal Court to be constituted entirely of High Court judges, and the Constitution did allow the Oireachtas stipulate the make-up of the court. However, the judgment appears naïve in the extreme; to describe the make-up of the court as an accidental circumstance, and the failure to acknowledge the realities of the situation is unfortunate.

There are examples of the ordinary courts being more stringent in their approach to the Special Criminal Court. In *The People (AG) v. Kennedy*[62] the Court of Criminal Appeal returned a more favourable verdict. The case involved a relatively technical argument concerning the status of Emergency Powers Orders. The court held that these Orders did not possess the same

57 [1945] IR 339, 350. **58** [1941] IR 83, 83. **59** Ibid., 85–6. **60** Ibid., 90. **61** [1945] IR 339, 350. **62** [1946] IR, 517.

authority in law as a statute and, therefore, it was necessary that they be proved in court. Although copies of the Orders had been produced by the prosecution, they had not been formally proved.[63] Furthermore, in asking that his client be acquitted at trial, Kennedy's solicitor had specifically pointed to the fact that the Orders had not been proved.[64] On the basis of this technical objection, the conviction was set aside by the Court of Criminal Appeal and the Supreme Court refused to hear an appeal by the AG against the acquittal. There are a number of points of note in the case. Firstly, the appeal court was highly distinguished, consisting, as it did, of Chief Justice Sullivan, the President of the High Court, Maguire P, and Devitt J. Also, consideration appear to have been given to the fact that, although Kennedy was not represented by counsel at trial, his solicitor had raised the objection during the original hearing and, therefore, there had been no unreasonable delay on the part of the defence.[65] Finally, the court noted that the Documentary Evidence Act, 1925 provided 'two very convenient methods of giving *prima facie* evidence' in support of the Orders, and it viewed it as regrettable that the prosecution had failed to employ these.[66] The case of *White*[67] concerned an appeal against a conviction for the murder of a Detective Garda. In *In re McGrath & Harte* the accused were sentenced to death by shooting. In *White*, the Court of Criminal Appeal overturned the conviction for murder on the facts, and substituted the lesser offence of manslaughter; a sentence of twelve years' penal servitude was imposed. These cases are cited as evidence that the Special Criminal Court was not free from review and that the ordinary courts did, on occasion, overturn its decisions on appeal.[68]

Although the Emergency officially continued until 1976[69] the wartime Special Criminal Court sat for the last time in December 1946.[70] The period 1939–1946 was central to the development of the court, and its impact has had a profound effect on the present-day institution.[71] Given the existence of broad powers of internment and a non-reviewable military tribunal where

63 Ibid. 64 Ibid., 519. 65 Ibid. 66 Ibid.,521. 67 *The People (AG) v. White* [1947] IR 247. 68 It is interesting to note that judgments of the appeal courts in both *Kennedy* and *White* were delivered after the end of WWII. In *Kennedy* the Court of Criminal Appeal delivered its judgment on 21 December 1945 and the Supreme Court heard the case in January 1946. *White* was considered by the Court of Criminal Appeal in January and February of 1947 although the shooting of Detective Garda Mordant, for which White had been convicted, occurred in October 1942. 69 *Committee to Review the Offences against the State Acts, 1939–1998*, para. 4.26, footnote 111. 70 However, as we shall see in the next chapter, the court was not in fact disestablished, which was to lead to some confusion. Department of An Taoiseach, file S11387 B, Department of Defence, Memorandum for the government. Members and registrar of the Special Criminal Court, dated 3 November, 1951. 71 In 1986, for example, the courts used the precedent of the black market cases to justify the trial of an individual not associated with an unlawful organization by the Special Criminal Court. See *The People (DPP) v. Quilligan* [1986] IR 495. Further consideration shall be given to these issues in subsequent chapters.

government and prosecutors could act in an unfettered manner, it is possibly disappointing the courts were not more wary of the Special Criminal Court. Significantly, the Military Court handled a mere thirteen cases and did not sit after 1943; it is pure speculation, but if the ordinary courts had engaged in a more robust examination of the Special Criminal Court they might have driven the executive to pursue more trials before the 'cruel and sinister' Military Court.

5

Whither the Special Criminal Court, 1946–1962?

The Special Criminal Court has been employed on three occasions. Firstly, it was extensively utilized during the Emergency, as was discussed in the last chapter. Most significantly, a government proclamation in 1972 created a Special Criminal Court which continues to exist to the present day (this will be examined in subsequent chapters). The court also operated for a brief few months in 1961 and 1962. It is unsurprising that the major development of the court occurred during its lengthier periods of service; however, the years 1946 to 1962 betray some features worthy of examination.

5.1 The Special Criminal Court and economic cases

We have already noted that when the Minister for Justice, introduced the Offences against the State Bill, 1939 in Dáil Éireann, he made it clear that the impetus behind the legislation was the subversive threat posed by the IRA.[1] In April 1947 the cabinet was informed that the Minister for Justice and Minister for Industry and Commerce were engaged in consultation concerning the future use of the Offences against the State Act (OAS), 1939 and the Special Criminal Court. The involvement of the Minister for Industry and Commerce confirms that the government now viewed the court as a suitable location for the prosecution of offences associated with rationing. In fact the ministers were scrutinizing the possibility of

> preparing legislation enabling offences, such as contraventions of the control and rationing of commodities, to be made scheduled offences for the purposes of Part V of the Offences against the State Act, 1939, in circumstances and subject to a procedure to be specified, without a declaration that the ordinary courts are inadequate to secure the effective administration of justice.[2]

It had been the practice since 1942 to issue a declaration that the ordinary courts were inadequate, and prosecute breaches of the Emergency Power Orders before the Special Criminal Court; ministers were now seeking to schedule these offences and thereby avoid having to make a declaration in

1 Dáil Éireann, *Parliamentary Debates,* 8 February 1939, vol. 74, col. 90. 2 Department of An Taoiseach, file S14068, Extract from cabinet minutes, G.C. 4/252, 25.4.1947, item 3, Pr Sec. M.I. & C., Finance, Justice advised 26/4/1947 (that is 26 April 1947).

each case. Rather than reducing the state's dependence upon the court in such situations, the government was, in effect, formalizing the practice.

While the AG recognized the need for swift prosecutions and severe penalties in rationing cases, he nevertheless opposed the use of the Special Criminal Court. He pointed out that the 'basis of resort to the Special Criminal Court is that the ordinary courts are inadequate to secure the effective administration of justice' and he suggested that 'the first cases … should be sent to the District Court with a request for a prompt hearing and that they should be prosecuted by Senior Counsel' who would press for severe sentences. Indeed, he argued that the 'injustice to the community' caused by such offences should be highlighted in order to ensure these severe penalties. Finally, he recommended that only if the District Court displayed an unwillingness to respond to the situation should the Special Criminal Court be utilized. He was of the opinion that 'conviction and severe sentences obtained in ordinary courts are less likely to be interfered with on appeal than convictions and sentences by the Special Criminal Court.'[3] This position would appear to be more acceptable than the scheduling of such offences. After all, as is implicit from the advice of the AG, the option of scheduling would remain available if the District Courts proved unwilling to impose severe sentences, and the method of transferring cases, as had been adopted from 1942 onwards, would still be available if the need arose.

The advice of the attorney general appears to have been influential and by October there seems to have been a consensus that it would be 'undesirable, if not dangerous to avail of … [the OAS, 1939] provisions for dealing with economic offences.'[4] Still, a further reference to the legislation occurs in November 1947; this time the responsibility for the matter is placed squarely upon the shoulders of the Minister for Industry and Commerce. Reference is again made to the AG's view that use of the OAS, 1939 for dealing with economic offences was undesirable. The memorandum suggests that, in light of that advice, the minister should reconsider the addition of the Control of Fuel Orders and Fuel Price Orders to the Schedule. The memorandum continues:

> if, however, the Minister considers that the existing practice in this regard should, nevertheless, be continued, he will no doubt, bring the view of the Attorney General on the matter to the notice of the government in the next submission being made by him [your

3 Department of An Taoiseach, file S14068, Department of the Attorney General, Dublin, to Mr Wiliams, signed Cearbhall Ó Dálaigh, Ard-Aighne. 4 Department of An Taoiseach, file S14068, Runai, Roinn an Taoisigh, signed M. Ó Muinneadhaigh, 6 October 1947. 5 Department of An Taoiseach, file S14068, An Runai, An Roinn Tionscail agus Trachtala, signed M. Ó Muimhneachain, 8 Deireadh Fomhair 1947 (that is 8 November, 1947).

> Department] to the government containing a proposal to add contraventions of any such Order to the Schedule to the Act of 1939.[5]

It is clear from the correspondence that the Minister for Industry and Commerce was the driving force behind these moves. Following the strongly worded advice of the AG the rest of government seems to have lost its appetite for these developments, and the measure was dropped.

The Minister for Industry and Commerce's desire to employ the Special Criminal Court in economic cases must be placed in context. The court had been available for such trials during the Emergency; furthermore, thanks to the position of the Taoiseach, the AG and the minister in 1942[6] there were controls on the nature of cases sent for trial before that court. The vast majority of black market cases were handled by the District Court. In 1945, for example, the District Court had disposed of some 1,500 prosecutions for breaches of the Emergency Powers Acts, while the Special Criminal Court had dealt with forty-two.[7] It is arguable that if the government felt it was necessary to continue to use Emergency Powers Orders, it should, also, have continued to employ the same trial procedures.

The period after the end of World War II was one of economic uncertainty. Although concerns that the mass return of Irish emigrants from Britain would spark social revolution never materialized, largely because 'British post-war reconstruction kept the potentially troublesome Irish emigrants in Britain',[8] other examples of social unrest were evident and the period saw bitter Labour disputes. Government refusal to meet the pay demands of national teachers resulted in a strike from March to October of 1946, and June 1947 was marked by a threatened strike at the country's flourmills. De Valera's handling of the flourmill dispute, meeting the leaders and so forth, has been described as flexible.[9] However, on 16 May 1947 the government decided 'as a matter of urgency' to amend the Protection of the Community (Special Powers) Act, 1926 in order to provide for 'the prohibition of a strike or lock-out of workers of any class; to prohibit any person from inciting, maintaining or subsidising such strike and to provide that, where a trade union is involved, a financial penalty may be imposed on the trade union funds'.[10] Such measures would have involved substantial interference with the right to assembly and would have greatly disrupted the trade union movement. This provision provides further evidence of the government's

6 Department of An Taoiseach, file S13069, Attorney general's Office, Memorandum to Mr M Moynihan, 22 December 1942, signed PP O'Donoghue. 7 Department of An Taoiseach, file S13069, Roinn an Taoisigh, Special Criminal Court, trial of offences against the Emergency Powers Acts, 26/6/46 (that is 26 June 1946). 8 Coogan, *De Valera,* p. 631. 9 Ibid., p. 636. 10 Attorney General's Office file 22/47, from Department of Industry and Commerce, to the Attorney General, signed (illegible), 17 May 1947.

readiness to impose drastic restrictions upon citizen's rights due to economic conditions within the state.

5.2 Who should pay for the Special Criminal Court?

Although the Special Criminal Court did not sit after 1946, the government spent much of 1947 discussing it and apparently viewed it as a living institution. In fact, the members of the Special Criminal Court were still being paid and the rates of remuneration were not reviewed until June 1948, a full eighteen months after the court last sat. The members of the court were paid £450 a year from August 1939 to August 1948, and £150 a year after 1 August 1948. The registrar of the court was paid 7*s.* 6*d.* a day, reduced in 1948 to 2*s.* 6*d.*; when Commandant Felly, the registrar of the court, retired from the Armed Forces he agreed to continue in the post of registrar and received £100 per annum for his services.[11] These seem substantial levels of payment for a court which was not, in actual fact, functioning. Astonishingly, the Minister for Justice was of the opinion that the members of the court had been badly treated when their rates of remuneration, which were additional to their army salaries, were reduced.[12] Unsurprisingly the Minister for Finance disagreed.

A second interesting development arose from the court's continued existence when some of its members retired. On 24 August 1939 the government appointed the following members: Colonel Francis Bennett; Colonel Daniel McKenna; Major John Vincent Joyce; Major Cornelius Whelan; and Major Patrick Tuite. Colonel McKenna was later promoted to the rank of Chief of Staff and was, at his own request, removed from the Special Criminal Court; he was replaced by Major Felix Devlin on 29 January 1940.[13] Colonel Bennett was retired from the Forces on 2 September 1949 and his degree of disability was adjudged, for pension purposes, to be 100 per cent. Colonel Tuite retired, on the grounds of age, in 1950.[14] Initially, the government assumed that, upon retiring, an officer ceased to be a member of the court, since he was no longer qualified as per s.39(3) of the OAS, 1939.[15] In June 1950, however, the AG stated the opinion that the retired officers were still members of the Special Criminal Court, and, therefore, the Minister was obliged to continue to pay them.[16] A debate as to the desirability

11 Department of An Taoiseach file S11387B, Department of Defence, 3 November 1951, Memorandum for the government, members and registrar of the Special Criminal Court, para. 5. **12** Ibid., para. 10. **13** Ibid., para. 3. **14** Ibid., para. 6. **15** Offences against the State Act, 1939, s. 39(3) states 'No person shall be appointed to be a member of a Special Criminal Court unless he is a judge of the High Court or the Circuit Court, or a justice of the District Court, or a barrister of not less than seven years' standing, or a solicitor of not less than seven years' standing, or an officer of the Defence Forces not below the rank of commandant'. **16** Department of An Taoiseach file S11387B, Department of Defence, 3, November, 1951, Memorandum for the government, members and registrar of the Special Criminal Court, para. 8.

of retaining the retired members of the court ensued.[17] Attention was drawn to the fact that Colonel Bennett, who was now deemed a member of the court, was also considered to have a 100 per cent disability. The situation was far from satisfactory.

Three separate views developed. As we have seen, the Minister for Justice was of the opinion that the members' salaries should not have been reduced in 1948. He also thought that the court should be retained and he saw no reason why an officer who retired should be removed from the court.[18] The Minister for Finance, naturally, opposed this view; he felt it was undesirable to have non-military personnel as members of the court, unless they satisfied the other criteria of s.39(3); and he expressed a particular objection to the retention of an ex-officer who was in receipt of a disability pension.[19] The final view was that of the Minister for Defence, who made an interesting observation,

> as all members and the registrar of the Court were officers of the Defence Forces, the expenses of the Court have ... been borne on the Vote for defence. If it is decided that the Court, which is really part of the civic judiciary, should have non-military members, the Minister for Defence considers that all matters affecting the Court should be taken over by the Department of Justice.[20]

There are a number of points to consider. Firstly, this was the first occasion that this court, or any court like it, had been staffed by non-military personnel. Admittedly this was not a cause for celebration, since it resulted in unqualified individuals staffing such an important institution. Secondly, the view of Defence, namely, that the court was part of the civic jurisdiction, is important. Although this argument was advanced in order to transfer the cost of the court to another department, it does merit serious examination. After all, the association of the court and Defence is a result, not only of its personnel, but also of its caseload. The court was originally envisaged as trying those suspected of committing violent subversive offences; it is understandable that Defence might have a role in such cases. However, from 1942 onwards the court became involved in economic as well as subversive cases and much of 1947 was spent discussing the possibility of increasing the court's use in black market cases. If the court was going to be staffed by non-military personnel and trying non-subversive cases, the Minister for Defence could surely argue that Justice and Industry and Commerce were more logical paymasters.

17 Ibid., para. 9. **18** Ibid., para. 12. **19** Ibid., para. 13. **20** Ibid., para. 14.

5.3 The 'normalization' of the Special Criminal Court

By 1945 the Minister for Justice, Gerald Boland, had announced that the IRA was dead;[21] therefore, the original rationale for employing the court (to combat the activities of subversives) no longer applied. The use of the court for black market cases can be described as a classic 'normalization effect': an emergency measure, introduced to deal with a specific threat, is utilized over time against a different group until it becomes normal to use it in this altered fashion. This normalization thesis is reinforced by the financial debate that arose in 1951. Some of the members of the court were no longer active members of the Defence Forces, and the court was no longer hearing subversive cases, nor was it contemplated that it should hear subversive cases; even so, the government did not disestablish the court. The Department of Defence, rather than calling for its abolition, simply asserted that this emergency institution was in fact part of the civic jurisdiction and should, therefore, be paid for out of the Justice vote. It is interesting that when in 1986 the Supreme court upheld the use of the OAS, 1939 in cases of a non-subversive character, it referred to the fact that, 'in the years during the late war and the years following it, the Special Criminal Court was frequently engaged in the trial of what were called "black market" cases'.[22] Thus, the court's use in economic cases set a precedent which still resounds today.

5.4 The rebirth of the IRA

The 1950s saw the re-emergence of the IRA which had been declared dead in 1945; however, hard-line republicanism continued to exist. In 1947 a new party, Clann na Poblachta, secured two out of three seats in bye-elections held on 29 October.[23] The following year that same party was to poll well and form part of the first inter-party government.[24] 'Clann na Poblachta ... presented itself as a seriously "republican" party, spiced up with a liberal dash of social and economic reform'.[25] The party was described by the *Irish Times* as representing 'something new, although its declared policy is as old as Sinn Féin, and its economic programme scarcely deserves to be taken seriously'.[26] The founder and leader of the highly successful Clann na Poblachta was Seán MacBride, leading senior counsel and former chief of staff of the IRA, who, in 1937, had accepted the new Constitution and declared that the IRA had no further role.[27] Although MacBride, and the Clann, were no longer associated in any way with the IRA, they did represent a form of republicanism recog-

21 J. Bowyer Bell, *The secret army: the IRA* (Dublin), p. 235. 22 *The People (DPP) v. Quilligan* [1986] IR 495, *per* Walsh J. 23 E. MacDermott, *Clann na Poblachta,* (1998), p. 52. 24 Clann na Poblachta, gained ten seats and went on to form a coalition government with Fine Gael, Clann na Talmhan, Labour, National Labour and eleven independent TDs. MacDermott, *Clann na Poblachta,* pp 64–7. 25 MacDermott, *Clann na Poblachta*, p. 102. 26 Ibid.,p. 62. 27 Patterson, *The politics of illusion*, p. 81.

nizable to that organization: 'the initial success of Clann na Poblachta encouraged the remnants of the IRA … to equip themselves with a political arm by re-establishing the link with Sinn Féin – by taking over the moribund organization'.[28] Thus the success of this constitutional, yet 'serious' republican party, encouraged the IRA to reorganize Sinn Féin. This reorganization preceded the IRA's resurgence.[29] The link is established by Patterson who comments that, 'for many like … [Thomás] MacGiolla, enthused and mobilized in 1949–50 and observing the lack of results from the campaign of the constitutional parties, membership of Sinn Féin was a natural progression, as was support for the armed assault on Northern Ireland'.[30] The first step in the rebuilding of the IRA was the reorganization of Sinn Féin; however, when that party failed to deliver a united Ireland it was predictable that matters would escalate.

A further point in the development of the IRA was to arise from the policies of the newly elected inter-party government. It will be recalled that during the 1930s the de Valera government went about the piecemeal destruction of the Free State Constitution. Much to the frustration of de Valera, the IRA did not accept the new 1937 Constitution as legitimate and escalated their activities with a bombing campaign on mainland Britain. After de Valera's reforms of the Free State Constitution, including the External Relations Act, 1936 and even the adoption of the new Constitution in 1937, Ireland was left in a somewhat ambiguous constitutional position vis-à-vis Great Britain and the Commonwealth. This position, or more accurately lack of a position, was derisively referred to as the 'dictionary republic' and was generally felt to be unacceptable.[31] In similar fashion to Fianna Fáil in the 1930s, Fine Gael hoped that 'the adoption of a clear-cut constitutional position might satisfy republicans and "take the gun out of politics"'.[32] Given the earlier rebuff to de Valera, this view appears extraordinarily naïve.

Ignoring the lessons of history, the inter-party government pursued a policy of repealing the External Relations Act, 1936 and declaring a Republic.[33] The Republic of Ireland Act, 1948 came into force on Easter Monday, 1949;[34] shortly thereafter the Minister for External Affairs, Seán

28 Ibid., p. 86. 29 Murphy, *Ireland in the twentieth century*, p. 128. 30 Patterson, *The politics of illusion*, pp 88–9. 31 Murphy, *Ireland in the twentieth century*, p. 125. 32 Ibid., p. 125. 33 In truth to say that the government pursued a policy may be an overstatement. The Taoiseach, Costello while touring Canada announced that Ireland was to leave the Commonwealth. There is no record of the cabinet having agreed in advance to that announcement and there is some dispute as to whether or not the cabinet had, in fact, agreed to it. Furthermore it appears that he felt pressured into the announcement following an article in the *Sunday Independent* stating that the government was about to repeal the 1936 Act. Some evidence exists to suggest that MacBride was behind the story in the *Sunday Independent*. For a more in-depth analysis of the circumstances surrounding the declaration of a Republic see, MacDermott, *Clann na Poblachta*, chapter 7. 34 Easter Monday is, of course, a significant day in Irish republican calendar, associated as it is

MacBride, signed the Statute of the Council of Europe on behalf of Ireland.[35]

> Despite the enactment of the Republic of Ireland Act, 1948, which severed the last remaining constitutional and political link with Britain, and membership of the Council of Europe, which gave Ireland a voice in European affairs, the lull in IRA activities was merely a prelude to a resurgence of political violence.[36]

The response of the British government to these events was to guarantee that 'in no event will Northern Ireland or any part thereof cease to be a part of His Majesty's dominions and of the United Kingdom without the consent of the parliament of Northern Ireland'. Clann na Poblachta may have been a constitutional and republican party but, rather than bringing about a united Ireland, the policy of the inter-party government had made it less likely. This perceived failure of constitutional politics contributed to the 'natural progression' from Sinn Féin membership to support for an armed assault on Northern Ireland.[37]

5.5 The Border Campaign

As with Mark Twain, reports of the passing of the IRA had been greatly exaggerated.[38] On 3 June 1951, a raid was conducted on the Ebrington Territorial Barracks in Derry. A considerable haul of twenty Lee Enfield rifles, twenty Sten guns, two Brens, six BESA machine guns and ammunition was taken. Indeed the raid was so successful that the IRA had to release a statement to the press before the British army and RUC were even aware that it had taken place.[39] Between 1951 and 1954 the IRA conducted a series of similar raids, mainly focusing on British army installations in Northern Ireland;[40] still the 'Border Campaign' proper is considered to have begun in 1956 and was to continue until 1962 (it is argued that 'within less than a year of its launch the border campaign had clearly failed ... yet it dragged on').[41]

The Border Campaign was a source of serious disruption, though it has been argued that it did not truly disrupt normal life and did not constitute a 'threat to the life of the nation'. Indeed, the lord mayor of Dublin, at the time, stated that 'there has been for many years now a complete absence of public

with the Proclamation of Easter Monday 1916. The choice of this day for the coming into force of the Republic of Ireland Act, 1949, is further evidence of the government's desire to portray this development as the natural conclusion of republican desires. 35 Doolan, *Lawless v. Ireland*, p. 2. 36 Ibid., pp 28–9. 37 Patterson, *The politics of illusion*, p. 88–9. 38 Mark Twain, *New Journal*, 2 June 1897. See N. Sherrin (ed.), *The Oxford dictionary of humorous quotations* (1995), p. 89. 39 Bell, *The secret army*, pp 250–1. 40 for a detailed account of these events see Bell, *The secret army*, pp 253–73. 41 Patterson, *The politics of illusion*, p. 89.

disorder, riots, civil commotion or other grave disturbances of the public peace arising out of political issues of any nature'.[42] In Northern Ireland, however, a total of six members of the RUC were murdered and a further thirty members of the RUC and Ulster Special Constabulary were injured between 1956 and 1962.[43] Department of Justice files reveal the level of disorder:

> Illegal meetings, parades, drilling and practice with arms, etc., went on frequently throughout 1956 but it was not until November that any serious incident took place involving the use of firearms or explosives in which 26-County activists were involved. Then an attempt was made to blow up the Gough Monument, Phoenix Park, and several British customs huts on the Border were blown up. A month later, (on December 12) ... a series of armed attacks on RUC. barracks and military posts, etc., in the Six Counties ... [were launched].[44]

The 12 December 1956 raids referred to involved 150 men in attacks on ten targets;[45] 1957 saw some 340 incidents in Northern Ireland and was the busiest year of the campaign.[46] The Brookeborough raid on 1 January 1957 resulted in the deaths of Seán South and Feargal O'Hanlon, who became republican martyrs within a week.[47] In the elections of 1957 Sinn Féin, contesting their first election since 1927, succeeded in winning four Dáil seats, which, in line with party policy, they refused to take.[48] The possibility that attacks would be launched on Northern Ireland from the South had been a source of real concern during the Emergency; the reality of such attacks during the 1950s caused a great deal of tension between Britain and Ireland. The situation could not be allowed to deteriorate any further.[49]

Although the IRA and likeminded republicans did not approve of Clann na Poblachta's approach, the party's continued existence was potentially beneficial to them. Clann's success had encouraged the IRA to reorganize Sinn Féin, and the revitalization of that party had led to a resurgence in the IRA itself. Furthermore, a sympathetic republican party in government might be worth its weight in (green, white and) gold. 'The participation of

42 Doolan, *Lawless v Ireland*, p. 38. 43 Sir John Hermon, *Holding the line: an autobiography* (1997), p. 45. 44 The words 'This was the work partly of "Saor Uladh", a Six-County body which was acting jointly with a "splinter group" of the IRA from the 26-Counties' and 'so called "Official IRA"' have been struck through in the original file. It is, however, an interesting recognition, both of the cross border cooperation which existed in republican circles during the campaign, and of the split in the IRA. See Department for Justice, file JUS 8/1040 'Dáil Motion for release of Offences-against-the-State-Prisoners, notes for minister's speech' undated, though it appears to be from late 1957. 45 Patterson, *The politics of illusion*, p. 91. 46 Hermon, *Holding the line*, p. 37. 47 Bell, *The secret army*, p. 299. 48 Murphy, *Ireland in the twentieth century*, p. 138. 49 Ibid., p. 300.

Clann na Poblachta in "Free State" politics alienated republican sentiment while the presence of republicans in government made firm handling of the IRA difficult.'[50] The influence of Clann is evident from the inter-party government's attempts to play down the significance of the IRA. The events of 12 December 1956, however, forced it to react. On 6 January 1957 the Taoiseach, John A. Costello, promised that action would be taken against the IRA.[51] Groups existed, he claimed, that were willing to defy the authority of the government and the Dáil; these groups set Irishmen against Irishmen; it was the government's duty to protect the people from the 'evils which followed when men take the law into their own hands'.[52] Any such government crackdown created a difficulty for Clann na Poblachta, since the association of Clann and republicanism made their position in government untenable. Such links were not merely ideological. Liam Kelly, a Senator appointed by the Taoiseach at the behest of MacBride, led a raid on the Roslea RUC barracks.[53] On 29 January 1957, MacBride and his party withdrew their support from the inter-party government.[54]

The general election of 1957 is one of the critical events in twentieth-century Irish history. Although not directly relevant to this book, it is interesting that Clann na Poblachta were essentially wiped out, losing two of their remaining three seats. Having burst onto the scene in 1946, and been viewed by many as a possible source of rejuvenation on the Irish political landscape, they were gone within a decade.[55] Sinn Féin, in this, their first election since 1927, secured four seats. This success can be attributed to the party's 'commitment to a radical social policy in a period of economic crisis as well as support for the border campaign'.[56] This combination of a radical social policy and republican values had been the cornerstone of the Clann na Poblachta manifesto ten years earlier; Sinn Féin, who had been reorganized following Clann's success, were now imitating that party's overall strategy. A significant difference between the parties was that Sinn Féin Deputies would not take their seats. O'Leary notes that because the IRA campaign had aroused some sympathy with the electorate, 'both Fianna Fáil and Fine Gael tried to avoid the delicate problem of what policy to adopt in regard to the IRA after the election'.[57] In the end the significant victors were Fianna Fáil, who, despite avoiding a definite policy on the Border Campaign, gained a total of seventy-seven of the 147 seats and an overall majority in Dáil Éireann.[58] The only question remaining was: how would they approach the IRA?

From January 1957 onwards, in an effort to thwart the IRA, attempts were

50 Murphy, *Ireland in the twentieth century*, p. 137. 51 Cornelius O'Leary, *Irish elections 1918–1977: parties, voters & proportional representation* (1979), p. 44. 52 Doolan, *Lawless v. Ireland*, p. 31. 53 Coogan, *De Valera*, p. 669. The Roslea raid took place on 27 January 1961 see Bell, *The secret army*, p. 331. 54 O'Leary, *Irish elections*, p. 44. 55 Lee, *Ireland, 1912–1985*, p. 327. 56 Ibid., p. 327. 57 O'Leary, *Irish elections*, p. 44. 58 Lee, *Ireland, 1912–1985*, p. 327.

made to prosecute individuals for membership of an unlawful organization or failing to give an account of their movements. 'Regrettably, the maximum punishment for such offences was two years' imprisonment on indictment, or six months in prison if – as often happened – they were treated as summary offences. They had, therefore, little, if any, deterrent effect on committed IRA activists.'[59] On 20 March 1957, when the new Fianna Fáil administration

> came into office there were fifty-three Offences-Against-the-State-prisoners under sentence in Mountjoy Prison ... By the month of July, 1957 103 men had been committed by the District Court to serve terms of imprisonment, ranging from up to six months, for Offences-Against-the-State-activities ... Forty-one of these men had served their sentences, however, *and were again at large* and almost all were known to be making preparations to resume their activities. Within a month or so the sentences of all but two of the sixty-two men still serving sentences in Mountjoy would have expired.[60]

De Valera's new government, with its sizeable Dáil majority, took firm action against the IRA[61] and on 5 July the government issued a Proclamation introducing internment without trial.[62] 'In the post-war years the only difference in the response of the inter-party and the Fianna Fáil governments to IRA provocation was that the latter proved firmer.'[63]

5.6 Internment without trial – 1957

The government of Northern Ireland had introduced internment in January 1957[64] and in the Republic between 8 July 1957 and 11 March 1959 a total of 206 individuals were interned.[65] The initial internment sweep appears to have been well organized. Bowyer Bell says that 'on Saturday, July 6, Dublin seemed to be teeming with Special Branch men ... That evening the police swooped ... By Sunday morning, sixty-three republicans had been picked up around the country.'[66] It is highly likely that intelligence gathered since January, when a policy of prosecutions for membership of an unlawful organization had been employed, assisted the Gardaí at this stage. Overall, the policy of internment was a success. Although 'the Northern campaign was to

59 Hermon, *Holding the line*, p. 37. **60** Department for Justice, file JUS 8/1040 'Dáil Motion for release of Offences-against-the-State-Prisoners, notes for minister's speech' undated. **61** Murphy, *Ireland in the twentieth century*, p. 139. **62** Department for Justice, file JUS 8/1040 'Dáil Motion for release of Offences-against-the-State-Prisoners, notes for minister's speech' undated. **63** J Bowyer Bell, *The gun in politics: an analysis of Irish political conflict 1916–1986* (1987), p. 221. **64** Hermon, *Holding the line*, p. 38. **65** Department of An Taoiseach, file S3785B, Memorandum for the government – return for Dáil and Seanad under Section 9 of the Offences against the State (Amendment) Act, 1940, 20 Samhain, 1959 (that is 20 November 1959), para. 2. **66** Bell, *The secret army*, p. 305.

continue nominally until 1962, the threat of violence had been effectively dealt with in the South by the end of 1957'.[67] If the purpose of internment was to reduce the levels of violence, then it clearly had worked. There were 27 and 26 incidents in 1959 and 1960 respectively. These figures are comparable to the month of December 1956 alone, when 25 incidents occurred. In the busiest year of the campaign, 1957, there were 341 episodes.[68]

Despite the success of internment in facing down the threat posed by the Border Campaign, questions regarding the policy remain. The government obviously had to take firm action against the IRA. However, the decision to introduce internment without trial in July 1957 was problematic, involving as it did a leap from prosecutions before the District Court to internment, without any intermediary steps. The decision is all the more remarkable, given the alternatives that were available. On 28 July 1957 Gen. Seán MacEoin TD, a former Minister for Defence and Minister for Justice in the inter-party governments, made a speech criticizing the new policy. He said:

> How long are we going to intern people? Will they repent while in confinement? The Minister for Lands is reported as saying that the government 'will be prepared to fill every jail and barracks in the state' in order to deal with these people. But I want to warn the Minister and the government, that threats and internments are no solution to the problem ... Offenders should be tried in court and given a chance to defend themselves. Let them know the charge, and, if found guilty, let there be punishment to fit the crime.[69]

Gen. MacEoin was a member of Fine Gael and a committed pro-Treatyite; he was in no way a supporter of the IRA and its campaign.

The previous government's policy of summary prosecutions on the relatively minor charges, such as membership of an unlawful organization, was incapable of deterring the IRA due to the short sentences which were imposed. A return to any such policy would have been foolish in the extreme. Besides, the majority of serious offences committed during the Border Campaign occurred outside the jurisdiction of the Republic of Ireland, in Northern Ireland, and at the time the law did not provide for the prosecution of a person found in the Republic for an offence committed elsewhere, so it was not possible to convict individuals for offences that merited lengthier sentences.[70] The Circuit Court and trial by jury in subversive cases had been

67 Murphy, *Ireland in the twentieth century*, p. 139. 68 Bell, *The secret army*, p. 329. 69 General MacEoin, at a public meeting after mass in Granard and Abbeylara, Co. Longford, reported in the *Longford Leader*, 3 August 1957. See Department for Justice, file JUS 8/1040, Dáil Motion for release of Offences-against-the-State-Prisoners, notes for minister's speech, undated. 70 Doolan, *Lawless v. Ireland*, p. 37.

problematic in the past, as we saw, so it would have been very surprising if the executive had attempted to pursue a policy of trial before it.

The problem of inadequate deterrent would also have reduced the possibility of re-instigating trial before the District Court since that court is limited in jurisdiction. Furthermore, the Department of Justice was suspicious 'that some members of the District Court judiciary harboured latent support for IRA activists'.[71]

> The single proven incident of such support was by District justice Michael Lennon when he remarked, after a copy of Iris Oifigiúil was handed to Court showing that Part V of the Offences against the State Act 1939 had been brought into force, that 'this proclamation does not end with God save the King'. The government later requested, and received, the judge's resignation because his conduct was calculated to bring the law into contempt.[72]

The Department's suspicions contrast starkly with the recommendations of Roche to the Constitution Review Group of 1934;[73] he had wanted to grant District justices and Circuit Court judges a central role in the declaration of a state of emergency, believing that,

> these judges and justices have a strong incentive to shift the burden of dealing with organized crime from their own shoulders, they see at close quarters the inadequacy of ordinary police and court methods in semi-revolutionary periods, they even run definite personal risks, and they are in the main sensible decent men, so that I have some hope that in any real emergency they will not be obstructive.[74]

By 1957, suspicion had shifted from the senior to the more junior ranks of the judiciary. In light of such suspicions it was highly unlikely that the District Court would be utilized.

Although it is possible to discount the utilization of the District and Circuit Courts, it is still difficult to understand why the government chose to introduce internment without trial, rather than employ the Special Criminal Court; particularly given that the members of the court were still being paid despite having not heard a case since 1946. The government had, ten years previously, discussed its possible use in black market cases, yet it does not appear to have engaged in any discussion about the possibility of using it against a substantial subversive threat. I have been unable to locate any

71 Ibid., p. 37. 72 Ibid., p. 45, fn 18. 73 See Chapter 3. 74 Department of An Taoiseach file S 2979, 'Inter-departmental committee on the Constitution, note with special reference to Article 2A', by Mr Roche (Justice) signed and dated 16/6/34.

discussion of the Special Criminal Court's use in 1957. Perhaps the government merely mimicked the policy of the Northern executive. The introduction of internment there, in January, may have provided a ready model for Dublin. The legislation was in place, and all it took was a proclamation. The Special Criminal Court would not have required any proclamation since technically it was still in existence (but it would have required political explanation). It is also possible that the status of the court may have been viewed with suspicion. The government had initially presumed that retired members of the Defence Forces were no longer members of the court. Maybe the government was nervous about the legal position of the court's members, but this could have been rectified by simply removing the old members and appointing new ones, as was done in 1961 when the court's vacancies were filled.[75]

The government, of course, had reason to fear the use that the IRA might make of any public trials as propaganda. During earlier trials before the District Court, defendants had taken the opportunity to express republican views from the dock. Typically, this involved stating the defendant's non-recognition of the court. Doolan cites such an example from one of Gerard Lawless' trials. Lawless, who was later interned,[76] was arrested with a group of other men. In court one of those men stated,

> as a soldier of the Irish Republican Army and as leader of these men here I do not wish to have any part in the proceedings of this Court.

The same individual later added:

> on behalf of my comrades and myself I wish to state that any arms and ammunition found on us were to be used against the British forces of occupation to bring about the re-unification of our country and no Irishman or woman of any political persuasion had anything to fear from us. We hold that it is legal to possess arms and also to believe it is the duty of every Irishman to bear arms in defence of his country.[77]

The government may have wished to avoid such public pronouncements. For whatever reason, or combination of reasons, the Fianna Fáil administration preferred internment to any trial process.

75 Robinson, *The Special Criminal Court*, p. 23. 76 Lawless subsequently challenged the internment regime before the European Court of Human Rights. This was, in fact the first case to heard by that Court. The case of *Lawless v. Ireland (no. 3)*, (1979) 1 EHRR 1, will be considered later. 77 Doolan, *Lawless v. Ireland*, p. 30.

5.9 Internment without trial – a general comment

At this stage it is appropriate to consider the principled objections which exist toward a policy of internment. That there has been a lengthy debate about the universality of human rights is undeniable.[78] Cicero stated that 'true law is right reason in agreement with nature; it is of universal application, unchanging and everlasting ... We cannot be freed from its obligations by senate or people.'[79] Locke was of the opinion that the law of nature imposed an obligation on everyone and that 'no one ought to harm another in his life, health, liberty or possession'.[80] It is not possible to consider the universality of human rights in any detail here, but it is obvious that this theory, if accepted, places a heavy burden on our legal system.[81] It should be apparent that a fundamental component of human rights is the universality of the right to liberty. Support for this proposition can be found in the work of Hume, who, for example, insisted 'that for a judgment to be a moral one it must be made from a general, disinterested point of view stemming from a "sentiment common to all mankind"'.[82] On the basis of this theory, for the right to liberty to be universal, it must, at the very least, be based on a view widely accepted. In this context it is important to note that a general right to liberty has been enunciated in a series of bills of rights.[83] A notable example is the US Declaration of Independence,

> We hold these truths to be *self-evident*, that all men are created equal, that they are endowed by the Creator with certain unalienable rights, that among these are life, *liberty* and the pursuit of happiness.[84]

The concept is also referred to in the most fundamental rights documents. Article 9 of the International Covenant on Civil and Political Rights (ICCPR) states that 'Everyone has the right to liberty and security of the person. No one shall be subjected to arbitrary arrest or detention.'[85] The ICCPR is of particular importance since it is 'the most comprehensive and well established UN Treaty on civil and political rights'[86] and it has received considerable

78 Passim, Gewirth, *Reason & morality* (1978). 79 Cicero, *De Republica*, see Lord Lloyd of Hampstead, *Introduction to jurisprudence* (1979), p. 108. 80 Locke, *Civil government*, see Lloyd, *Introduction to jurisprudence*, p. 114. 81 For further comment on this issue see: Gewirth, *Reason & morality*; Dworkin, *Taking rights seriously* (1978); and Rawls, *A theory of justice* (1973) amongst others. 82 Gewirth, *Reason & morality*, p. 6. 83 for example see, Article 6 *African Charter on Human and Peoples' Rights* (1981); Article 9.1, *International Covenant on Civil & Political Rights* (1966); Article 5.1 *European Convention for the Protection of Human Rights and Fundamental Freedom* (1953); Article 2(1) *Basic Law for the Federal Republic of Germany* (1949); Article 40.4.1°, *Bunreacht na hÉireann – The Irish Constitution* (1937), among others. 84 *The United States Declaration of Independence,* Adopted in Congress July 4 1776. 85 Article 9.1, *International Covenant on Civil & Political Rights* (1966). 86 S. Joseph et al., *The International Covenant on Civil & Political Rights: cases, materials & commentary* (2000), p. 4.

international recognition.[87] Also, Article 5 of the European Convention of Human Rights (ECHR) guarantees liberty and security of the person.[88] These texts are referred to due to their importance and to illustrate the nature of the right to liberty as a human right, with universal effect, which has been widely recognized and accepted.

The ICCPR secures the right to liberty and provides that anyone arrested or detained on a criminal charge must be brought promptly before a judicial authority.[89] Some human rights advocates argue that the right to a fair trial is fundamental and should be guaranteed even in times of emergency.[90] However, a competing view exists which recognizes that 'constitutional states are ... obligated to protect themselves and their citizens against political violence, not only because it constitutes a challenge to the current constitutional order, but also because its persistence handicaps the process of reconstruction'.[91] This conflict between the need to uphold human rights and the need for states to protect themselves, and by extension their citizens, during times of national emergency is accommodated through the process of derogation.

The specific derogation clause within the ICCPR is Article 4 which states that

> In time of public emergency which threatens the life of the nation and the existence of which is officially proclaimed, the states parties to the present Covenant may take measures derogating from their obligations under the present Covenant to the extent strictly required by the exigencies of the situation, provided that such measures are not inconsistent with their obligations under international law and do not involve discrimination solely on the ground of race, colour, sex, language, religion, or social origin.[92]

This clause contains a number of interesting provisions. Firstly, it explicitly provides for limitations on the rights protected by the Covenant. However, such limitations may only be imposed during a 'time of public emergency which threatens the life of the nation'; the measures taken must be propor-

87 As of 17 August 2004, there were 152 State Parties. See, <http:www.unhchr.ch/html/menu3/b/a_ccpr.htm> accessed 17 August 2004. 88 'Everyone has the right to liberty and security of person' Article 5.1, *European Convention for the Protection of Human Rights and Fundamental Freedoms*, (1953). 89 Article 9, *International Covenant on Civil & Political Rights* (1966). 90 See for example Amnesty International, 'Israel/occupied territories, administrative detention: despair, uncertainty and lack of due process' (April 1997), 3. 91 John E. Finn, *Constitutions in crisis: political violence & the rule of law*, (1991), p. 84. 92 Article 4.1, *International Covenant on Civil & Political Rights* (1966). It should be noted that Article 4.2 states that 'No derogation from articles 6, 7, 8 (paragraphs 1 and 2), 11, 15, 16, and 18 may be made under this provision'. However this does not prohibit derogation from the relevant provisions of Article 9 and 14.

tionate to the threat and must not be based on discriminatory grounds. Unfortunately, the Human Rights Committee (HRC)[93] has not addressed the issue of Article 4 very often;[94] however, in one important early decision it did consider the issue of derogation. In *Landinelli v. Uruguay*[95] it examined the necessary ingredients for a 'public emergency'. The government of Uruguay had attempted to establish the existence of an emergency simply by stating that one existed and citing the existence of a number of 'Institutional Acts.' Crucially, 'however, no factual details were given ... The note confined itself to saying that the existence of the emergency situation was "a matter of universal knowledge".'[96] Thankfully, the HRC rejected this approach, stating that it required adequate information to enable itself to make an objective assessment of the emergency.[97] The Committee then considered the issue of proportionality and argued that,

> even on the assumption that there exists a situation of emergency in Uruguay, the Human Rights Committee does not see what grounds could be adduced to support the contention that, in order to restore peace and order, it was necessary to deprive all citizens, who as members of certain political groups had been candidates in the elections of 1966 and 1971, of any political right for a period for as long as 15 years.[98]

Despite the provisions of Article 4 the actions of the government of Uruguay were considered to be inconsistent with the ICCPR.

The jurisprudence of the ICCPR is, obviously, not applicable to the situation in 1957; however, it is instructive. Essentially, even operating within the Human Rights 'norms' established under that document, internment without trial is acceptable in certain circumstances. However, all actions must be proportionate, and it is at this point that the question of Ireland's use of internment arises. Given the grave restriction on the right to liberty which internment involves and given the existence of an alternative trial process, it would have been preferable to employ the Special Criminal Court. The justi-

93 The HRC has a number of distinct functions. Firstly, under Article 40 of the ICCPR it considers and studies national reports submitted by States parties on measures they have adopted to implement the rights guaranteed by the Covenant. Secondly, under Articles 41 and 42 an inter-State complaints procedure exists and finally, under the Optional Protocol the HRC may receive communications from persons under the jurisdiction of a State Party whose Covenant rights have been violated. For a detailed analysis of the role and function of the Human Rights Committee see, McGolderick, *The Human Rights Committee: its role in the development of the International Covenant on Civil & Political Rights* (1991), pp 47–51. **94** Joseph, *The International Covenant on Civil & Political Rights*, p. 624. **95** Communication No. 34/1978, 8 April 1981. **96** Ibid., para. 8.2. **97** Ibid., para. 8.3. **98** Ibid., para. 8.4.

fiability of the internment procedures was challenged in the celebrated *Lawless* case.

5.8 Lawless v. Ireland[99]

The ECHR was signed by the Minister for External Affairs, Seán MacBride, on behalf of Ireland on 4 November 1950.[1] Ireland's detention policy was subsequently challenged by Gearóid Ó Láighléis[2] on the basis that the internment procedures violated the ECHR. In an interesting twist, Ó Láighléis was represented by Seán MacBride (who had, of course, represented many republican claimants throughout his career). Ó Láighléis was a member of the Irish army reserve, Forsa Cosanta Aitiúil (FCA), who became involved in the IRA; he later joined the more violent IRA splinter group.[3] He appeared before the courts on firearms charges and by 11 December 1956 he had been discharged from the Defence Forces.[4] On 11 July 1957, as he was about to board a boat to Britain, he was arrested on suspicion of being a member of an illegal organization, under s.30 of the OAS, 1939.[5] The following day, the Minister for Justice issued a warrant under s.4 of the OAS (Amendment) Act, 1940, providing for the detention without trial of Gerard Richard Lawless.[6] These events set in motion a process which would transform Gearóid Ó Láighléis from an activist in an IRA splinter group into Gerard Lawless, the first claimant to have a case heard before the European Court of Human Rights.

Although Ó Láighléis always intended to seek redress under the ECHR,[7] he began the challenge against his detention through the traditional process of an application for *habeas corpus* before the High Court. This was necessary for two reasons; firstly, before any application may be made to the European Court of Human Rights all domestic remedies must be exhausted;[8] and secondly, the European Court did not yet exist.

> The establishment of the Court, and the first election of members, could not take place until the jurisdiction of the Court had been accepted by eight states ... At the time Lawless submitted his claim, in

99 *Lawless v. Ireland (no. 3)*, (1979) 1 EHRR 1. The case was decided on July 1 1961 but was not reported until 1979. 1 Doolan, *Lawless v. Ireland*, p. 6. This text has provided interesting background material regarding the ECHR and in particular Ireland's position in relation to it. It has also proved to be an invaluable source of information regarding the *Lawless* case itself. 2 Ó Láighléis was also known by the English language version of his name, that is, Gerard Lawless. It is the Irish version which was used in the domestic courts while Lawless was employed before the European Court of Human Rights. It might be thought that the translation to 'Lawless' was an auspicious beginning to the case. 3 Doolan, *Lawless v. Ireland*, p. 29. 4 Ibid., pp 30–1. 5 Ibid., p. 47. As Doolan comments, 'those involved in the saga must ... have occasionally wished that the police on that fateful summer's day had literally missed the boat.' 6 Ibid., p. 49. 7 Doolan, *Lawless v. Ireland*, p. 49. 8 Ibid., p. 49.

> November 1957, the jurisdiction of the Court had been recognized by only five states. Subsequently, this condition was fulfilled on 3 September 1958, which enabled the first election to take place on 21 January 1959 ... The Court had to wait almost a year for a case, that of *Lawless v. Ireland*, to be referred to it.[9]

The attitude of the domestic courts was relatively straight-forward and formalistic; Article 29.6 of the Constitution stipulated that 'no international agreement shall be part of the domestic law of the state save as may be determined by the Oireachtas'.[10] Since the Convention had not, in fact, been incorporated by the Oireachtas, its provisions could not overrule domestic legislation. As Davitt P noted, 'if this principle were not to be observed it would follow that the executive government by means of an international agreement might, in certain circumstances, be able to exercise powers of legislation contrary to the letter and the spirit of the Constitution'.[11] Therefore, the issue was judged solely on the basis of the Irish Constitution, and all arguments based upon the Convention were discounted. The OAS (Amendment) Act 1940 had been referred to the Supreme Court under Article 26. After that case had been heard, Article 26 was amended to ensure that any legislation referred to the Supreme Court and deemed to be constitutional is immune from further constitutional challenge. This amendment was introduced to ensure constitutional certainty. Although such an interpretation attributes a level of retrospective effect to the amendment, it is widely accepted that the OAS (Amendment) Act, 1940 is immune from challenge.[12] The internment procedure was upheld by the domestic courts.

The ECHR has a derogation clause which is broadly similar to that of the ICCPR.[13] It states that, 'in time of war or other public emergency threatening the life of the nation any High Contracting party may take measures derogating from its obligations under this Convention to the extent strictly required by the exigencies of the situation'.[14] Importantly, the position of the Irish government vis-à-vis the Council of Europe at this point appears somewhat confused. The *Kerryman* lamented that the British government

9 Doolan, *Lawless v. Ireland*, pp 9–10. 10 Bunreacht na hÉireann, Article 29.6. 11 *In re Ó Láighléis* [1960] IR, 93, 103. 12 Doolan, *Lawless v Ireland*, p. 22. see chapter 3. 13 The origins of this clause are interesting. As Jaime Oraá notes, 'The first multinational treaty dealing with a wide range of human rights was the European Convention, which was signed in Rome in 1950 and came into force in 1953, while the ICCPR was signed in 1966 and entered into force ten years later. However, the drafting of the Covenant had started much earlier, in fact in 1947. At that time, the UK forwarded to the Drafting Committee (1st session) a proposal for an International Bill of Rights which already contained a derogation clause ... The European Convention then borrowed the derogation clause form the draft Covenant.' Oraá, *Human Rights in states of emergency in international law* (Oxford: 1992), 7/8. 14 Article 15.1, *European Convention for the Protection of Human Rights & Fundamental Freedoms*, (1953).

had derogated from the Convention and had thereby shed its responsibilities under the ECHR. The paper's main concern, however, was that while,

> in normal circumstances, such British action might be expected to call forth bitter protests from our own representatives ... the fact that the internment powers invoked in the territory of the Republic clearly contravene the Human Rights Convention and that nobody is quite sure how we have contrived to 'regularise' that situation with the Council of Europe, introduces a factor of very great complexity.[15]

It is difficult to ascertain whether the *Kerryman* was upset because the Irish government had employed such measures; because the government may have failed to derogate correctly from the ECHR; or because the situation prevented Irish representatives calling forth bitter protests upon Britain.

In 1961 the European Court of Human Rights considered the circumstances of Ó Láighléis and the Republic of Ireland's policy of internment. This was, as was noted earlier, the first case to be heard by the new European Court. The court referred to the 'renewed outbreaks of IRA activity ... in 1954 and 1956'.[16] Having outlined the situation, the judgment concluded that

> in the general context of Article 15 of the Convention, the natural and customary meaning of the words 'other public emergency threatening the life of the nation' is sufficiently clear; they refer to an exceptional situation which affects the whole population and constitutes a threat to the organized life of the community of which the state is composed.[17]

Therefore, in the specific context of IRA violence the majority of the court held that the Republic of Ireland was entitled to derogate and employ a policy of internment. The European Court did not consider the alternatives available to the Irish parliament, namely, the pre-existing and paid-for Special Criminal Court.

5.9 The return of the Special Criminal Court

It was noted earlier that although 'the Northern campaign was to continue nominally until 1962 the threat of violence had been effectively dealt with in the South by the end of 1957'.[18] Internment without trial was discontinued in 1959. It is somewhat surprising, therefore, that 1961 saw the reintroduction, or reactivation, of the Special Criminal Court. Bell argues that the court was reintroduced because it appeared that the campaign was going to

15 *The Kerryman,* 19 October 1957, see Department for Justice file JUS 8/1040. 16 *Lawless v. Ireland (no. 3),* (1979) 1 EHRR, 1, 18. 17 Ibid., 31. 18 Murphy, *Ireland in the twentieth century*, p. 139.

drag on into 1961.[19] The Roslea barracks raid of 27 January 1961 certainly put the campaign back on the front pages,[20] and the government decided to act swiftly rather than waiting as it had done previously. Séan Lemass, the successor to de Valera, as leader of Fiann Fáil and Taoiseach, was of the view that Northern unionists needed to be attracted and not coerced into a united Ireland, and this position influenced many of his policies.[21] This stance surely encouraged him to crack down on the IRA before they got out of hand. Furthermore, it was Lemass as Minister for Supplies who had been so keen on utilizing the Special Criminal Court in black market cases; he was therefore familiar with the body. This revival of the Border Campaign did not result in a groundswell of support for Sinn Féin; in the general election of October, 1961 that party had a dismal showing and gained a mere three per cent of the vote.[22] Indeed, when the Taoiseach referred to the reintroduction of the court in Dáil Éireann he referred to the 'emphatic repudiation of those who supported' the campaign of violence across the border in the general election.[23]

For whatever reason, 'on November 23 the Irish government reintroduced the military tribunals [*sic*], so effective in the 1940's ... The cabinet simply announced that the tribunals were again functioning – in some cases with the same aged personnel.'[24] The 'military tribunals' referred to was, in fact, the Special Criminal Court; the use of military personnel was entirely consistent with that body's previous engagement; and the aged personnel had, of course, been retained for some time. Robinson is more accurate in noting that on 22 November three vacancies in the membership of the court were filled and it sat again on 27 November 1961.[25] The simplicity of reintroducing the court in 1961 once again begs the question: why was internment preferred in 1957? The statements of the Taoiseach only add to the confusion. He explained that

> the bringing of offenders before the District Court does not permit of sentences being imposed appropriate to the gravity of the offences and may have occasioned some misunderstanding amongst those concerned with them as to the seriousness with which the government view the position and their determination to deal with it.[26]

No mention of prosecution on indictment before a jury in the Circuit Court was made and one assumes that the nature of the offences made that unsafe. What is fascinating is that the reasoning for introducing internment in 1957 was the same justification for reactivating the Special Criminal Court in 1961.

19 Bell, *The gun in politics*, p. 221. 20 Bell, *The secret army*, p. 331. 21 Lee, 'Séan Lemass' in Lee (ed.), *Ireland 1945–70*, (Dublin: 1979), pp 16–26 at p. 22. 22 Bell, *The secret army*, p. 332. 23 Dáil Éireann, *Parliamentary Debates*, 23 November 1961, vol. 192, col. 838. 24 Bell, *The secret army*, p. 333. 25 Robinson, *The Special Criminal Court*, p. 23. 26 Dáil Éireann,

It is also interesting that when Lemass assured the Dáil that 'the only cases which will be brought before the Court will be those arising from this armed conspiracy of violence' he was virtually repeating the words used in 1939.[27]

During its previous incarnation the Special Criminal Court was extensively utilized in cases of a non-subversive nature; that did not occur in 1961. On 15 February 1961, the then Minister for Justice, C.J. Haughey TD, outlined the number of convictions under the OAS, 1939, the Firearms Act, 1925 and the Explosive Substances Act, 1883, 'where the evidence suggests these offences were connected with the activities of illegal organistions'.[28] The minister's response was in tabular form and included the name of the individual, the offence and the sentence. Part I displays the convictions before the District Court. Unsurprisingly these individuals attracted the relatively light sentence of six months, overall sentences ranging from six to twelve months when account is taken of consecutive sentences. As Sir John Hermon noted, such sentences would not act as a deterrent.[29] Part II of the minister's statement provides the same details for convictions before the Special Criminal Court. It is interesting to note that the most severe sentence imposed by the Special Criminal Court was five years. The preponderance of cases before both courts concern a 'failure to account for movements' and possession of ammunition.[30] The Special Criminal Court was imposing sentences of a similar severity to the District Court in most cases; it was, however, capable of imposing more severe penalties, and that may have been seen as its strength.

It might be supposed that the relatively light sentences imposed by both the District Court and the Special Criminal Court would have been insufficient to alter IRA policy. During its brief period in operation, between 1961 and 1962, thirty people were convicted by the Special Criminal Court; 'under an amnesty in 1962, twenty-four of these convicted persons were released'.[31] The truth is that the IRA campaign had been in steady decline since the introduction of internment, North and South, in 1957. The re-introduction of the Special Criminal Court was the straw that broke the camel's back. 'On February 3 [1962] ... the Army Council met again and formally and unanimously voted to end the campaign.'[32] The Border Campaign had been defeated. On 2 October 1962, the Special Criminal Court, which had been first established in 1939, was finally disestablished by a government proclamation under Part V of the OAS, 1939.[33]

The period 1946–1962 at first appears to be a mere footnote in the court's

Parliamentary Debates, 23 November 1961, vol. 192, col. 839. **27** Ibid., col. 839. **28** Dáil Éireann, *Parliamentary Debates,* 15 February 1962, vol. 108, col. 376. **29** Hermon, *Holding the line*, p. 37. **30** Dáil Éireann, *Parliamentary Debates,* 15 February 1962, vol. 108, col. 377/380. **31** Robinson, *The Special Criminal Court*, p. 24. **32** Bell, *The secret army*, p. 334. **33** Robinson, *The Special Criminal Court*, p. 23.

history; it did not sit for fifteen years and, when a credible terrorist threat emerged, it was ignored in favour of internment. The court's reactivation and use solely against violent subversives ensured that it was re-associated with its 'core business' of prosecuting terrorists. The year 1961 paved the way for the court's introduction, eleven years later, as a response to 'the Troubles.'

6

1969–1972: countdown to the Special Criminal Court

There are a number of contenders for the title of 'most significant date in the history of the Special Criminal Court': the introduction of Article 2A, in 1931; the Constitution Review Group of 1934; the Constitution of 1937; and the Offences against the State (OAS) Act, 1939 all played significant roles. However, 26 May 1972 has to be considered the odds-on favourite for the honour. On that day the government issued a proclamation activating Part V of the OAS, 1939 which brought the Special Criminal Court back into existence[1] and heralded the beginning of the court's longest period of employment.

6.1 The Troubles[2]

It is difficult to establish the exact date on which the Northern Ireland 'Troubles' began;[3] some might even argue as to which century saw the beginning of the Irish 'Troubles'.[4] But what is clear is that by 1969 the situation had deteriorated dramatically. In 1967 the Northern Ireland Civil Rights Association (NICRA) was formed. In the two years that followed riots involving members of the NICRA and the police were so prevalent that on 6 May 1969 the prime minister of Northern Ireland 'announced an amnesty that covered most of the offences arising from the demonstrations, including charges against the RUC'.[5] On 15 August 1969 the first member of the IRA had died in the Troubles, and by 6 February 1971 the first British soldier had been killed by the IRA.[6] Eventually, over 3,000 people were to die as a result of political violence in Northern Ireland.[7] Events there were to have profound impact upon the politics of the Irish Republic. Jack Lynch was elected Taoiseach on 6 November 1966[8] and ultimately his government would

1 Department of An Taoiseach, file 2003/16/93, Statement Issued by the government information bureau, issued as 4.55pm P O'S 26/5/72. 2 It is not possible or desirable to conduct a review of the history of the Troubles here. Instead a number of key responses to the increasing violence in, and associated with, Northern Ireland will be examined. For a history of the Troubles see Bell, *The Irish Troubles: a generation of violence, 1967–1992;* Murphy, *Ireland in the twentieth century;* and others. 3 Bloomfield, *We will remember: report of the Northern Ireland victims commissioner* (1998), para. 2.1. 4 In this context, for example, three dates from the 1600's are of great importance to Northern Irish unionists. '1641 represents a time of betrayal and death, 1689 marks a famous siege, while 1690 is the date of a great military victory'. Brian Walker, *Dancing to history's tune: history, myth & politics in Northern Ireland* (1996), p. 1. 5 Bell, *The Irish Troubles: a generation of violence, 1967–1992* (Dublin, 1993), 92. 6 Bew & Gillespie, *Northern Ireland: a chronology of the Troubles, 1968–1993* (1993). 7 Ibid., p. v. 8 Murphy, *Ireland in the twentieth century,* p. 151.

respond to the continued threat of violence by introducing the Special Criminal Court.

6.2 The arms trial

The incidents surrounding the 'arms crisis' are complicated and confused, involving claim and counter-claim. For the purposes of this chapter a few salient facts are important. On 28 May 1970, Ministers 'Haughey and Blaney were arrested and charged with conspiracy to import arms and ammunition.'[9] This was a highly sensitive issue since it appeared that ministers of the Irish government were involved in the illegal importation of arms to Northern Ireland. To make matters worse, Haughey always insisted 'that he acted only on the authority of the cabinet and of Lynch himself'.[10] A 1971 Department of Finance Memorandum refers to the allegation that certain moneys paid, through the Irish Red Cross, to the Belfast Fund for the Relief of Distress was used in whole or in part to finance the purchase of arms.[11] During the trial of the ex-ministers it was alleged that the Fianna Fáil government had engaged in 'some training for Six County people in the techniques of defensive street fighting'.[12] It is important to realize that the ministers were acquitted on the charges. However, allegations that ministers were involved in such activities were grave enough; the suggestion that those activities may have been government-sanctioned was frankly explosive.

6.3 Invasion, the UN and internationalization

It may be surprising at this distance, but the Lynch government appears to have considered the possibility of an armed response to the Troubles, at least in a 'doomsday' scenario. Strangely, former Fianna Fáil minister Gerald Boland, who had used internment and other measures against the IRA during the Emergency, publicly stated in 1970 that, 'in the existing circumstances the government should be training commando type groups to operate in support of the besieged nationalist community in the Six Counties.'[13] These comments are mentioned because it might be expected that the introduction of internment or trial by Special Criminal Court would have been viewed as a more acceptable alternative to the quasi-invasion of Northern Ireland, but at the time a respected former minister, who had once claimed to have defeated the IRA, now felt it was appropriate to train commandos to operate in the North. In the interests of clarity it should be clear that Kevin Boland, a government minister at the time, has stated categorically that 'at no time … was there the slightest suggestion of intervention by the army. The

9 Lee, *Ireland, 1912–1985*, p. 459. 10 Ibid., 460. 11 Department of An Taoiseach 2003/26/1, Department of Finance 6 January 1971 memorandum concerning 'Northern Ireland relief expenditure (grant-in-aid) 1969/70.' 12 Boland, *The rise & decline of Fianna Fáil* (Dublin, 1982), 31. 13 Ibid., p. 31.

suggestion was that it was the merest prudence to put ourselves in a state of preparedness.'[14] This appears to put the point beyond any doubt: the government was not planning an invasion but it felt it should be ready in case the circumstances dictated that such action was necessary. This begs the question: In what circumstances did the Lynch government consider it would be necessary to invade Northern Ireland, thereby bringing itself into conflict with Britain? Boland explains that the government

> appreciated the fact that, while effective protection against the attackers[15] could be given in Derry, Newry and other Border towns, the people in Belfast and in isolated areas could be wiped out . . . There was then completely unanimous realisation that there could be no suggestion of any crossing of the Border unless the situation was already so bad that no action of ours could make it worse – in other words unless we had Gibbon's[16] 'doomsday situation'.[17]

Boland resigned from Jack Lynch's government during the 'arms crisis' and his loyalty to the government of the time is more than questionable; however, the above comments are still of some value. The government was concerned that a 'doomsday' situation could arise and was preparing for it; this was no mere hypothetical worst-case scenario, but rather an event worth considering and planning for. The government clearly felt that it was possible for the situation to deteriorate so much that invasion would be a proportionate response; Boland even states that consideration was given to recalling Irish troops who were serving with the UN in Cyprus.[18]

The government also examined the possibility of internationalizing the conflict. A Department of An Taoiseach memorandum from 1972 outlines the 'possibility of invoking the Geneva Convention [*sic*] against Britain for violence and torture of detainees'.[19] Mr Seán Donlon of the Department for Foreign Affairs (the memorandum continues) stated that the Department had 'considered using the Convention but a difficulty arises in the lack of any convenient court or forum in which to prosecute the matter whereas the European Court of Human Rights is being availed of and is therefore more attractive'.[20] It is significant that, in its effort to bring the issue of Northern Ireland to the world stage, the government was willing to classify the

14 Boland, *We won't stand (idly) by* (1973), p. 50. 15 this is presumably a reference to Protestant, loyalist militia such as the UDA. 16 the then Minister for Defence. 17 Boland, *We won't stand*, p. 50. 18 Ibid., pp 49–50. 19 Department of An Taoiseach, file 2003/16/476, memorandum to Rúnaí Cúnta, dated 15 Márta 1972 (that is 15 March 1972). 20 Ibid. The reference here is to the Irish government's attempts to oppose the British government policy of internment in Northern Ireland. The policy of internment will be outlined later, for the time being the important factor is the willingness of the Irish government to seek out a suitable international venue in which to oppose the British policy.

Northern Irish Troubles as being an 'armed conflict not of an international character' as per Common Article 3 of the Geneva Conventions. Furthermore, it was willing to utilize the fledgling European Court for Human Rights.

A further element of this policy is evident from the government response to the European Convention on the Suppression of Terrorism. Foreign ministers (of the actual and acceding members of the European Economic Community) adopted a communiqué calling for concerted action in the fight against terrorism.[21] While most countries were said to view the Convention in light of the Arab-Israeli conflict, the government was concerned that Britain 'may regard it as an opportunity to raise IRA activities'.[22] The document identifies a difficulty in promoting cooperation in tackling political violence; it states that 'as regards "political" offences and particularly as regards co-operation with the police in the North in the prosecution of such offences, it has been the policy that the giving of assistance would require special consideration and would be refused as a rule'.[23] The document goes on:

> If the British seek to broaden the subject by raising the North and IRA activities ... the Irish representative could say that the British have always argued against bringing the issue into the international arena. We, however, could allow the matter to be raised and then call for examination of the causes and of the methods adopted to deal with it. It would seem reasonable to suggest that if one seeks to condemn acts as terroristic, one must also seek to remove unjust conditions which give rise to such acts.[24]

The approach of the Irish government, once again, illustrates its desire to raise the issue of Northern Ireland in the international arena.

The attempts of the Irish government to differentiate between Irish terrorism and terrorism in the context of the Arab-Israeli conflict are not novel. Defining terrorism is a complex task (in a survey of leading academics 109 alternative definitions of terrorism were proposed).[25] Forging international agreement on what constitutes terrorism has proved to be extremely

21 Department of an Taoiseach 2003/16/580, 'European control of terrorism' 18 September 1972. The communiqué was proposed by the Foreign Minister of West Germany and was a response to the terrorist attacks on the Munich Olympics. 22 Ibid., para. 4. 23 Ibid., para. 6. 24 Ibid., para. 9. 25 Ganor, 'Defining terrorism: is one man's terrorist another man's freedom fighter?' http://www.ict.org.il/articles/define.htm accessed 28 April 2003. For a detailed analysis of the issues involved in defining terrorism see Schmid & Jongman *Political terrorism: a new guide to the actors, authors, concepts, data bases, theories and literature* (1988), chapter 1. The authors provide a lengthy and comprehensive definition of terrorism and analysis of the terms employed.

difficult; as recently as 1998 the Rome Conference which led to the Statute of the International Criminal Court could not agree on a definition and as a result that court does not have jurisdiction over the specific crime of terrorism.[26] One of the more generally supported definitions is that of the US State Department: 'the term terrorism means premeditated, politically motivated violence perpetrated against non-combatant targets by subnational groups or clandestine agents, usually intended to influence an audience'.[27] This definition includes a number of the key criteria laid down by Schmid and Jongman which can be described as the gold standard of terrorism definitions.[28] Although this book is not concerned by the complex issues involved in defining terrorism, the desire of the Irish government to distinguish between IRA violence and terrorism is interesting.

A number of methods can be employed to distinguish the actions of a group from terrorism. In a similar fashion to the Irish government, President Hafez el-Assad of Syria stated, in 1986, that his government had always opposed terrorism 'but terrorism is one thing and a national struggle against occupation is another'.[29] Salah Khalef of the Black September group, which carried out the attack on the Munich Olympics in 1972, differentiated between terrorism, which he said he was opposed to, and revolutionary violence, which he claimed was acceptable.[30] The problem with such an approach is that it seeks to excuse terrorists by describing them as revolutionaries or national liberators. An example of the difficulties associated with such an approach is evidenced by the 1979 Convention against Hostage Taking. This should have been relatively uncontroversial since the taking of civilian hostages is surely never acceptable; however, a clause was inserted stating that the Convention did not apply in armed conflicts 'in which peoples are fighting against colonial domination and alien occupation and against racist regimes in the exercise of their right to self determination'.[31] It is a matter of grave concern that international law now formally recognizes hostage taking as a legitimate tactic in these circumstances, circumstances which any terrorist is likely to claim are applicable to their own cause. In order to avoid such problematic outcomes an objective definition of terrorism is required.[32]

26 Robertson, op. cit., p. 311. 27 The US government has employed this definition since 1983. See US Department of State, *Patterns of global terrorism 2003* (2004), xii. http://www.state.gov/s/ct/rls/pgtrpt/2003/ accessed 5 September 2005. 28 The definition provided by Schmid & Jongman is lengthy and complicated. It is not necessary to consider it in any detail here. Those interested should consult, Schmid & Jongman, *Political terrorism*, p. 1. 29 Ganor, 'Defining terrorism'. 30 Ibid. 31 Article 12, UN International Convention against the taking of hostages, (New York, 1979). <http://www,unodc.org/unodc/terrorism_convention_hostages.html> accessed 5 September 2005. 32 For a detailed discussion on the need to define terrorism see Ganor, 'Defining terrorism'; Netanyahu, *Fighting terrorism: how democracies can defeat the international terrorist network* (2001); and most authoritatively Schmid & Jongman, *Political terrorism*.

The final example of attempted internationalization can be seen in the repeated references to the possibility of UN involvement in Northern Ireland. The Department for Foreign Affairs was of the view that the suspension of normal laws in Northern Ireland in 1971 would have benefited from a full-scale UN debate on internment.[33] Deputy Dr John O'Connell asked the Taoiseach in 1972 if he would consider seeking British government support for the setting up of an impartial peace-keeping force in Northern Ireland. The Taoiseach's replied, 'as the Deputy is aware, the consent of the British government is necessary if a United Nations peace-keeping force is to operate in Northern Ireland. They have repeatedly refused to give their consent and I do not intend to pursue the matter with them at present.'[34] The government had pursued a policy of attempting to involve the UN as an impartial peace-keeping force; they had pursued this policy with the British government and had now abandoned it because they had failed to secure British support.

6.4 Kidnap and internment in 1970

On 5 December 1970 the government issued a proclamation introducing interment. The *Irish Press* reacted with 'surprise and puzzlement'; it reviewed the state of republicanism at the time and judged it to be quite weak:

> it appears that the main IRA grouping is split between 'Provisionals' and 'Officials' and considerably weakened, so much so that the 'Officials' are rumoured to be considering a proposal to change their title to the 'Irish Citizens Army'. The Saor Éire group are also reported to be split and it is difficult to see where, on this side of the Border, there is the strength to stage the sort of action which somebody in the Department of Justice is obviously worried about.[35]

On the next day the *Sunday Press* provided a review of Saor Éire, commenting that one body styling itself Saor Éire had merged with the Limerick Brigade of the Official IRA, while a second group had been formed in Cork, consisting of expelled IRA members. This second group had disbanded and joined the Irish Communist Organization.[36] (The Saor Éire of the 1970s will be considered in greater detail in Chapter 9.)[37]

The government announcement about internment referred to a serious and impending threat from extremists. When internment was last employed,

33 Department of An Taoiseach, file 2003/16/476. 34 Dáil Éireann, *Parliamentary Debates*, 15 June 1972, vol. 261, col. 1683. 35 Department of An Taoiseach, file 2001/61/7, *Irish Press*, 5 December 1970. 36 Department of An Taoiseach, file 2001/61/7, *Sunday Press*, 6 December 1970. 37 O'Ruaric, 'A little known Republican militant group: Saor Eire', *The Blanket*, 13 January 2005. <http://lark.phoblacht.net/ lor1401051g.html> accessed on 2 August 2005.

it was a *response* to the Border Campaign;[38] on this occasion it was being introduced *pre-emptively*. The Taoiseach and Minister for Justice issued the following statement:

> Garda authorities have informed the government that reliable information has come into their possession to the effect that a secret armed conspiracy exists in the country to kidnap one or more prominent persons. Connected with this conspiracy are plans to carry out armed bank robberies which the police believe may involve murders or attempted murders.[39]

The kidnap threat was said to have been directed against staff of the British embassy.[40] The British Foreign Office commented that 'protection is being provided by the Irish police authorities and they must have their reasons'.[41] Implicit within this statement is a recognition that extra security was being provided and that the British government accepted that it must have been necessary. In the absence of the actual intelligence it is impossible to confirm whether the threat was real or imagined; either way, the government was clearly concerned.

There are three final points concerning the December 1970 internment announcement. Firstly, it was made to the press. The *Irish Times* noted that,

> it is odd that Mr Lynch should come to the news media to make his announcement. What was so pressing on Thursday that the Dail [*sic*] could not have been informed of the grave situation which the Taoiseach now announces? ... It may be that Mr Lynch does not want his warning on the record of the Dail [*sic*]. He may feel that the record carries enough for one year.[42]

The re-introduction of the Special Criminal Court two years later was similarly made through the media and not the Dáil. Secondly, the government acted in accordance with its international obligations and informed the Secretary-General of the Council of Europe of its desire to derogate from the European Convention for Human Rights.[43] Finally, it considered that the introduction of internment in the South would 'facilitate the introduction of similar measures in the North ... If this happened, many areas of Belfast would be deprived of their defence against British troops and

38 See Chapter 5. 39 Department of An Taoiseach, file 2001/61/7, Official Statement, *Irish Times*, 5 December 1970. 40 Department of An Taoiseach, file 2001/61/7, *Irish Independent*, 5 December 1970. 41 Ibid. 42 Department of An Taoiseach, file 2001/61/7, *Irish Times*, 5 December 1970. 43 Department of An Taoiseach, file 2001/61/7, Official Statement, *Irish Times*, 5 December 1970.

unionist extremists'.[44] Internment was introduced in Northern Ireland and it was certainly not welcomed by the politicians or population of the Republic.

6.5 Internment in the North

Internment in the North, was initially activated by the Stormont parliament, under the Civil Authorities (Special Powers) Act (1922) (Northern Ireland) (SPA)[45] on 9 August 1971. Regulation 12 of the SPA authorized the Minister for Home Affairs to issue an internment order against any person 'who is suspected of acting or having acted or being about act in a manner prejudicial to the preservation of the peace and the maintenance of order in Northern Ireland'.[46] The stated aim of internment in Northern Ireland was to detain active members of the IRA and to obtain more information about their activities and organization, with a view to protecting the public.[47] Despite these ambitious aims, 'the initial internment sweep on 9 August, 1971 was, militarily, a complete failure. The IRA had known of it for some time, and as a result virtually every senior IRA man was billeted away from home. Of the 342 men arrested … 116 were released after 48 hours.'[48] The RUC seems to have acted upon intelligence concerning those interned during the 1950s; however, since then the IRA had split, and the authorities appear to have had little information about the new Provisional IRA.[49]

Violence soared following the introduction of internment.[50] The British government replaced the Northern Ireland parliament with 'direct rule',[51] but continued a policy of internment; however, the SPA was replaced by the new Detention of Terrorists (Northern Ireland) Order, 1972.[52] At the same time an independent inquiry (the Diplock Commission) was established to consider 'what arrangements for the administration of justice in Northern Ireland could be made in order to deal more effectively with terrorist organizations by bringing to book, otherwise than by internment by the executive, individuals involved in terrorist activities'.[53] It accepted the principle of internment; its report acknowledged that, in the climate prevailing at the time, dangerous terrorists existed who could not be tried effectively in the courts; internment was cited as the only effective means of re-establishing order.[54] In light of these conclusions the internment procedure was translated

44 Department of An Taoiseach, file 2001/61/7, 'Internment protests in Dublin', *Irish Times,* 18 January 1971. 45 hereinafter the SPA. 46 Spjut, 'Internment without trial in Northern Ireland 1971–1975: ministerial policy & practice' (1986) 49 *Modern Law Review*, 712, 713. 47 Ibid., p. 715. 48 McGuffin, *Internment!* (1973), p. 86. 49 Spjut, 'Internment without trial in Northern Ireland 1971–1975', 715. 50 'Prior to internment there had been thirty-four deaths in 1971; between internment and the end of the year there were 139.' Patterson, *The politics of illusion*, p. 151. 51 The Northern Ireland Parliament was prorogued on 16 March1972. Spjut, 'Internment without trial in Northern Ireland 1971–1975', 712. 52 Hogan & Walker, *Political violence & the law in Ireland* (1989), p. 86. 53 *Diplock Report*, para. 1. 54 Ibid., para. 27. In a frank statement the report concluded that 'until the current terrorism by extremist organizations of both factions

from the 1972 Order into the Emergency Provisions Act, 1973.[55] Internment without trial operated between 1972 and 1975.[56] Its end was signalled in April 1974 and on 6 December 1975, forty-six of the remaining detainees were released. A further twenty-seven detainees were held on criminal charges, a move which pointed toward a new policy of 'criminalization'.[57] This new policy sought 'to downplay the political character of Irish terrorism by emphasizing its criminality ... One consequence of this policy was ... to rely instead upon modified versions of the criminal law to cope with terrorism.'[58]

The reaction of the Irish government to internment in the North was astonishing: they were opposed to it. Given that the Taoiseach and Minister for Justice had announced the introduction of internment in the Republic in December 1970, their opposition to its introduction in the North the following August appears somewhat hypocritical. The files of 1972 refer repeatedly to the Taoiseach's abhorrence of internment.[59] Internment in Northern Ireland was extremely unpopular; it lead to increased levels of violence in the North and was opposed in the Republic. There was a common perception that internment was being targeted at the political opponents of unionism:[60] initially, arrests were confined to Catholics. The number of republican detainees continually exceeded loyalists, as table 6.1 illustrates.

There were reasons for this apparent discrimination. Firstly, as Prime Minister Faulkner was to explain, loyalists were not as well organized as the IRA and therefore, proof of involvement in terrorism was more difficult to establish.[61] Secondly, internment was implemented, largely, by the army, who operated mainly in republican areas. It has been stated that the police could have employed internment as well as prosecutions against loyalists but chose not to.[62]

As part of the policy of internationalisation, the Republic's government sought to challenge the UK's internment policy before the European Court of Human Rights; the issue of internment in Northern Ireland was

in Northern Ireland can be eradicated, there will continue to be some dangerous terrorists against whom it will not be possible to obtain convictions by any form of criminal trial ... The only hope of restoring the efficiency of criminal courts of law in Northern Ireland to deal with terrorist crimes is by using an extra-judicial process.' **55** hereinafter the EPA, 1973. Hogan & Walker, *Political violence*, p. 87. **56** In 1975 the Gardiner Commission conducted a further review of internment. It was critical of the quasi-judicial role of the Commissioners and made a series of recommendations regarding the operation of internment. The recommendations formed the basis of the Emergency Provisions Act, 1975, however, this alternative system of internment was never actually implemented and therefore no discussion of it is necessary at present. **57** Hogan & Walker, *Political violence*, p. 92. **58** Finn, *Constitutions in crisis*, p. 85. **59** Department of An Taoiseach 2003/16/476 makes repeated reference to the Taosieach's abhorrence of internment. **60** See McGuffin, *Internment!*, p. 87 and Spjut 'Executive detention in Northern Ireland: the Gardiner report and the Northern Ireland (Emergency Provisions) (Amendment) Act 1975' (1975) 10 *Irish Jurist*, 272, 275. **61** Wilson, *Ulster: conflict & consent,* (Oxford: 1989), 169. **62** This might be seen as institutional bias. Hogan & Walker, *Political violence*, p. 94.

Table 6.1
Northern Ireland internment figures[63]

	Republicans			Loyalists			Total
Year ending	*Intake*	*Releases*	*Still held*	*Intake*	*Releases*	*Still held*	
1971	783	129	651	–	–	–	651
1972	551	899	294	–	–	–	294
1973	448	191	547	64	17	47	594
1974	267	295	517	45	67	25	542
1975	11	529	–	–	25	–	–

considered by the court in 1978. It accepted that an emergency existed and upheld the right of the UK government to utilize a policy of internment; on the specific allegation of sectarianism it justified the difference in treatment. It is worth quoting the judgment:

> There were profound differences between loyalist and republican terrorism ... The IRA, with its far more structured organization, constituted a far more serious menace than the loyalist terrorists ... [Also] it was as a general rule easier to institute criminal proceedings against loyalist terrorists than against their republican counterparts ... Accordingly although loyalist terrorists were not extrajudicially deprived of their liberty, they do not appear to have been able to act with impunity.[64]

The allegation of sectarianism was a serious one and the acceptance by the court that differing treatment did not imply discrimination is important. The facts, as accepted by the court, show that the differing treatment was based on the different status of loyalist and republican paramilitaries, as such no discrimination contrary to Article 14 was established. Northern Ireland's internment provisions were held to be in violation of Article 5, however, as in *Lawless v. Ireland*,[65] it was recognized that derogation was permissible 'in times of war or other public emergency'. The court concluded that the situation satisfied the conditions necessary for an emergency to be declared.

6.6 Bloody Sunday – infection by the Northern virus?

Protests were organized in response to the introduction of internment in Northern Ireland. 'On 22 January 1972, a march took place to Magilligan Prison Camp in Derry ... It was a peaceful march supported by the sort of

63 These figures are compiled from a Table in Hogan & Walker, *Political violence*, p. 93. 64 *Republic of Ireland v. The United Kingdom* [1979] 2 EHRR, 25, para. 228. 65 *Lawless v. Ireland (no. 3)* (1979) 1 EHRR 1. See chapter 5.

people who had come out in favour of civil rights, and by relatives of the interned.'[66] As the march approached the camp it was confronted by a squad from the First Paratroop Regiment who fired rubber bullets. This regiment was 'only brought back to a sense of discipline when the NCO's began wielding their batons fiercely on their own men.'[67] Eight days later, on Sunday 30 January, an incident occurred at a civil rights march in Derry which remains a source of controversy to this day. The event, which became known as 'Bloody Sunday,' involved the shooting dead of thirteen men, 'all apparently unarmed,' by the Parachute Regiment.[68] Such controversy surrounds these events that two judicial inquiries have been set up – the Widgery Inquiry which never satisfied the nationalist community of Derry[69] and then the Saville Inquiry, which has yet to report.[70] Two days after Bloody Sunday a crowd marched in protest on the British embassy in Dublin and it was burned to the ground[71] – this showed how Northern events could rock the Southern body politic and lead to public disorder. The mounting violence in Northern Ireland, the reaction of people in the Republic and the other events mentioned above ensured that the Lynch government had to take action if chaos was to be averted.

It is remarkable that the Lynch government was not entirely destabilized by these events. Murphy notes that

> the absence of any positive Dublin policy on the North became painfully evident. Lynch's dismissal of two cabinet ministers on suspicion of arms-running, the resignation of another minister and the setting up of a splinter party, Aontacht Éireann, the sensational arms trial of the ex-ministers, the James Bond like atmosphere of espionage and intrigue, the convulsions caused in the South by Bloody Sunday, January 1972 in Derry, the burning of the British Embassy in Dublin – all these earth-shaking events still left Jack Lynch and Fianna Fáil solidly in office.[72]

The ability of the government to retain power seems to have had little to do with its ability to control the terrorist problem associated with Northern Ireland. Indeed, in 1972 the then Minister for Justice, Mr Desmond O'Malley, informed the Dáil that between 1 January and 31 May 1972, there were 172 bomb threats reported to the Garda Siochána as compared to 25 in

66 Coogan, *The Troubles: Ireland's ordeal, 1966–1995 and the search for peace* (1995), p. 133. **67** Ibid., p. 134. **68** Bew & Gillespie, *Northern Ireland*, p. 44. **69** Vincent Kearney, 'Bloody Sunday soldiers "allowed to change stories"', *Sunday Times*, 8 August, 1999. **70** Clive Walker, 'The commodity of justice in states of emergency,' (1999) *Northern Ireland Legal Quarterly*, vol. 50, no. 2, 164, 170. **71** Department of An Taoiseach 2003/26/6, Report of Superintendent B. Clinton. **72** Murphy, *Ireland in the twentieth century*, p. 151.

the corresponding period in the previous year. He saw this increase as being connected with 'activities in the northern part of the country.'[73] Joe Lee comments that, 'the Northern virus inevitably infected the Southern body politic. The wonder is that it infected it so little for so long.'[74] Economics and Ireland's bid to join the European Economic Community[75] took centre stage in the 1973 election campaign[76] and although Fianna Fáil argued that it had succeeded

> in keeping the Northern troubles from spilling over into the South ... what concerned the southern electorate was not so much the trauma of the North as inflation and rising prices and the universal feeling that it was time for a change after sixteen years of rule by a party which showed many of the signs of an irritating complacency if not of arrogance.[77]

73 Dáil Éireann, *Parliamentary Debates,* 15 June 1972, vol. 261, col. 1762. 74 Lee, *Ireland, 1912–1985*, p. 458. 75 A referendum on membership of the then EEC was held on 10 May 1972, 83% voted in favour of joining. Murphy, *Ireland in the twentieth century,* p. 150. 76 O'Mahony, *Jack Lynch: a biography* (Dublin, 1991), 107. 77 Murphy, *Ireland in the twentieth century,* p. 152.

7

The re-introduction of the Special Criminal Court

By 1972 it was painfully obvious that the government needed to respond: tensions were continuing to rise in Northern Ireland; the South faced increasing bomb threats; and some Dáil Deputies were even concerned that the Baader Meinhof terrorist group was operating in Ireland.[1] In 1970 the government had flirted with the possibility of introducing internment,[2] but it now rejected that proposal.[3] The *Irish Times* commented that, 'internment is abhorred by everyone and is hardly feasible even if the government were so minded';[4] internment was no longer a politically viable option.

7.1 Announcing the Special Criminal Court

As with the announcement of internment in 1970 the declaration that a special criminal court was to be established appears to have taken people by surprise. The idea of a special criminal court was mooted in the Dáil only two days before the court was re-established. On 24 May 1972 Minister O'Malley stated on the Dáil record that

> The Taoiseach made it perfectly clear yesterday ... that we had no intention of introducing military courts in this country, but in order that neither he nor I nor anybody else can be accused of misleading anyone, I want ... to say that the government do not rule out the possible introduction of special criminal courts, and in fact the government have under active, and very active, consideration at this moment the question as to whether or not to introduce special criminal courts.[5]

Deputy Cluskey inquired as to what exactly a special criminal court was and Deputy Desmond asked: 'Would this require legislation? You would have to bring in a bill?'[6] Since the Offences against the State Act, 1939 was still active,

1 Deputy Dr O'Connell asked the Minister if he was, 'aware of the existence in Dublin of any members of the extreme militant Baader Meinhof group;....' The Minister dismissed the speculation. Dáil Éireann, *Parliamentary Debates,* 15 June 1972, vol. 261, col. 1763. 2 Department of An Taoiseach, file 2001/61/7, Official Statement, *Irish Times,* 5 December 1970. See Chapter 6. 3 *Irish Times,* 'Special criminal courts now being considered', 25 May 1972. 4 *Irish Times,* 'Very active consideration', Editorial Comment, 25 May 1972. 5 Dáil Éireann, *Parliamentary Debates,* 24 May 1972, vol. 261, cols. 256–7. 6 Dáil Éireann, *Parliamentary Debates,* 24 May 1972, vol. 261, col. 257.

the government did not require legislation of any sort to reintroduce the court and the Deputies' lack of awareness of the measure can be taken as evidence of the surprise nature of the move.

On 25 May the front page of the *Irish Times* informed the public that while, 'the announcement created the impression that the introduction was imminent . . . it was stated *most authoritatively* last night that the government had not taken any decision yet on the matter and that such courts would *not be set up in the immediate future*'.[7] On Friday 26 May 1972 the same paper made it clear that there was 'no pressure from Britain to bring in the courts', and it argued that the government would be more than satisfied by the 'lack of any important public feeling against the announcement'.[8] On the very same day, a proclamation was made by the government bringing Part V of the Offences against the State Act back into effect. Four days later, on 30 May 1972 a further Order was made establishing a Special Criminal Court and appointing judges to sit on it.[9]

7.2 A different Special Criminal Court

From the moment the re-establishment of the court was first suggested in the Dáil it was clear that this Special Criminal Court would be unlike its predecessors. On 24 May 1972 Minister O'Malley stated quite categorically, 'if those special criminal courts are introduced, there will, be no military officers on them'.[10] Previous emergency court models had been staffed by members, or retired members, of the Defence Forces.[11]

> On the 30 of May, an Order was made establishing a Special Criminal Court and determining that the court would consist of three members, a judge of the High Court, Mr Justice Griffin, a judge of the Circuit Court, Judge Conroy; and the President of the District Court, Mr Justice Cathal O'Floinn.[12]

The appointment of members of the judiciary was progressive. Earlier courts had always had the appearance of military tribunals; on this occasion, however, there could be no such accusations.

Significantly, the government did not amend the legislation to prevent the appointment of non-judges. As has already been noted s.39(3) of the 1939 Act provides for the appointment of

7 McInerney, 'Government gets plans for special courts ready', *Irish Times*, 25 May, 1972. 8 *Irish Times*, 'Prisons bill signed by President', 26 May 1972. 9 Robinson, *The Special Criminal Court*, pp 25–6. 10 Dáil Éireann, *Parliamentary Debates*, 24 May 1972, vol. 261, col.256/7, 24 May 1972. 11 See Chapter 5. 12 Robinson, *The Special Criminal Court*, pp 25–6. Peadar O'Reilly an officer of the Circuit Court was appointed as the registrar of the Special Criminal Court. Department of An Taoiseach, 2003/16/93, Draft of Government Minutes 30.5.72 – item 1.

> a judge of the High Court or the Circuit Court, or a justice of the District Court, or a barrister of not less than seven years' standing, or a solicitor of not less than seven years' standing, or an officer of the Defences Forces not below the rank of commandant.[13]

The government retains the power to appoint any of the above to the court, although it should be stated that since 1972 all of its members have been judges or former judge of the ordinary courts; 'moreover, since 1986, all members of the court have been actually serving judges'.[14] The independence of the members of the court has been affirmed in *Eccles v. Ireland.*[15] S.39 provides that members of the Special Criminal Court shall be appointed and removable at will by the government. The Minister for Finance is given the power to set the remuneration of the members of the court as he sees proper. In *Eccles* it was alleged that this provision could allow for interference with the independence of the court. Finlay CJ stated that although 'the Special Criminal Court does not attract the express guarantees of judicial independence contained in Article 35 of the Constitution, it does have, derived from the Constitution, a guarantee of independence in the carrying out of its functions'.[16] Thus, the judicial independence of the court has been secured. Given the difficulty of its dual role as arbiter of fact and of law, the independence of the court could be furthered guaranteed by amending s. 39(3) to ensure that the law falls in line with the practice; in other words, the legislation could be improved by excluding the appointment of all non-judges to the court.

The government's stance on the appointment of judges to the court should be viewed as an attempt to ensure that the Special Criminal Court was acceptable to the public. These attempts at ensuring the legitimacy of the court appear to have been taken seriously. When Deputy Dr David Thornley referred to the court as a 'three member judicial tribunal' in the Dáil on 30 May 1972, the description was strongly rejected by the Minister for Justice: 'it is not a judicial tribunal' he protested. 'It is a court of law expressly provided for in the Constitution.'[17] He also emphasized that 'the ordinary laws of evidence will and must apply' in the court.[18] The government wanted to avoid any attempt to portray the court as a military tribunal or sinister emergency power. Of course, these assertions were not uncontroversial; while the appointment of the members of the judiciary was to be welcomed one cannot gainsay the fact that the Special Criminal Court is extraordinary. After all, the issue of the rules of evidence before the court had been a source of

13 section 39(3) Offences against the State Act, 1939. 14 Hogan & Whyte, *Kelly*, para. 6.5.335. 15 [1985] IR 545. 16 [1985] IR 545, 549. 17 Dáil Éireann, *Parliamentary Debates*, 30 May 1972, vol. 261, col. 599. 18 Ibid., col. 600.

controversy during the Emergency, as has already been commented upon.[19] The relevant section of the Act is s.41(4). It states that

> the practice and procedure applicable to the trial of a person on indictment in the Central Criminal Court shall, *so far as practicable,* apply to the trial of a person by a Special Criminal Court, and the rules of evidence applicable upon such trial in the Central Criminal Court shall apply to every trial by a Special Criminal Court.[20]

This issue was also referred to in the *Irish Times.*[21]

The purpose of s.41(4) has been described as to ensure that 'the Special Criminal Court will operate its jurisdiction according to the known pattern of the Central Criminal Court, and thus escape the hazards of the unknown and the uncertainty that would beset a new court'.[22] However, it has been noted, that

> to some extent, the adaption of Central Criminal Court practice and procedure is effected by the Special Criminal Court rules ... [T]hese rules cover miscellaneous matters such as court sittings, access of members of the public and press, witnesses, extension of time and legal aid.[23]

Furthermore, the ordinary courts have accepted that 'it is impracticable – indeed impossible – to import a rule ... governing the conduct of jury trial by a non-jury court'.[24] It appears, therefore that the rules applicable before the Special Criminal Court are not the same as those applicable before the Central Criminal Court and as a result, the rights of the accused are being affected. However, 'while some allowance must, admittedly, be made for the fact that a trial before the Special Criminal Court does not take place before a jury, s.41(4) should not be construed as abrogating fundamental principles'.[25] Thus, the Special Criminal Court is restricted by the rules of the Central Criminal Court, but practical consideration is given to the fact that some alterations are necessary because the Special Criminal Court does not have a jury. It is tempting to overemphasize the amount of latitude granted to the court by s.41, but it appears reasonable to say that that section merely allows for practical modifications rather than wholesale amendment. Indeed, there is authoritative support for the view that 'if legislation did ... provide for special rules of evidence in the Special Criminal Court ... such

19 See Chapter 4. 20 s.41(4) The Offences against the State Act, 1939. 21 McInerney, 'Special courts now established', *Irish Times*, 27 May 1972. 22 *The People (DPP) v. Rice* [1979] IR 15, 18. 23 Hogan & Walker, *Political violence*, p. 230. 24 *The People (DPP) v. McMahon* [1984] ILRM, 461, 467. 25 Hogan & Walker, *Political violence*, p. 231.

arrangements would be unconstitutional'.[26] As the OAS Review Group has noted, the decision in *Cox v. Ireland*[27] puts this matter beyond any doubt: the Supreme Court held that s.34 of the OAS, 1939, which provided for the loss of office and pension for all public servants convicted of a scheduled offence before the Special Criminal Court, was unconstitutional:

> Having regard [to] the varying gravity of the range of scheduled offences and the fact that the operation of s.34 is triggered by the venue of the trial ... which in turn is primarily selected by the fact that the offence is scheduled, the Court concluded that the section was invalid as 'impermissibly wide and indiscriminate'.[28]

By extension, if the Special Criminal Court cannot employ extra punitive measures based solely on its selection as a trial venue, it is highly unlikely that any special rules of evidence would be accepted.

The Lynch government emphasized the similarity of the rules of procedure and evidence applicable before the Special Criminal Court in an attempt to curb the level of criticism that could be legitimately levelled at it. With public feeling on the issue of the Northern Troubles palpably high in the wake of 'Bloody Sunday', the government clearly attempted to ensure that its response was viewed as measured, proportionate and just.

7.3 Opposition to the government's measures

Although the government may have quelled some opposition to the Special Criminal Court by underlining its normality, other legislative provisions were strongly condemned. Particular opposition was directed toward the Offences against the State (Amendment) Act 1972, s.3(2) which states that 'where an officer of the Garda Síochána, not below the rank of Chief Superintendent ... states that he believes that the accused was at a material time a member of an unlawful organization, the statement shall be evidence that he was then such a member'. The constitutionality of this provision was challenged over twenty years later in *O'Leary v. AG.*[29] Costello J held that

> s.3(2) of the 1972 Act merely made admissible in evidence in certain trials statements of belief which would otherwise be inadmissible; the court remained free to evaluate such evidence and was not required to convict in the absence of exculpatory evidence, so that the presumption of innocence still operated.[30]

26 *Committee to Review the Offences against the State Acts, 1939–1998*, para. 9.9. **27** [1992] 2 IR 503. **28** Hogan & Whyte, *Kelly*, para. 6.5.57. **29** [1993] IR 102. **30** Hogan & Whyte, *Kelly*, para. 7.5.211.

In 1972, however, the provision was viewed with a deep suspicion. Thirty-eight academics of Trinity College Dublin, including Professor Mary Robinson, who would go on to write authoritatively on the subject of the Special Criminal Court,[31] lodged a letter of protest with the office of the Taoiseach[32] in which they stated: 'we take particular exception to Section 3, which transfers the onus of proof to the accused and invests Chief Superintendents ... with powers which are wholly repugnant'.[33] 'Citizens for Civil Liberties' produced a memorandum on the Act, which described s.3 as being the heart of the bill and objected to it in forceful terms.[34] In comparison to the outcry that greeted the introduction of internment in Northern Ireland, however, these objections to the 1972 Act and the muted response to the introduction of the court must have been seen as a triumph for the government. They had essentially succeeded in taking action against a subversive threat without inspiring a popular backlash.

7.4 Diplock and the beginnings of a common policy

As we have seen, the government of the United Kingdom had introduced internment to Northern Ireland at a time when the Irish government felt unable to do so. This policy proved to be highly unpopular with the nationalist population of Northern Ireland and led to a widespread campaign of civil disobedience. Indeed, it has been argued that internment which had been introduced to 'stem the flow of violence had merely contributed to an intensification of the "troubles"'.[35] By 1972 the UK government was seeking an alternative approach.

The haste with which the Special Criminal Court was introduced in Ireland has been commented on earlier in this chapter. When the government of the UK came to consider alternative responses to the violence in Northern Ireland, it decided to establish a commission (under Lord Diplock) to review the situation and propose measures suitable for the circumstances. Unlike the Lynch government, it found this necessary because its legislative arsenal did not include a measure similar to the Offences against the State Act, 1939. One contemporary commentator suggested that Lord Diplock's (eventual)

> recommendations have provided the main basis for the Northern Ireland (Emergency Provisions) Bill, which has strong claims to be considered the most draconian measure to be put before parliament at Westminster since the Emergency Powers (Defence) Act 1939.[36]

31 Robinson, *The Special Criminal Court*. 32 Department of An Taoiseach file, 2003/16/590. 33 Ibid. 34 Ibid. 35 Jackson & Doran, *Judge without jury: Diplock trial in the adversary system*, (1995), p. 8. 36 Twining, 'Emergency powers & criminal process: the Diplock report' [1973] *Criminal Law Review*, 406, 406–7.

The UK government accepted the Diplock recommendations on 20 December 1972,[37] and prepared the Northern Ireland (Emergency Provisions) Act, 1973, which came into force on 25 July of that year. The central provision of the Act is that 'a trial on indictment of a scheduled offence shall be conducted by the court without a jury'.[38]

Therefore, by 1973 both jurisdictions had introduced trial without jury, although the approaches were different. The non-jury courts in Northern Ireland are widely referred to as 'Diplock courts'. It is important to realize that 'the term "Diplock court" is ... misleading in so far as it suggests a special criminal court in a special courthouse ... In fact the single judge trials are heard in Belfast Crown Court.'[39] The Northern Ireland model simply utilizes a division of the Belfast Crown Court to hear cases without a jury; it is not a separate court in the way that the Special Criminal Court is. A second difference in the approaches is that, while the Special Criminal Court has trial by a panel of three judges, the Diplock model involves trial by a single judge sitting alone.

A feature common to these two court systems is the scheduling of offences. Both contain a list or 'schedule' of offences which are to be tried by these courts. Essentially in the North the schedule creates 'a presumption against jury trial'[40] due to the structure of the scheme whereby the attorney general may certify that a scheduled offence be heard outside of the Diplock system if he chooses. However, until he takes that positive action these offences will be tried by a non-jury court. It is important to understand that the AG 'certifies out an offence if he is satisfied in the individual case that it was not terrorist or security related, although this test is not specified in statute'.[41] Therefore, the AG has a rather unfettered discretion in relation to the trying of these offences. The scheduling system in the Republic is similar in its operation: if the offence is scheduled then the case is transferred to the Special Criminal Court unless the director of public prosecutions (DPP) directs otherwise; if it is not a scheduled offence, it may still be transferred if the DPP certifies that the ordinary courts are inadequate.[42] The acceptability of this power has been questioned, and a review of it has been called for.[43] Robinson has argued that 'to channel persons charged with purely criminal offences to the Special Criminal Court is to abolish trial by jury by the back

37 Aitken, 'New laws will tighten net on terrorists', the *Guardian*, 21 December 1972. 38 Northern Ireland (Emergency Provisions) Act, 1973, s.2(1). 39 Jackson & Doran, *Judge without jury*, p. 9. 40 Jackson, 'Diplock & the presumption against jury trial: a critique' (1992) *Criminal Law Review*, 755, 755. 41 Secretary of State for the Home Department & the Secretary State for Northern Ireland, *Legislation against terrorism*, cm 4178, (1988), para. 13.4, henceforth *Legislation against terrorism*. 42 Hogan & Walker, *Political violence*, p. 232, and Offences against the State Act, 1939, s.45(2) and s.46(1). 43 Ibid., p. 238.

door'.[44] A 'scheduling in' procedure[45] designed to combat these problems will be discussed in detail later.

The comparability of the two regimes did not go unnoticed at the time. 'A source close to the Belfast brigade of the Provisional IRA dismissed the [Diplock Commissions'] report as similar to Mr Lynch's amendment to the Offences against the State Act. "The only difference', he added, 'is that the one in Dublin is written in Irish".'[46] On the same day the editorial in the normally liberal *Guardian* commented that the Diplock report had 'followed Dublin in proposing trials without jury. In current circumstances this will probably be no great loss of protection to accused men.'[47] The Irish model had been in existence since 1939, and there is no evidence to suggest that the UK was guided by the Republic. The Diplock Commission probably examined the Irish legislation, but there are enough differences between the approaches to show that the regimes were conceived independently of each other. What is interesting is that both governments chose a similar response to the problem.[48]

7.5 Justifying the abolition of the jury

Both governments had to justify their respective decisions to remove the right to trial by jury for certain, scheduled offences. The Diplock Commission has been criticized for not forwarding enough quantitative evidence to support its conclusions. In 1973, before the Northern Ireland (Emergency Provisions) Bill had been passed into law, Professor W.L. Twining stated:

> the Commission adduced very little evidence, statistical or otherwise, in support of some of its main factual premises – for instance, that there is a real danger of a significant number of convictions or acquittals against the evidence by juries, that there is a serious risk of widespread intimidation of jurors as well as witnesses, or that the relatively liberal Northern Ireland provisions for granting bail were in fact being widely abused.[49]

The reason for this lack of evidence has been explained: 'one problem with evaluating the jury system in the United Kingdom is that researchers are forbidden from examining what goes on in the jury room, with the result that

44 Robinson, *The Special Criminal Court*, p. 35. 45 Jackson, 'Diplock & the presumption against jury trial: a critique', 764. 46 Aitken, 'New laws will tighten net on terrorists', *Guardian*, 21 December 1972. 47 Editorial, 'Keeping some law in Ulster', *Guardian*, 21 December 1972. 48 As was previously discussed in chapter 1, other Governments have also turned to the non-jury trial model when faced with terrorist problems. For example 'in Israel criminal cases are tried by a judge sitting alone or in the most serious cases by a panel of three judges.' See Jackson & Doran, *Judge without jury*, pp 1–2. 49 Twining, 'Emergency powers & criminal process: the Diplock report', 413.

we know very little about how juries actually operate'.[50] The decision to remove the jury from these trials was taken in the belief that juries were unable to guarantee truthful results; however it is practically impossible to establish that that was, in fact, the case. The lack of quantitative evidence to support the findings of the Diplock Commission in Northern Ireland was highlighted by the existence of a public report which could be studied and commented upon. In the Republic no such report existed, and, as a result, the criticism appears to have been somewhat more muted.

Under the Constitution and the Offences against the State Act, 1939, the government may introduce special criminal courts when it is of the opinion that the ordinary courts are inadequate. This test appears clear enough; however, the government was faced with the same difficulty that confronted the Diplock Commission. Deputy Michael O'Leary raised the issue with the Minister for Justice in Dáil Éireann on 15 June 1972, inquiring as to whether the minister would 'cite the cases on which the government based their opinion that the ordinary courts are inadequate'. Dr Noel Browne made a similar inquiry.[51] Unfortunately, though predictably, the minister was unable to provide an adequate answer. He stated:

> I am precluded from referring to individual cases in which persons have been acquitted. I would, however, draw attention to the fact that, when a jury verdict has to be unanimous, each member of the jury that brings in a verdict of guilty is known to have supported the verdict and is thus a potential target for attack by associates of the convicted person. The possible threat of retaliation assumes new proportions when court-houses are picketed by persons in a barely-veiled atmosphere of intimidation.[52]

The minister's reasoning needs to be complemented. The existence of unanimous verdicts does make it obvious that every member of the jury supported a conviction; it is problematic, however, that the only evidence to support the view that jury intimidation was resulting in wrongful acquittals in 1972 is the conjecture of a government minister that such intimidation was occurring. When asked directly if there was any evidence of jury intimidation, the minister responded, 'one can, I think, fairly draw conclusions from verdicts that were brought in over a period of months'.[53]

The law makes it impossible to determine if intimidation played a role in a jury's verdict because 'it is part of a juror's oath that he will not [later] disclose anything connected with the case'.[54] So, evidence of jury intimidation did not

50 Jackson & Doran, *Judge without jury*, p. 4. 51 Dáil Éireann, *Parliamentary Debates*, 15 June 1972, vol. 261, col.s 1764–65. 52 Ibid., col. 1765. 53 Ibid. 54 Dáil Éireann, *Parliamentary Debates*, 15 June 1972, vol. 261, col. 1766.

exist; however, support for the view that juries may have suffered intimidation can be deduced from the 'declared intention of certain groups to embark on a policy of picketing the homes of members of the judiciary'.[55] If groups were willing to picket the homes of judges then they would surely have been willing to intimidate jurors. In these circumstances, the introduction of the Special Criminal Court was justifiable despite the lack of direct evidence of jury intimidation.

55 Department of An Taoiseach, file 2003/116/93.

8

The Special Criminal Court under review

8.1 The legislative framework

The basis for the Special Criminal Court is to be found in Article 38.3 of Bunreacht na hÉireann which states that 'special courts may be established by law for the trial of offences in cases where it may be determined in accordance with law that the ordinary courts are inadequate to secure the effective administration of justice and the preservation of public peace and order'. Part V of the Offences against the State Act (OAS), 1939 provides the legislative framework to give effect to this constitutional provision. Section 35(2) of the Act lays down the mechanism by which Part V of the Act can be activated; essentially it restates the Article 38 test, stating that the government may publish a proclamation declaring that it is satisfied that the ordinary courts are inadequate and ordering that Part V be brought into force. The government issued such a proclamation in May 1972. This proclamation, however, did not and cannot

> of itself seise the Special Criminal Court with jurisdiction to try any particular offence. The offence in question must be scheduled by the government under s.36 (1) of Part V (and where triable summarily, the necessary direction has been given under s.45 (1) of that part) or, alternatively, form the subject of a charge against an accused in respect of whose trial on such charge a certificate in writing has been issued by the director of public prosecutions under ss.46, 47 or 48 of Part V.[1]

In fact Part V of the Act provides that the power to certify such issues vests in the attorney general; under s.3 (1) of the Prosecutions of Offences Act, 1974 these functions have been transferred to the director of public prosecutions. This power has resulted in a number of alternative routes via which a case can reach the Special Criminal Court; these will be examined individually.

Where a person is charged before the District Court the case may be transferred for trial to the Special Criminal Court in four circumstances. Scheduled offences are dealt with in one of the following two ways:

- Section 45(1) sets down the procedure to be followed when the offence is a scheduled offence which the District Court has jurisdiction to deal with

1 Pye, 'Judicial Review of Discretionary Powers under Part V of the Offences against the State Act 1939', (1985) 3 *Irish Law Times*, 65, 65.

summarily, 'the District Justice must, if so requested, send the accused for trial before the Special Criminal Court'.[2]

- In the case of an *indictable* and scheduled offence where 'the District Justice finds that there is a case to answer following a preliminary examination, then s.45 (2) requires that the accused be transferred to the Special Criminal Court unless the DPP otherwise directs'.[3]

The regime is slightly different for non-scheduled offences.

- 'Section 46(1) provides that in the case of a non-scheduled offence which is triable *summarily,* then the District Court must send the accused for trial before the Special Criminal Court where the director . . . certifies that the ordinary courts are inadequate to secure the effective administration of justice'.[4]
- *Indictable* non-scheduled offences must be sent forward for trial before the Special Criminal Court following a preliminary examination where the DPP again certifies that the ordinary courts are inadequate.[5]

Alternatively, if an accused has been returned for trial to the Circuit Court or Central Criminal Court, the trial may be transferred to the Special Criminal Court, in which case the DPP must again certify that the ordinary courts are inadequate and must then apply to the High Court. 'Once the necessary certificate has been produced, it appears that the High Court has no option but to accede to the request. Although s.48 is not frequently invoked, it has been held that the mandatory nature of the section does not infringe the separation of powers'.[6] Furthermore, 'the DPP may . . . have a person charged directly before the Special Criminal Court with a scheduled offence, thereby eliminating the possibility of a preliminary examination in the District Court (see s.47 (1).[7] However, 'where non-scheduled offences are involved the requisite certificate as to the adequacy of the ordinary courts is necessary'.[8] Clearly, the DPP is given a broad discretion in determining the trial venue for both scheduled and non-scheduled offences. A certificate as to the inadequacy of the ordinary courts can result in almost any trial being heard by the juryless Special Criminal Court. Given the central position of the jury system within our body of law, it is important, to examine the limitations which have been placed on this discretion.

2 Hogan & Walker, *Political violence,* p. 232. 3 Ibid. 4 Ibid. 5 Ibid. 6 Ibid., see also *O'Reilly & Judge v. Director of Public Prosecutions* [1984] ILRM 224, 230. 7 Pye, 'Judicial Review of Discretionary Powers under Part V of the Offences against the State Act 1939', 66. 8 Hogan & Walker, *Political violence,* p. 232.

8.2 Judicial review of the executive

It is no surprise that the OAS has been the subject of litigation and much of that has centred on the role of the AG (and more recently the DPP) in certifying that the ordinary courts are inadequate. The High Court and Supreme Court, however, have been slow to review the decision of the DPP.

Two cases provide the jurisprudence on the reviewability of the decision of the DPP to certify that the ordinary courts are inadequate. In the case of *Savage & McOwen v. DPP*[9] the plaintiff had been returned for trial by the District Court to the Special Criminal Court pursuant to a certificate of the DPP. The plaintiff argued that the opinion of the DPP which was the basis of the certificate issued under s.46 of the Act of 1939 'could not have been reached on reasonable grounds or if reached on reasonable grounds was in error and was reached on insufficient grounds'.[10] In reviewing the decision of the DPP Finlay P, in the High Court, took a very narrow view of the role of the courts. He stated:

> The Courts ... are of course concerned to ascertain as to whether in any particular case the attorney general's certificate was valid in the sense that it was a certificate issuing from the attorney general and it would be concerned as to whether the attorney general had reached an opinion as expressed in that certificate but it seems to me ... that the opinion of the attorney general is not reviewable by the courts.[11]

This view suggests that unless the certificate is a forgery, or is purporting to express an opinion that the AG had not, in fact, reached, the certificate is immune from review. Furthermore, Finlay P established that s.45 of the Act 'does not appear to envisage any review by the courts'[12] thereby, almost entirely excluding the possibility of judicial review of the opinion of the DPP.

The reasoning of Finlay P was to be followed two years later by Carroll J in *O'Reilly & Judge v. DPP*,[13] where the plaintiff based his claim on a number of points. It was argued that the right to jury trial is a positive right and therefore there had to be a 'decisive process to take it away'; it was suggested that this could only be done by a member of the judiciary. It was also contended that the substitution of the DPP for the AG was unconstitutional since the AG was a constitutional officer, whereas the DPP was merely a civil servant. Perhaps the most interesting ground raised before the court was that,

> The plaintiff is not in a position to investigate the grounds on which the DPP issued the certificate. Once the plaintiff has raised the issue

9 [1982] 2 ILRM 385. 10 [1982] 2 ILRM 385. 11 [1982] 2 ILRM 385, 388. 12 [1982] 2 ILRM 385, 387. 13 [1984] ILRM 224.

> whether there were any or any adequate or reasonable grounds for the issue of the certificate, the court is entitled to and should investigate the grounds on which the DPP issued the certificate. It was suggested that this should be akin to the supervision exercised by the courts over a claim of privilege by the government. The plaintiff did not require that the grounds should be revealed in open court but did say there should be judicial supervision.[14]

This approach could be described as a compromise between the need for national security, and those of the accused to a fair trial.[15]

In relation to the need for judicial intervention in determining the trial venue and the constitutionality of substituting the DPP for the AG, the court was clear. Carroll J referred to three earlier precedents[16] and concluded that the Supreme Court had already decided,

1. that the Constitution authorizes the legislature to choose the method by which the question of the inadequacy of the courts is to be determined.
2. the determination does not have to be a judicial determination.
3. the legislature formerly chose the method of certification by the attorney general.
4. the legislature has now chosen that it is to be the DPP who certifies.[17]

This approach effectively dismissed those issues and again established that the determination of venue was not a judicial function and that the role of the AG and now the DPP was constitutional and acceptable.

On the further question of reviewing the reasons of the DPP for issuing a certificate, the High Court referred to the judgment of Finlay P in *Savage & McOwen v. DPP*.[18] In a lengthy passage worth quoting, Carroll J approved of that decision and followed it. She went on to hold that,

> the revealing of information in open court under conditions in which persons are seeking to overthrow the established organs of the state would be a security impossibility ... The plaintiff does not in this case seek revelation in open court but does seek a private investigation by the court into the certificate of the DPP.

14 *O'Reilly & Judge v. DPP* [1984] ILRM 224, 227. 15 The Offences against the State Review Committee made a recommendation based on a similar form of reasoning in their 2002 report. This recommendation will be considered in more detail later. See *Committee to Review the Offences against the State Acts, 1939–1998*, paras 9.60–9.77. 16 Namely, *In re MacCurtain* [1941] IR 83, *The State Bollard v. The Special Criminal Court*, High Court Unreported, 20 September 1972, and *In re the Criminal Law (Jurisdiction) Bill, 1975*, [1977] IR 129. 17 [1984] ILRM 224, 228. 18 [1982] 2 ILRM 385.

> Even though the Supreme Court in *re the Criminal Law (Jurisdiction) Bill 1975* [1977] IR 129 at p151 left open the question of the circumstances, if any in which the courts would be entitled to review *inter alia* a certificate by the DPP as to the inadequacy of the courts, I am of opinion, based on the terms of Article 38.3.1° of the Constitution and the authorities to date, that the opinion of the DPP is not reviewable by the courts, whether in open court or as a private investigation …
>
> The Oireachtas has determined the method under Article 38.3 by which the inadequacy of the ordinary courts is to be determined, i.e. the opinion of the DPP evidenced by his certificate. The courts do not have power to set that opinion aside, for to do so would be to substitute in a negative way their opinion as to the adequacy of the grounds on which the opinion was based.[19]

The main difficulty involved in reviewing that decision are reasons of national security. As Carroll J points out, when parties are attempting to overthrow the state it may be impossible to reveal the reasons behind the decision of the DPP in open court. She also notes, however, that the plaintiff was not seeking a review in open court. She then referred to the decision of the Supreme Court in *In re the Criminal Law (Jurisdiction) Bill 1975*. On the issue of reviewing the decision of the DPP, the court stated that, 'it is not necessary in this case for the Court to express an opinion on the circumstances, if any, in which the courts would be entitled to review any such proclamation, declaration or certificate – and it does not seek to do so'.[20] Therefore the issue of reviewing the decision of the DPP was left unresolved by the Supreme Court. Carroll J was free to consider the issue herself and referring to precedent and Article 38.3, she concluded that the decision of the DPP could not be reviewed either in open court or private session. The decision of Carroll J, like that of Finlay P in *Savage & McOwen v. DPP*, has been criticized.

These High Court judgments mean that the decision of the DPP is immune from review. While, the recent case of *Eviston,*[21] has seen a decision of the DPP successfully challenged; nevertheless, the majority of the case law has affirmed the position in *Savage & McOwen.* Barrington J in the High Court, while considering a somewhat unrelated matter, stated that 'it clearly

19 [1984] ILRM 224, 229. **20** *In re the Criminal Law (Jurisdiction) Bill, 1975* [1977] IR 129, 151. **21** *Eviston v. the DPP* [2002] 3 IR 260. While this case did not concern the Special Criminal Court it is a rare example of the Appeal Courts granting a successful review of a decision of the Director of Public Prosecutions, as such it may provide precedent which could be applied to the decision to certify the ordinary courts inadequate. At the very least it confirms that the decisions of the Director of Public Prosecution can be reviewed by the courts.

would be impracticable and dangerous, in the circumstances envisaged by the Offences against the State Act, to force the AG or the DPP to disclose in court the circumstances which had led him to the opinion that the ordinary courts were inadequate'.[22] The case of *The State (McCormack) v. The DPP*[23] is also of interest. This case arose from the Criminal Law (Jurisdiction) Act, 1976. McCormack had been returned for trial at Belfast Crown Court and wanted to opt for trial in the Republic, so, he requested that the respondents issue a warrant for his arrest; but the DPP refused to issue such a warrant. The case is unusual in that the applicant was seeking to force the DPP to issue a warrant for his arrest, and he was not attempting to avoid the jurisdiction of the Special Criminal Court. Barr J in the High Court stated:

> I respectfully concur with the reasoning of the President and the conclusions which he arrived at in *Savage & McOwen's* case that the Court has no power to review an opinion expressed by the director in a certificate issued by him under s.46 (2) of the Act of 1939. It seems to me that his function in deciding whether or not to prosecute a particular person for allegedly having committed a criminal offence is no different ... Both functions are executive in nature.[24]

On appeal in the Supreme Court, Finlay CJ laid down the grounds on which a decision of the DPP could be reviewed: 'if, of course, it can be demonstrated that he reaches a decision *mala fides* or influenced by an improper motive or improper policy then his decision would be reviewable by a court'.[25] The 'Catch 22' of this approach was explained by Walsh J when he commented:

> As the defendants have chosen not to offer any evidence in this case the court does not know what are the reasons which warranted the DPP's conclusion ... Be that as it may there is nothing before this court from which it could be reasonably inferred that, the opinion was either perverse or inspired by improper motives.[26]

Since the DPP has given no indication of his reasons, the court cannot determine if the opinion was based on *mala fides* or improper motive.

22 *The State (Smith & Fox) v. The Governor of the Curragh Military Detention Barracks* [1980] ILRM 208, 211. This case concerned the Prison Act, 1972. Section 2(3) of that Act provided that a Minister could direct that a prisoner be transferred to military custody where he had certified that he was 'of the opinion that prison accommodation or prison staff as insufficient to provide secure and reasonable conditions of custody...' As a result there are clear differences between the two cases, one concerns the reviewability of the DPP under the Offences against the State Act, 1939; the other considers the role of a Minister. Barrington J's support of the decision in *Savage & McOwen* is, however, interesting. 23 [1987] ILRM 225. 24 *The State (McCormack) v. The DPP* [1987] ILRM 225, 232. 25 Ibid., 237. 26 Ibid., 238/9.

Given the reluctance of the courts to review the decision of the DPP, it is unsurprising that they have been even less willing to entertain the possibility of reviewing the decision of government to maintain Part V of the OAS, 1939 in operation. In *In re the Criminal Law (Jurisdiction) Bill, 1975*[27] the Supreme Court appeared to leave the issue of review open. This Act, which also grew out of what the Supreme Court referred to as 'the intercommunal violence and killing in Northern Ireland',[28] provides that, 'when a person does in Northern Ireland an act which, if done in the state, would constitute an offence specified in the schedule of the bill, [that person] shall be guilty of an offence';[29] the details of the Act are not of interest here; but, it is interesting that the Supreme Court, during the course of their judgment in that case, confirmed that 'it was constitutional for the Oireachtas to have provided by the Act of 1939 that the question of the inadequacy of the ordinary courts should be determined by the government or by a certificate of the Attorney General'.[30] In *Savage & McOwen,*[31] Finlay P had noted that the Oireachtas had vested in the government the power to determine when special courts were required.[32] He further noted that there was a resultant right in Dáil Éireann to annul the government's proclamation. He then argued that the Act 'did not vest in the courts ordinarily sitting any power as it seems to me either to decide that in any particular circumstances special courts were necessary or on the other hand that they had, under any circumstances, ceased to be necessary.'[33] Therefore, because the Act did not specifically provide for review, Finlay P rejected the possibility of reviewing the government's decision that such courts were necessary. Carroll J reiterated this point in *O'Reilly & Judge.*[34] As a result of these decisions the courts are obviously unwilling to engage in any form of review of a government's decision to proclaim that the ordinary courts are inadequate.

8.3 The 'organized crime' cases

In the 1990s a series of cases arose where it was argued that, since the cases had no connection with the terrorist threat emanating from Northern Ireland, the Special Criminal Court was the incorrect trial venue. These cases could, for the sake of simplicity, be referred to as 'organized crime cases'. The use of the Special Criminal Court in such instances is not all that remarkable when consideration is given to the European experience of anti-terror legislation. For example, *pentiti,* a form of witness protection scheme in Italy was initially employed against the Red Brigades but was later utilized against the Mafia;[35] and similarly, the Germen systems of *Staatszeugen* (state's witness)

27 [1977] IR 129. 28 *In re the Criminal Law (Jurisdiction) Bill, 1975* [1977] IR 129, 142. 29 Ibid., 143. 30 *In re the Criminal Law (Jurisdiction) Bill, 1975* [1977] IR 129, 151. 31 *Savage & McOwen v. DPP* [1982] 2 ILRM 385. 32 Offences against the State Act, 1939, s.35 (2). 33 [1982] 2 ILRM 385, 386. 34 *O'Reilly & Judge v. DPP* [1982] ILRM 224, 228. 35 Fyfe &

and *Kronzeuge* (crown witness) 'evolved out of earlier experiments in trials of those accused of terrorism'.[36] Fyfe and Sheptycki note that the German prosecution of the Baader-Meinhof group rested upon the testimony of a 'crown witness', Gerhard Muller; this type of evidence was later utilized in the prosecution of neo-Nazi groups and, having been employed against both ends of the political spectrum, it was adapted through the *Verbrechensbekämpfungesgestz* of October 1994 for use in cases involving organized crime.[37] So, legislative measures that have been employed against terrorists in one context are often adapted for use in cases of organized crime.

With reference to the Irish experience, the first of the 'organized crime' case to be considered is that of *Kavanagh*. Here the applicant was charged directly before the Special Criminal Court with the non-scheduled offence of false imprisonment following a certificate of the DPP under s.47 (2) of the Act of 1939. The applicant sought a declaration that there was no reasonable basis for the opinion of the DPP to the effect that the ordinary courts were inadequate. In the High Court Laffoy J stated:

> The director's certificate under s.47 (2), in my view, belongs to that category of decisions which the Supreme Court, on policy grounds, has held to be reviewable only to a limited extent and accordingly, in my view, on the authority of *State (McCormack) v Curran* and *H v. Director of Public Prosecutions* the Director's certificate is not reviewable in the absence of evidence of *mala fides* on the part of the Director or that he was influenced by improper motive or improper policy.[38]

That conclusion is not, in and of itself, surprising, for it merely restates the test previously developed.

The important theme of this case is that the applicant claimed that, since he was not involved in a subversive organization, the venue was unsuitable; but Laffoy J concluded that 'the applicant did not adduce any evidence in support of his contention that the proclamation of 1972 was designed and intended to deal and only deal with cases arising from or reasonably connected with the conflict and troubles in Northern Ireland.'[39] Therefore, although the history surrounding the reintroduction of the court in 1972 may have suggested that it was designed to deal with a terrorist threat, the High Court felt that it was not exclusively created for such purposes. As the Committee to Review the OAS noted, the government proclamation in 1972 did not expressly state that the Special Criminal Court was being created to tackle the threat emanating from Northern Ireland.[40] However, 'the original

Sheptycki, 'Facilitating witness co-operation in organized crime cases: an international review' (Home Office On-line Report 27/05), 20. **36** Ibid., 21. **37** Ibid. **38** *Kavanagh v. The Government of Ireland* [1996] 1 ILRM 133, 146–7. **39** Ibid., 148. **40** *Committee to review the*

justification for the establishment of the ... Court is commonly believed to be directly associated with the civil conflict in Northern Ireland'.[41] Such a belief is not without basis; on 23 June 1972 the Taoiseach, Mr Lynch, stated on RTÉ Radio:

> We want to make sure that we can continue to control any subversive activities here ... But these activities were, of course, related to the situation in the North of Ireland and as soon as that situation will have eased ... then there wouldn't seem to be any need for the continuation of the special courts and therefore we would have to look at the situation again.[42]

Interestingly, although the Taoiseach clearly justified the establishment of the Special Criminal Court by referring to the North, he expressly did not say that it would be disestablished once violent activities had ended. He appears to have left the door open for the continued use of the court with the phrase, 'we would have to look at the situation again'. If the court was solely established for the purpose of tackling subversives then there would be no need for re-examination.

The case was appealed to the Supreme Court. The applicant again argued that the government Order of 1972 was a response to the trouble associated with Northern Ireland:

> the appellant relied upon a representation alleged to have been made by the Irish attorney general to the Human Rights Committee of the General Assembly of the United Nations and referred to in a paragraph from the Report of the Human Rights Committee dated 7 October 1993. The paragraph in question is paragraph 575 and reads as follows:
>
> > 'With respect to the Special Criminal Court, the representative stressed that the court was needed to ensure the fundamental rights of citizens and protect democracy and the rule of law from the ongoing campaign related to the problem of Northern Ireland.'[43]

The AG had justified the continuing existence of the Special Criminal Court by reference to the ongoing terrorist threat but this case did not involve such a threat and the appellant argued that as such the court's use in this case was unjustifiable. Barrington J was unimpressed and the Supreme Court held that

Offences against the State Acts, 1939–1998, para. 9.31. **41** Ibid., para. 9.32. **42** Department of An Taoiseach, file 2003/16/93. **43** *Kavanagh v. The Government of Ireland* [1997] 1 ILRM 321, 326.

> It is clear … that under our system the question of whether Special Criminal Courts should be established is a matter for the legislature and the question of whether the part of the Offences against the State Act providing for the establishment of Special Criminal Courts should be brought into force or should cease to be in force is a matter for the government.
>
> Provided these powers have been exercised in a *bona fide* manner the ordinary courts have no function in relation to them. There is a certain logic in this as the question under consideration is the adequacy or otherwise of the ordinary courts.[44]

As was noted in Chapter 4, the Special Criminal Court was used in trials of a non-subversive nature during World War II, so there is precedent for this approach. Arguably, it was open to the court to review the basis of the director's decision in a case where no terrorist threat had been cited. In *Savage & McOwen* and *O'Reilly & Judge* the court referred to the impossibility of review in cases where parties were seeking to undermine the organs of the state. In a case where no such organization was alleged to be involved, the court may have felt it more proper to examine what *other* motive the director may have had for choosing this trial venue. It, however, did not pursue that approach.

In *DPP (Ward) v. The Special Criminal Court & the DPP*[45] the High Court offered a justification for the use of the Special Criminal Court in a case where terrorist involvement was not alleged. Carney J pointed out that, in the modern age,

> An Garda Síochána as well as having to deal with crime in its traditional forms now has in addition to deal with organized crime. Those engaged in such crime require a wall of silence to surround their activities and believe that its maintenance is necessary for their protection. They have at their disposal the resources including money and firearms to maintain this wall of silence and will resort to any means including murder in furtherance of this objective.[46]

Such an organization, it could be argued, poses as much of a threat of jury intimidation as a terrorist organization. The UK Home Office has also commented that 'in conducting their operations organized criminals frequently resort to extreme violence, intimidation and corruption … Organized crime groups and terrorist groups have many similarities in their ways of operating.'[47] If such a motive had inspired the decision of the DPP

44 Ibid., 327–8. 45 [1998] IEHC 48; [1999] 1 IR 60. 46 [1998] IEHC 48, para. 1. 47 The Home Office, *One step ahead; a 21st century strategy to defeat organized crime*, Cm 6167 (2004), p.

to certify the ordinary courts as inadequate, it could easily be upheld. Unfortunately, the DPP was not obliged to state this as his reason. In their dissent to the Report of the Committee to Review the OAS, Justice Hederman, Professor William Binchy and Professor Dermot Walsh note that 'no other common law jurisdiction has come to the conclusion that the risk of jury intimidation warrants non-jury trial'.[48] They also comment that

> while Ireland ... has experienced the growth of organized crime in recent years, it is not plausible to suggest that, in contrast to other common law jurisdictions such as the United States of America, England and Australia, Irish social conditions are so perilous as to warrant dispensing with jury trial.[49]

This argument, I feel, underestimates the importance of two points. Firstly, the existence of the Special Criminal Court prior to the emergence of the threat of organized crime coupled with its proven track record in the fight against terrorism, meant that it was logical for the Irish authorities to utilize it. Authorities in Germany and Italy (as we have seen) have also adapted anti-terror measures to combat organized crime.[50] Secondly, the comparison to the United States, England and Australia ignores the differences in population among these jurisdictions. Economies of scale operate in these larger jurisdictions which make it easier to maintain the anonymity of a jury. Disappearing unnoticed for the course of a criminal trial is more difficult in Ireland – a point recognized by the dissenting members of the Committee.[51] It is not my contention that only cases of a terrorist nature should be tried before the Special Criminal Court; but I do feel that while in terrorist cases the reason for the decision of the DPP is obvious, in other cases such as *Kavanagh* and *Ward* the courts should satisfy themselves that there is a reasonable basis for the transfer of trials to this venue. Robinson commented that 'to channel persons charged with purely criminal offences to the Special Criminal Court is to abolish trial by jury by the back door'.[52] Meaningful review would address these concerns; perhaps, in light of the decision in *Eviston,* such review will be possible in the future.

As a matter of practice, a reliable source has informed me, confidentially, that the office director of public prosecution has had a subtle change in policy and is now not generally in favour of trying cases of an 'organized crime' nature before the Special Criminal Court. As a result, there has been a drop in the number of organized crime cases being referred to the court. While

7. **48** *Committee to review the Offences against the State Acts, 1939–1998*, para. 9.93. **49** Ibid. **50** As was noted earlier. See Fyfe & Sheptycki, 'Facilitating witness co-operation in organized crime cases', 19–22. **51** *Committee to review the Offences against the State Acts, 1939–1998*, para. 9.95. **52** Robinson, *The Special Criminal Court*, p. 35.

welcoming any such development, the court's restrictive interpretation of their role in reviewing the decision of the DPP to certify the ordinary courts inadequate, remains a point of some considerable concern.

8.4 Alternative approaches available to the courts

Savage & McOwen and *Judge & O'Reilly* placed particular emphasis on the security implications of reviewing the decision of the DPP and on the executive nature of that decision. However, as Byrne noted,

> the decision of the Supreme Court in *Murphy v. Dublin Corporation* established that where a privilege is claimed by the executive regarding a piece of evidence required by the judiciary, and the privilege is based on that evidence being classified by the executive as sensitive from a security point of view, the courts may examine the material *in camera.*[53]

Murphy can be distinguished from *Savage & McOwen* and *O'Reilly & Judge* because it was a civil, not a criminal, case. For that reason, the Supreme Court stated: 'the court has not to review the considerations which might arise if in the course of a criminal prosecution an effort was made to obtain the disclosure' of certain documents.[54] However, Walsh J also noted that,

> It is clear that, when the vital interests of the state (such as the security of the state) may be adversely affected by disclosure or production of a document, greater harm may be caused by ordering rather than by refusing disclosure or production of a document. In such a case the courts would refuse the order but would do so at their own decision.[55]

Walsh J was clear that, although the courts might rarely disagree with the executive, they should not accept 'without question the judgement of the minister'.[56] This is a very different approach to that later taken by the courts when dealing with review of the DPP's certificate. An increased willingness on the part of the courts to review the DPP's decision would be welcome and an approach more akin to that in *Murphy* than that in *Savage* would allow at least a more meaningful if limited appraisal. To facilitate such a review, the Committee to Review the OAS recommended that independent counsel could be employed to argue on behalf of the applicant before an *in camera* sitting of the High Court. Under this proposal the High Court could examine the material without granting the accused access to sensitive information; it would also ensure that counsel for the accused would not be in possession of information which they were not at liberty to disclose to their client.[57]

53 Byrne, 'Judicial reviewability of a prosecutorial discretion' (1981) 16 *Irish Jurist*, 86.
54 *Murphy v. Corporation of Dublin* [1972] IR 215, 233. 55 Ibid., 234. 56 Ibid., 236.
57 *Committee to review the Offences against the State Acts, 1939–1998*, para. 9.65.

Following the decision in *Judge & O'Reilly* judicial review merely questions whether the DPP was acting *intra* or *ultra vires*. 'This means that, unless the court found that there was *no* evidence on which the DPP could have based his opinion, which triggers the referral of non-scheduled offences to the Special Criminal Court, it would still be possible for a valid opinion to be informed by him.'[58] Therefore, even if review were allowed it would be restricted, and, as long as there was some evidence supporting the opinion, the certificate could stand. Byrne notes that the courts are often willing to refer to possible justifications for the decision of the director. As he comments,

> In *State (Littlejohn) v. Governor of Mountjoy Prison*, the Supreme Court took the view that in exercising the power under the 1939 Act it was permissible to take account of the difference between a judge sentencing alone in the ordinary courts and the anonymity of three judges reaching a decision in the Special Criminal Court. Speaking for the Court Henchy J stated they were 'not entitled to speculate as to the grounds on which' the discretion was exercised, but that it was sufficient for the Court to support the sentencing basis where this was the only possible ground for its exercise.[59]

Although the court did not seek a reason from the DPP, it was willing to accept that the sentencing issue was valid and was the only reason on which the director could have based his decision. I suggest that rather than speculating as to the DPP's possible reasons it would be preferable if the courts developed a suitable means of reviewing his actual reasons.

In *Savage* and later in *O'Reilly* it was noted that the power regarding special criminal courts is vested in the Oireachtas who have delegated some of that authority to the government, however, this does not necessarily preclude judicial review. Pye refers to the common law presumption in favour of reviewability; only clear words precluding review can remove this right.[60] However, he also notes that 'the courts have not always been consistent in the application of this common law doctrine, particularly where legislation designed to cope with an emergency falls to be interpreted'.[61] So, it may be more useful to consider issues surrounding claims of privilege by the executive in Irish law. In the *State (Lynch) v. Cooney* the Supreme Court held that 'it could review an opinion of the Minister of Posts and Telegraphs reached under s.31(1) of The Broadcasting Authority Act, 1960, as amended, that "the broadcasting of a particular matter or any matter of a particular

58 Byrne, 'The Director of Public Prosecution's power to refer cases to the Special Criminal Court' (1984) 6 *Dublin University Law Journal*, 177, 179. 59 Ibid. 60 Pye, 'Judicial review of discretionary powers under Part V of the Offences against the State Act 1939', 67. 61 Ibid.

class would be likely to promote, or incite to, crime or would tend to undermine the authority of the state'".[62] The case concerned an Order made by the minister to the effect that the broadcasting authority should refrain from broadcasting material 'made by or on behalf of, or inviting support for, the Sinn Féin organization'.[63] O'Hanlon J stated forcefully in the High Court that he,

> was not aware of any case where the use of the expression 'is of opinion' has admitted of judicial review with regard to the reasonableness of the decision made. The decision of the Supreme Court in *In re the Offences against the State (Amendment) Bill, 1940* would appear to be conclusive against any such interpretation.[64]

If such an approach had remained, the possibility of review would be unlikely; however, the Supreme Court took an unexpected approach. Chief Justice O'Higgins stated that

> in the opinion of this Court the learned trial judge was mistaken in his conclusion. While the opinion of the former Supreme Court, expressed in 1940 and in 1957, reflected what was then current judicial orthodoxy, judicial thinking has since undergone a change. Decisions given in recent years show that the power of the courts to subject the exercise of administrative powers to judicial review is seen as having a wider reach than that delimited by those decisions of 1940 and 1957. In particular, it has been established by this Court in *McDonald v. Bórd na gCon* an *East Donegal Co-operative v. The Attorney General* that the correct approach in considering such questions is first of all to construe the statute. If the statute lends itself to more than one construction ... there is a presumption that the Oireachtas ... intended only the constitutional construction.[65]

This is important for a number of reasons. Firstly, it overturned the decision of the Court in *In re the Offences against the State (Amendment) Bill 1940*, and secondly, it permitted review of an executive decision in a case concerning an emergency provision. A curtailment of the right to free speech for the Sinn Féin Party and its members under the Broadcasting Authority Act, 1960 may be based on the same or similar information that caused the director to issue a certificate under the Offences against the State Act, 1939.[66] Both potentially involve security considerations; therefore, if one is reviewable, why not the

62 Pye, 'Judicial review', 69. **63** *The State (Lynch) v. Cooney* [1982] IR 337, 337. **64** Ibid., 347. **65** Ibid., 360. **66** Pye, 'Judicial review', 70.

other? The decision in *In re the Offences against the State (Amendment) Bill, 1940* (we will recall) concerned the operation of internment without trial. Since the Supreme Court was willing to overrule that decision, a review of the director's certificate might be possible. After all, 'there are more security type problems connected with the operation of the internment powers under this legislative scheme than with the DPP's venue choice power'.[67]

Further support is available for the view that the ordinary courts have a role to play in limiting the discretion of the DPP in relation to the selection of a trial venue. The case of *Eccles v. Ireland* concerned a challenge of the independence of the members of the Special Criminal Court. The plaintiff argued that the tribunal did not enjoy the appropriate level of independence largely because of the method of appointment of members of the court.[68] Finlay CJ stated the case succinctly when he said:

> The contention of the plaintiffs is that the terms of s.39 (2) are, as a matter of law, to be interpreted as meaning that the government could exercise an *unfettered* power to interfere with the proceedings and decisions of the Special Criminal Court by terminating the appointment of its members for the reason only that their decisions did not favour the interests of the executive ... This Court rejects these submissions as being incorrect in law.[69]

The chief justice went on to explain how and why the government did not have an unfettered discretion:

> The judgment of this Court in *East Donegal Co-operatvie Livestock Marts Ltd. v. Attorney General* [1970] IR 314 at p 341 of the report; states as follows:
>
> > 'At the same time, however, the presumption of constitutionality carries with it not only the presumption that the constitutional interpretation or construction is the one intended by the Oireachtas but also that the Oireachtas intended that proceedings, procedures, discretions and adjudications which are permitted, provided for, or prescribed by an Act of the Oireachtas are to be conducted in accordance with the principles of constitutional justice. In such a case any departure from those principles would be restrained and corrected by the courts.'
>
> This principle applies to the powers granted to the government

67 Byrne, 'The Director of Public Prosecution's power to refer cases to the Special Criminal Court', 181. 68 *Eccles v. Ireland* [1986] ILRM 343 and s.39 Offences against the State Act, 1939. 69 *Eccles v. Ireland* [1986] ILRM 343, 350.

> and to the minister respectively, by these subsections. If either of these authorities were to seek to exercise its power in a manner capable of interfering with the judicial independence of the court in the trial of persons charged before it would be attempting to frustrate the Constitutional rights of persons accused before that court to a trial in due course of law. Any such attempt would be prevented and corrected by the courts established under the Constitution.[70]

So, Finlay CJ felt that, in the above circumstances, executive discretion was open to review. These circumstances are similar to those under consideration since they involve the same court and therefore the same security implications. Despite the fact that the Supreme Court concluded that s.39 of the Act of 1939 was not repugnant to the Constitution, its willingness to review the government actions displays a belief that such issues can be reviewed despite Article 38.3.

A more recent, but unconnected, case is relevant since it shows the willingness of the courts to review government and executive actions despite concerns about the separation of powers. The facts of *DB v. Minister for Justice*[71] are unrelated to the Special Criminal Court. The applicant, a minor in need of secure accommodation, said, 'that whilst the High Court has made declarations concerning the obligations of the state towards young people with these special needs, the Minister of Health has failed to take timeous and effective steps to meet those needs.'[72] Kelly J, citing Ó Dálaigh CJ in *State (Quinn) v. Ryan*,[73] argued that the Constitution was designed to provide substantive fundamental rights; he concluded by saying,

> it is said that this Court does not have any entitlement to become involved in what was called matters of policy. I am by no means persuaded that this is so. If such an intervention were required in order for this Court to carry out its duties under the Constitution ... then, in my view, it would be open to it to do so.[74]

As a result, the High Court directed the minister to provide funds for the development of secure accommodation for *DB* and others in similar circumstances. Although this was not an emergency case, in the usual meaning of that phrase, it is interesting that the court was willing to interfere with the discretion of the minister to such an extent in order to protect individual rights. *DB* was overturned by *D (T) v. Minister for Education*.[75] Keane CJ noted:

70 Ibid., 351. 71 [1999] 1 ILRM 93. 72 *DB v. Minister for Justice* [1999] 1 ILRM 93, 96. 73 [1965] IR 70, 122. 74 *DB v. Minister for Justice* [1999] 1 ILRM 93, 103. 75 [2001] IESC 86.

> The ministers in the present case, in determining that particular resources should be allocated to the building and staffing of the units which are now the subject of the order, were beyond argument exercising the executive power of the state on behalf of the government as a whole. The monies required to provide and staff the units can only be made available to the ministers by Dáil Éireann under the appropriation machinery prescribed under Article 17.2 and then only on the recommendation of the government.[76]

The majority of the Supreme Court,[77] concluded that the decision in *DB* was an unjust interference with the separation of powers. If a fraction of the level of judicial activism displayed in *DB* were brought to bear on the issue of reviewing the decision of the DPP to certify the ordinary courts inadequate, meaningful review would be possible. The Supreme Court judgment in *D (T)* could be distinguished since review of the decision of the DPP would not concern the expenditure of public funds.

Perhaps most significantly, in *Eviston*[78] the courts revealed a willingness to review the decision of the DPP as to whether or not it was proper to proceed with a prosecution. The case concerned a fatal motor accident. On 28 June 1998 Linda Eviston had a puncture which she was unable to fix. Two men volunteered to change the wheel and shortly afterwards Eviston crashed into another car resulting in the death of Tony Moynihan. Eviston co-operated with the subsequent investigation and it was determined that the replacement wheel had suddenly deflated, causing the crash.[79] The office of the DPP considered the case and determined that there should be no prosecution.[80] Following these events, the father of the deceased wrote to the DPP stating, 'I have personally contacted the Minister John O'Donoghue in relation to this matter in the hope that he can use his good office to assist us in this most distressing matter' and appealing for the decision to be reconsidered.[81] The issue was reconsidered and proceedings against Eviston began; this decision to change opinion was challenged. Kearns J in the High Court noted that

> the courts in Ireland have shown considerable reluctance to apply the normal standards of judicial review to prosecutorial decisions … [concluding that] in a nutshell, it has been held that in decisions to prosecute or not to prosecute, the court can only intervene by way of judicial review where it is demonstrated that the respondent in making his decision did so *mala fide* or was influenced by an improper motive

76 [2001] IESC 86, 74. **77** With Denham J dissenting. [2001] IESC 86, 164. **78** *Eviston v. the Director of Public Prosecutions* [2002] 3 IR, 260. **79** [2002] 3 IR 260, 264. **80** [2002] 3 IR 260, 265. **81** [2002] 3 IR 260, 266.

> or was influenced by an improper purpose or had abdicated his functions.

Furthermore, reasons do not have to be given for any decision.[82] This, as we have seen, is an accurate summation of the previous case law in the area. In the current instance, however, the High Court was willing to depart from the previous orthodoxy. Kearns J stated that

> this case is not about a decision to prosecute or not to prosecute. It is about the reversal or unmaking of such a decision in particular circumstances ... The court cannot refrain from an assessment of those reasons and the circumstances in which the decision to reverse was made, always bearing in mind that it should only intervene on rare occasions and allow the respondent the widest possible margin of appreciation.[83]

Kearns J then applied a test similar to the famous test in *Wednesbury*[84] stating that 'no sensible person who applied his mind to the matters to be decided by the respondent could have arrived at the decision which he did';[85] significantly, Kearns J was adamant that he was not stating that the director had acted with *mala fides* or any form of improper motive.[86] In other words, he was not applying the test which had been laid down in previous cases. A high barrier to review remained, since Kearns J was applying a *Wednesbury* style test: namely the decision maker must reach a decision which no sensible (or in the case of *Wednesbury,* reasonable) decision maker would have reached. However, he had opened the door to effective judicial review of the merits of the decisions of the DPP.

Significant High Court rulings, like dissenting judgments, are of academic interest, but little practical importance, if they are overturned on appeal. The Supreme Court in *Eviston,* however, did not overrule Kearns J, although it did clarify a number of issues and in doing so probably lessened the impact of the case. Keane CJ concluded that Kearns J had erred in the High Court when he had concluded that the decision of the DPP was irrational.[87] Importantly, however, the chief justice noted that although

> it was undoubtedly open to the respondent in this case, as in any other case, to review his earlier decision and to arrive at a different conclusion, even in the absence of any new evidence ... The distinguishing feature in this case is the communication by the respondent of

82 [2002] 3 IR 260, 269/270. 83 [2002] 3 IR 260, 276/277. 84 *Associated Provincial Picture Houses Ltd. v. Wednesbury Corporation* [1947] 2 All ER 680. 85 [2002] 3 IR 260, 277. 86 [2002] 3 IR 260, 277. 87 [2002] 3 IR 260, 296.

> a decision not to prosecute the person concerned ... I am satisfied that the decision of the respondent was *prima facie* reviewable by the High Court on the ground that fair procedures had not been observed.[88]

The Supreme Court affirmed the decision of the High Court while adopting a different form of reasoning to justify it. Even McGuinness J, who dissented from the majority decision, commented that,

> whilst I believe Kearns J was incorrect on the particular grounds on which he granted the relief sought and I am unconvinced by the more extensive argument made in this court in support of his order, I confess to a sense of relief that my views have not prevailed.[89]

Despite the misgivings of McGuinness J, review of the decisions of the DPP now appears possible.

The Supreme Court decision is intriguing. The grounds for review adopted by Kearns J in the High Court set a high barrier for any future review of a decision of the director but nonetheless provided for some form of meaningful judicial review. The Supreme Court, unwilling to apply this test, instead adopted the approach of protecting 'fair procedures'; it is possible that future argument will centre on whether or not 'fair procedures' include a duty to give reasons which up until now, as we have seen, has been resisted. In the High Court, it was noted that 'the practice of the DPP is not to give reasons for his decisions not to initiate or to proceed with prosecutions. Casey has suggested that if judged by the broad standards of fairness, openness, accountability and efficiency, the Irish prosecution system is found wanting'.[90] It is not inconceivable that such a shift in emphasis, over time, might allow the procedures of the DPP to be challenged. The Supreme Court has certainly broadened the scope of judicial review of the decisions of the director and may have broadened it significantly.

I have repeatedly stated during the course of this book that in the field of emergency legislation the courts must balance the rights of the accused against the needs of national security.

> It is widely held in liberal democratic countries that the traditional institutions of adjudication, the courts, need to be independent of, and insulated from, politics in order to perform their function properly ... That is not to say that ... the actions of the courts do not form part of the process of government. What it does mean is that efforts are made

88 [2002] 3 IR 260, 298. **89** [2002] 3 IR 260, 303. **90** [2002] 3 IR 260, 271 citing Paul McDermot, *Res judicata & double jeopardy* (1999), para. 22.22.

> to enable the courts to function in an autonomous way in performing their duty of saying what the law is, even if this involves restraining governments themselves.[91]

There is an increased need for caution when the courts are asked to restrain the government in cases involving state security. The government may be better placed to assess the danger facing the state; however, the limited nature of judicial review does not necessarily endanger state security. In *Judge & O'Reilly* Carroll J exercised extreme restraint in rejecting the possibility of review; stating that review in open court would be a security impossibility, she went on to dismiss even *in camera* review.

There are genuine security concerns with reviewing the certificate of the DPP: if an accused succeeds in rebutting the presumption in favour of a certificate's validity, the onus of supporting the certificate would fall on the DPP. As Pye notes, in some cases this might cause the DPP 'to forego establishing his opinion's validity rather than put in evidence security sensitive information'.[92] Alternatively, the evidence, 'could form the subject matter of a private examination by the presiding judge himself to determine whether the DPP had discharged the onus of proving his opinion's validity'.[93] It is true that 'such a judicial determination in private of a substantive issue (as distinct from a procedural one concerning a claim of executive privilege or the admissibility of evidence in respect of an important state interest) would, no doubt, be novel'.[94] I suggest that a novel approach would be preferable to blind trust in the director's good faith. The proposal of the Committee to Review the OAS allowing for an *in camera* hearing with independent counsel is an ideal compromise between the competing interests of national security and justice for the accused. This proposal combined with the decision in *Eviston* allows some scope for the development of judicial review of the decisions of the DPP, including the decision to certify the ordinary courts inadequate. A private investigation would not provide the accused with the right to view the files and rebut the evidence, because that might compromise national security; however, a private investigation does ensure a greater level of protection for the accused by guaranteeing a judicial role in the supervision of the DPP's discretion.

8.5 Parliamentary review of the executive

While the courts have been unwilling to interfere with the executive in relation to the existence or operation of the Special Criminal Court, they have drawn attention to the role of the legislature in determining these issues.[95]

91 Chubb, *The Constitution & constitutional change in Ireland* (1978), p. 37. 92 Pye, 'Judicial review', 70. 93 Ibid., 71. 94 Ibid. 95 *O'Reilly & Judge* [1984] ILRM 224, 228.

S.35(5) of the OAS, 1939 provides that Dáil Éireann may annul the government proclamation. Despite the ending of the state of emergency under Article 28.3.3° by the Houses of the Oireachtas in February 1995,[96] the Dáil has not (at the time of writing) considered any resolution to rescind the government proclamation of 1972.[97] This is regrettable. The Department of Justice, Equality and Law Reform, the AG, the DPP and the Gardaí conducted reviews in 1997, 1998, 1999 and 2000 and these confirmed the continuing necessity of the Special Criminal Court. Welcome and all as such reviews might be, they are no substitute for parliamentary supervision of the executive arm of state. Furthermore, no subsequent reviews seem to have taken place since the publication of the Report of the Committee to Review the OAS.[98] To ensure regular parliamentary examination of the issues surrounding the Special Criminal Court the Committee recommended that a sunset clause (requiring a positive resolution to be passed by both Houses of the Oireachtas) be included in the OAS Acts.[99] This would have the added attraction of providing a public record (in the Dáil Debates) of the workload and use of the court and would help to avoid the 'normalization' of the court; it would be impossible to ignore the fact that the court is extraordinary.

8.6 Review of the executive by the Supreme Court of Israel

The example of Israel is instructive since that nation has faced both interior and exterior threats for most of its history.

> During its forty-eight year existence, Israel has gone to war seven times with its neighbors. It has also had to counter incessant threats of hostilities and terrorist attacks perpetrated by countries hostile to it, or organizations aimed at its destruction and replacement by a different political entity. Under such circumstances, Israel has developed a high level of war preparedness.[1]

An area of particular interest is that of 'administrative detention', which is in effect Israel's system of internment without trial.

96 *Committee to review the Offences against the State Acts, 1939–1998*, para. 4.40. 97 Ibid., para. 6.42. 98 In correspondence with the author in June 2004, David Walker, of the Security & Northern Ireland Division, Department of Justice, Equality & Law Reform, informed the author that annual reviews had occurred between 1997 and 2000. 'In 2001, it was decided to defer the review pending the report of the recommendations of the Committee to Review the Offences against the State Acts 1939–98. The final report of the Committee was published in August 2002 ... and its recommendations, including those pertaining to the Special Criminal Court, are currently under consideration'. It would appear that following the deferral of the annual review mechanism in 2001, it has not been reactivated. 99 *Committee to review the Offences against the State Acts, 1939–1998*, para. 9.43. 1 Hofnung, *Democracy, law & national security in Israel* (1996), p. 2.

Unlike Ireland, Israel does not have a written constitution; instead it has a series of Basic Laws which are developing into something akin to a constitutional code. In relation to administrative detention the relevant Basic Law is Basic Law: Human Dignity and Liberty of 1992, s.5 of which states that, 'there shall be no deprivation or restriction of the liberty of a person by imprisonment, arrest, extradition or by any other manner'; s.12 continues:

> This Basic Law cannot be varied, suspended or made subject to conditions by emergency regulations; notwithstanding when a state of emergency exists, by virtue of a declaration under section 9 of the Law & Administration Ordinance, 5708 – 1948, emergency regulations may be enacted by virtue of said section to deny or restrict rights under this Basic Law, provided the denial or restriction shall be for a proper purpose and for a period and extent no greater than required.[2]

Like Bunreacht na hÉireann the Basic Law provides a right, in s.5, and then limits that right in a later section; under s.12 deviation from the Basic Law is permissible when a state of emergency has been declared. '[F]inding the balance between security needs and adherence to the rule of law is central to any democracy under threat';[3] as early as 1949 the High Court of Israel had stated that 'while it is true that state security, which requires detaining an individual, is no less important than the need to preserve civil rights, whenever it is possible to achieve both aims, one should not ignore one or the other'.[4] This point was recognized during the Knesset[5] debate introducing the Emergency Powers (Detention) Law of 1979; the chairman of the Knesset Constitution, Law & Justice Committee, David Glass Member of the Knesset (MK), recognized it but argued that administrative detention was necessary as a last resort; Meir Vilner MK argued that

> Israel had been in a state of continuous emergency ever since its establishment. Thus his party proposed ... that rather than being in effect during emergencies ... the law should come into effect only when Israel was involved in actual war and only after the Knesset had decided to put it into operation.[6]

2 Zamir & Zysblat, *Public law in Israel* (1996), pp 154–56. 3 Hofnung, *Democracy, law*, p. 1. 4 *El Carbotliv v. Minister of Defense et al.*, High Court 48[8] P.D. 2, 1949, 106 see Sharfman, *Living without a constitution: civil rights in* Israel (1993), p. 96. 5 The Israeli Parliament. Members of the Knesset are referred to as MKs. 6 Sharfman, *Living without*, p. 149. 7 Despite the fact that the Special Criminal Court can exist in the absence of a state of emergency, it is a matter of fact that a declared state of emergency existed in Ireland from 1939 to 1976, whereupon a fresh state of emergency was proclaimed which continued to operate up until 1995. See *Committee to review the Offences against the State Acts, 1939–1998*, para. 5.5–5.14. It should be noted that 'despite the absurdity of this state of affairs, the artificial maintenance of this declaration of

This is interesting. In Ireland, the Special Criminal Court can be established whenever the government is of opinion that the ordinary courts are inadequate; the existence of a state of emergency is not necessary. The government felt that the ordinary courts were inadequate in 1972 and at that point Ireland was indeed in a state of emergency. However, when that official state of emergency ended, the Special Criminal Court was allowed to continue since the government continued to deem it necessary.[7] In Israel, the permanency of the state of emergency could also allow for the continuous employment of administrative detention; and Meir Vilner MK was fearful this of in 1979. These concerns were largely ignored, and the law of 1979 provides the framework for administrative detention in Israel.

The role of judicial review is to protect and vindicate the rights of citizens against executive abuse. A power such as internment without trial is a draconian one, and any abuse of it would have a grave impact on the party detained; so it needs to be exercised carefully and reviewed frequently. In 1994 the Supreme Court of Israel heard a case involving the administrative detention of a number of Lebanese citizens who had been detained under the Act of 1979.

> The appellants argued against the validity of their detention. Their argument was, that holding them as a 'bargaining chip' in the negotiations with the various organizations for advancing the release of navigator Ron Arad does not fall within the framework of 'reasons of state security' which appear in Clause 2A of the State of Emergency Powers Law.[8]

The Israeli government argued that the detention of the appellants was vital for advancing the release of Israeli prisoners of war (POWs) and missing in actions (MIAs) being held by hostile states. Therefore, the respondents argued that the phrase 'state security' included the goal of achieving the release of Israeli POWs. Chief Justice Barak stated in the court that administrative detention was the,

> fruit of the balance between two tendencies: one is granting the state appropriate means to defend itself in the face of organizations that pose a great danger, and against which there is no possibility of acting in the way of conducting a normal criminal trial; the second – guaranteeing, by means of judicial review, that the regime does not wrongfully or needlessly use the authorities that it was lawfully given.[9]

emergency had no real practical consequences …'. Ibid., para. 5.7. 8 *A.B. appellants v. Minister of Defense* Israeli Supreme Court, Administrative Detention Appeal 10/94. http://humrts.huji.ac.il/landau1.htm accessed 15 November, 2000. 9 Ibid.

Barak CJ continued that 'once it has been proved that the continued detention of the Appellants contributes to the release of the MIA's, indeed the proper balance has been achieved in the framework of the Law, and the detention of the Appellant is valid'.[10] The chief justice showed an unwillingness to interfere with the role of the executive despite the fact that those detained did not, themselves, pose a security risk.

In the circumstances of a national emergency and given the sensitivity of seeking the release of POWs, the stance of the chief justice might be viewed as regrettable but not unexpected. Given those circumstances, the view of Dorner J is all the more commendable. She dissented from the majority view and 'emphasized that [administrative detention] was directed to the detention of particular persons whose own conduct was damaging to state or public security'.[11] Dorner J candidly noted that the appellants were Lebanese citizens and that 'eight of them are members of the Hizbollah organization. The other two are members of organizations that fight against Israel alongside Hizbollah.'[12] Despite these factors, she could not concur with the ruling of Barak CJ; arguing that 'a fundamental principle of our system is that denying a person's freedom is limited to punitive reasons or to prevent a danger that derives from the person whose freedom it is proposed to deny'.[13] She cited Justice Minister Shmuel Tamir who, in introducing the 1979 Act to the Knesset, stated that the Act

> concerns ... people from the centre of terrorism and murder. They cannot be brought to trial in the normal judicial system due to evidence problems. And if the General Security Service learns, from a competent and official intelligence source which satisfies the Chief Justice of the District Court and on appeal – the Supreme Court, that a certain person – is at the centre of the murder tendencies ... would you set him free knowing that tomorrow another bomb might be placed in Zion Square or on Mughrabi Street or in the heart of the Carmel or in remote settlements as the direct outcome of that persons activity?[14]

This statement explicitly recognizes the role of the courts in reviewing the administrative detention orders. Having examined the above, Dorner J concluded that

> the position of my colleague, Chief Justice Barak, leads to an interpretation of the law that permits the detention, for an unlimited period, of any person, as long as the detention entails a benefit, albeit indirect, for state security. Such sweeping and unlimited authority is not recognized

10 Ibid. 11 Ibid. 12 Ibid. 13 Ibid. 14 Ibid., quoting Justice Minister Shmuel Tamir.

> even in the laws of war from the field of international law. I cannot recognize its existence according to Israeli law.[15]

This judgment, like that of Gavan Duffy J on the same issue, is a *tour de force.*

In April 2000, however, the Israeli Supreme Court again examined the issue of administrative detention and the 'bargaining chip' precedents. In this re-examination the Supreme Court reversed its previous decision and announced that

> the 1979 Emergency Prerogatives Law (Detention) does not grant the Defense Minister the authority to place a person in administrative detention if the person does not pose a threat to the security of the state. The court went further and decided that no danger to state security emanates from the eight Lebanese being held in administrative detention, and we must conclude from this that the state does not have the authority to continue to hold them in administrative detention.[16]

This decision did not receive universal approval. While Zehava Galon MK of the Meretz Party[17] welcomed the ruling, the Defense Ministry stated that, 'although the prime minister believes that Israel should continue to hold the detainees for a certain period, it will act in accordance with the Supreme Court ruling'.[18] Indeed, it was later stated that the government intended introducing new legislation, 'to get around' the Supreme Court decision.[19] The important issue from our current perspective is that the Israeli Supreme Court was willing to review the role of the executive in the implementation of emergency legislation of a highly sensitive nature; where the Irish courts have been unwilling to introduce a meaningful examination of the reasons behind the DPP's decision to certify the ordinary courts inadequate in cases of a non-terrorist, non-subversive nature.

8.7 Diplock and the scheduling-in proposal

The establishment of the Diplock courts in Northern Ireland and the similarity of the two procedures was noted in previous chapters. Unlike the Special Criminal Court, which is a separate institution, the Diplock courts are a branch of the Belfast Crown Court.

15 Ibid. 16 Izenberg, 'Supreme Court orders Lebanese hostages freed', *Jerusalem Post*, 13 April, 2000. 17 a political party toward the left of the political spectrum. In December 2003 Meretz merged with two other parties of the left to form a new party YAHAD which means 'Together' but is also an abbreviation of 'Democratic Social Israel' in Hebrew. http://www.fact-index.com/m/me/meretz.html accessed 30 July 2004. 18 Izenberg, 'Supreme Court orders Lebanese hostages freed'. 19 'Israel Seeks to Codify Detention of Hostages', *Washington Post,* 18 April, 2000, http://washingtonpost.com/wp-dyn/articles/A37757–2000Apr18.htm accessed 15 November 2000.

> The term 'Diplock courts' is ... misleading in so far as it suggests a special criminal court in a special courthouse where special judges deal with special kinds of cases. In fact the single judge trials are heard in Belfast Crown Court, in the same building in Crumlin Road where ordinary Crown Court jury trials continue to be held, and they are presided over by High Court and County Court judges who also conduct normal court business in Northern Ireland.[20]

Despite this, the two legislative models are remarkable similar. Like the OAS, 1939 the legislation in Northern Ireland includes a Schedule of Offences. Scheduled Offences are described as 'terrorist and security offences';[21] however, the schedule 'also includes several statutory offences, such as wounding with intent and causing grievous bodily harm; robbery and aggravated burglary; and arson and criminal damage'.[22] Naturally, many of these offences may be conducted by, or in the support of, terrorist organizations but they may also be committed in other non-subversive circumstances. As a result,

> built into the legislative scheme is a mechanism which is designed to redirect to jury trial those cases which the Diplock system was not meant to cater. The key figure in this process is the attorney general. By note 1 of the schedule he is given a discretion to certify that any scheduled offence which is subject to that Note is not to be treated as a scheduled offence and is therefore to be dealt with by jury trial ... [However] there are no formally prescribed criteria governing the exercise of the Attorney-General's discretion.[23]

This discretion is wide-ranging and corresponds to the discretion of the Republic of Ireland's DPP discussed above.

The scheduling system has some identifiable problems. Jackson & Doran note that

> the most obvious and enduring criticism of the scheduling system is that it operates in such a way as to draw too many 'ordinary' cases within the Diplock net. Reference is often made to Walsh's survey of 111 cases tried in Diplock courts in 1980, from which the author concluded that around forty *per cent* of the alleged offences had no observable connection with the emergency situation.[24]

20 Jackson & Doran, *Judge without jury*, p. 9. **21** *Legislation against terrorism*, para. 13.4. **22** Jackson & Doran, 'Diplock & the presumption against jury trial: a critique' [1992] *Criminal Law R*eview 755, 757. **23** Ibid., 758. **24** Ibid., 759.

A scheduling-in procedure has been proposed as a solution to this problem; this would compel the AG to issue a certificate for all cases going before the Diplock courts; in the absence of a certificate there would be a presumption in favour of jury trials.[25] 'Proponents concede that the actual numbers of cases going for trial in Diplock courts would probably not be dramatically reduced but the symbolic force of such a move ought not to be underestimated'.[26]

The scheduling-in procedure appears to be compatible with the recommendations of the Committee to Review the OAS. The scheduled/non-scheduled distinction was felt to be unhelpful; the Committee noted that the distinction did not provide a transparent means of assessing which cases were directed before the Special Criminal Court.[27] Indeed, it was of the opinion that the scheduling procedure might contravene Article 38.3 of the Constitution since it did not provide for a determination that the ordinary courts were inadequate in each individual case.[28] The Committee recommended that the schedule be scrapped and replaced by a system whereby the DPP would have to certify in each case that the trial should be heard by the Special Criminal Court. While some members of the Committee were concerned that such a proposal might increase the remit of the court, that view appears unsubstantiated. Under the procedure for non-scheduled offences operating at present in the Republic of Ireland, there is a presumption in favour of jury trial which can be reversed by a certificate of the DPP, similar to the scheduling-in proposal of Jackson and Doran. As has been noted, that system does not necessarily safeguard the accused. The scheduling-in procedure can only be valuable if the reasons for scheduling a case 'in' are reviewable by the appellate courts. If the ordinary courts remain unwilling to review that certificate, as in the case of non-scheduled offences, then extending that procedure to scheduled offences would be unlikely to alter the practical consequences for an individual accused. The issue of reviewing the exercise of the DPP's discretion remains a central dilemma.

8.8 The Human Rights Committee (HRC)

The Human Rights Committee is an institution established under the International Covenant on Civil and Political Rights. It

> is not, strictly speaking, a United Nations organ. It is a treaty based organ created by the states parties to the Covenant ... Realistically, however, it must be recognized that in practice the HRC[29] is, in effect, in the position of a United Nations organ ... They are totally financed

25 Ibid., 764. 26 Ibid. 27 *Committee to review the Offences against the State Acts, 1939–1998*, para. 9.57. 28 Ibid., para. 9.58. 29 Human Rights Committee.

> from the United Nations budget ... [and] the Annual Report of the HRC is submitted to the General Assembly, through ECOSOC.[30] In practice the Annual Report is considered in some detail by the Third Committee of the General Assembly.[31]

The HRC has a number of distinct functions. Firstly, under Article 40 of the Covenant it considers and studies national reports submitted by states parties, 'on the measures they have adopted to give effect to the rights recognized in the Covenant';[32] secondly, Articles 41 and 42 provide for an inter-state complaints procedure; and finally, under the optional Protocol, the HRC may 'receive and consider communications from individuals subject to the jurisdiction of a state Party to the Protocol who claim to be victims of a violation of any of the rights set forth in the Covenant'.[33] The HRC has considered the issue of the Special Criminal Court on a number of occasions.

In the *Kavanagh* case, referred to earlier, the appellant relied on a submission made by the Irish attorney general to the HRC. The HRC's Annual Report of 1993 noted that 'with respect to the Special Criminal Court, the representative stressed that the court was needed to ensure the fundamental rights of citizens and protect democracy and the rule of law from the ongoing campaign related to the problem of Northern Ireland'.[34] The Irish Supreme Court was not swayed by the argument that since the AG had justified the court's existence on the basis of the Northern problem, the only grounds for the DPP's issuing a certificate as to the inadequacy of the ordinary courts was if the case pertained to the problem emanating from Northern Ireland. The HRC, however, stated that

> it did not consider that the continued existence of [the Special Criminal Court] ... is justified in the present circumstances. The measures referred to ... are of a character that normally fall to be notified under article 4 of the Covenant. The Committee notes, however, that the state party has failed to inform other states parties of any state of emergency ... as required under article 4, paragraph 3, of the Covenant.[35]

Clearly, the HRC considered deviation from the ordinary mode of trial to be an emergency power and it was critical of the Special Criminal Court's continued existence in the absence of such an emergency.

30 The Economic & Social Council. 31 McGolderick, *The Human Rights Committee*, pp 52–3. 32 Ibid., p. 50. 33 Ibid., pp 50–1. 34 Report of the Human Rights Committee to the General Assembly of the United Nations, 7 October 1993, para. 575, see *Kavanagh v. DPP* [1997] 1 *ILRM* 321, 326. 35 Human Rights Committee, *Concluding Observations of the Human Rights Committee: Ireland. 03/08/93*. CCPR/C/79/Add.21. 3 August 1993, para. 11, http:// www.unhchr.ch tbs/ doc.nsf/(Symbol)/10cef6e66dedc39e41256324003c32cc?Opendocument accessed 9 September 2004.

In 1998 the HRC considered the *Kavanagh* case under the third procedure outlined above, examining a number of issues arising from the case, including an outline of the proceedings undertaken by Kavanagh in the Irish courts. The 'author ... [that is, Mr Kavanagh] alleges to have been arbitrarily restrained and unequally treated in his procedural rights, since the DPP has not given any reasons or justification for his decision'.[36] Kavanagh also complained that the decision of the DPP was

> without any reason or justification and thereby violated the guarantee of Article 14, paragraph 1, to a public hearing. The state party's highest court ... had held in *H v. Director of Public Prosecutions*,[37] that the DPP cannot be compelled to give reasons for the decision short of exceptional circumstances such as *mala fides* being shown. The author claims that a crucial decision in relation to his trial, namely the choice of procedure and forum, was made in secret and on the basis of considerations which were not revealed to him or to the public and which therefore were not open to any rebuttal.[38]

Furthermore Kavanagh argued that the Order of 1972 providing for the reintroduction of the court was made in response to the increasing violence in Northern Ireland and not to deal with non-terrorist cases.[39] It could be said that Kavanagh brought the main issues under consideration in this chapter before the HRC for examination. Therefore, the decision of the HRC should be very instructive.

In response to these submissions, the state argued that there was a continuing threat to national security. Unlike in 1993 when it was contended that the basis of this threat was the political violence emanating from the North, it argued instead that there was a continuing threat to state security posed by the rise of organized crime and criminal gangs which could undermine the administration of justice and engage in jury intimidation.[40] The HRC concluded that trial in a venue other than the ordinary courts was not, in and of itself, a violation of the rights protected under the Covenant.[41] Specifically, the HRC was of the opinion that non-jury courts were not, per se, a violation of the rights of the accused.[42] The main conclusion of the HRC, however, was unfavourable from a government standpoint:

> The Committee regards it as problematic that, even assuming a truncated criminal system for certain serious offences is acceptable so

36 *Kavanagh v. Ireland* CCPR/C/71/D/819/1998, 26 April 2001, para. 4.1. 37 [1994] 2 IR 589. 38 *Kavanagh v. Ireland* CCPR/C/71/D/819/1998, 26 April 2001, para. 4.3. 39 Ibid., para. 4.4. 40 Ibid., para. 7.1. 41 Ibid., para. 10.1. 42 *Committee to review the Offences against the State Acts, 1939–1998*, para. 9.62.

> long as it is fair, parliament through legislation set out specific serious offences that were to come within the Special Criminal Court's jurisdiction in the DPP's unfettered discretion ... and goes on to allow ... any other offences also to be tried if the DPP considers the ordinary courts inadequate. No reasons are required to be given for the decision that the Special Criminal Court would be 'proper', or that the ordinary courts are 'inadequate', and no reasons for the decision in the particular case have been provided to the Committee. Moreover judicial review of the DPP's decision is effectively restricted to the most exceptional and virtually undemonstrable circumstances.[43]

Thus, the Committee concluded that Kavanagh's rights under Article 26 had been violated. This decision of the HRC can be broken down into three points: it was considered unreasonable that any offence, scheduled or not, could be directed for trial before the Special Criminal Court on the basis of a certificate from the director; furthermore, the lack of reasons given by the DPP for this decision was criticized; finally, the unreviewability of the director's certificate and reasons was felt to be in violation of the Covenant. I submit that these issues could be resolved by three reforms: the adoption of a scheduling-in procedure; the incorporation of independent counsel and *in camera* hearings for the review of sensitive material; and a more proactive form of judicial review similar to that employed in *Eviston*. As we have seen, these reforms would allow meaningful review of the DPP's decisions without jeopardizing national security.

43 *Kavanagh v. Ireland* CCPR/C/71/D/819/1998, 26 April 2001, para. 10.2.

9

Recent developments

9.1 The Court of Criminal Appeal

A significant difference between the present Special Criminal Court and its predecessors is that it provides for a right of appeal to the regular courts;[1] this increases its legitimacy. In the case of *The People v. Madden*[2] O'Higgins CJ reviewed the function of the Court of Criminal Appeals (CCA) in proceedings arising from trial by the Special Criminal Court noting that, 'in the appeals now before this Court, we have the transcripts of the rulings of the Special Criminal Court made in the course, and at the end, of the trial on questions of law and findings of facts'.[3] These transcripts are required by law[4] and could be said to provide an extra protection for the defendant. At present the Special Criminal Court provides a reasoned judgment as a matter of practice,[5] and a majority of the Committee to Review the OAS recommended that this practice be placed on a statutory footing.[6] The Special Criminal Court's reasoned 'judgment ... will set out the findings of fact and the inferences drawn from those facts ... The Court of Criminal Appeal will be able to examine the court's detailed findings of fact and inferences drawn from those facts when considering the soundness of the conviction'.[7] Such an examination would be impossible in cases of trial by jury because it is impossible to accurately determine the reasons behind a jury's verdict. [8] In *Madden* the Supreme Court concluded that

> the function of this Court [is] to consider the conduct of the trial as disclosed in the stenographer's report to determine whether or not the trial was satisfactory in the sense of being conducted in a constitutional manner with fairness, to review so far as may be required any ruling on matters of law, to review so far as may be necessary the application of the rules of evidence as applied in the trial, and to consider whether any inferences of fact drawn by the court of trial can properly be supported by the evidence; but otherwise to adopt all findings of fact, subject to the admonitions in the passages cited above.[9]

1 See s. 44, Offences against the State Act, 1939. For further discussion of this point see chapter 3. 2 [1977] IR 336. 3 [1977] IR 336, 340. 4 The Offences against the State Act, 1939–1972 Special Criminal Court Rules, 1975, Rule 25 and Rules of the Superior Courts, Order 86, Rule 14. 5 Walsh, *Criminal* Procedure, p. 1010. 6 *Committee to review the Offences against the State Acts, 1939–1998*, para. 14.1–14.2 7 Ibid. 8 Walsh, *Criminal procedure*, p. 1011. 9 [1977] IR 336, 340.

Thus, the role of the CCA is limited to considering matters of law, but it may also consider whether or not the evidence produced at the trial supports the inferences drawn by the court; a reasoned judgment and court transcript would obviously be of great assistance in this undertaking.

In the case of Liam Campbell,[10] the accused was tried before the Special Criminal Court for membership of an unlawful organization contrary to s.21 of the Offences against the State Act (OAS), 1939. At the trial he had not contested the evidence, and the trial court 'noted that this approach had saved a considerable amount of court time and expense'.[11] Following his conviction Campbell sought leave to appeal on the sole ground that 'the court erred in holding that the Real IRA was a prescribed organization'.[12] (The validity of this point will be examined later in this chapter.) The CCA cited, with approval, the decision in *The People (DPP) v. Moloney*[13] where O'Flaherty J stated that

> if an appeal is brought before this Court on a point that has not been canvassed at trial this Court will regard any person making such a point as having an obligation to explain why it is sought to made on appeal when not made at the trial. That is not to say that if the essential justice of the case calls for its intervention we have an obligation to so intervene.

Thus, the CCA will be reluctant to hear an appeal based on grounds which were not argued at trial. In the case of *Campbell,* the CCA concluded that the failure to raise the ground for appeal at trial

> was not an error or oversight but rather a strategic or tactical decision made by the appellants advisers who evidently decided that they might obtain a more lenient sentence for the appellant in the court of trial and perhaps thereafter succeed in persuading this Court that they should be allowed to raise a legal argument that was never made in the court below.[14]

Such a position appears reasonable. One cannot allow an individual secure a reduced sentence on the basis that they have saved the court time by not contesting evidence and then allow them to contest that evidence on appeal.[15]

10 *The People (DPP) v. Campbell* [2005] IE CCA 27. 11 Ibid. 12 Ibid. 13 *ex tempore,* Unreported, Court of Criminal Appeal, 2 March, 1992. 14 *The People (DPP) v. Campbell* [2005] IE CCA, 27. 15 There is a separate argument concerning the justness of allowing reduced sentences in such circumstances. From a Kantian perspective such an approach violates the principle of 'punishment as a categorical imperative' and is therefore highly objectionable. Such considerations are beyond the scope of this work but it will be asserted that plea and sentence bargaining of this sort is common place and appears to be accepted for practical, if not for philosophical, reasons. For a detailed examination of the these concepts see Christopher, 'The

So, the CCA takes a necessarily strict view of its function and does not exercise its appeal function lightly.

The decision of the CCA in *Murphy*[16] is also instructive. Murphy was 'convicted of conspiracy to cause an explosion of a nature likely to endanger life'.[17] The explosion in question was the 15 August 1998 bombing of Omagh, Co. Tyrone, and Murphy was said to have handed a number of mobile phones to dissident republican terrorists for the purpose of assisting them 'to move explosives to Northern Ireland for the purpose of bombing targets there'.[18] There were three key pieces of evidence in the case. Firstly, the accused made a series of admissions and Patrick Terence Morgan gave evidence to the effect that Murphy had borrowed his phone prior to the bombing; phone records established a similar pattern of phone calls before the Omagh and Banbridge bombings; and the trial court considered Murphy's prior convictions for similar offences. On the issue of Murphy's prior convictions the CCA was unequivocal. The accused had not put his good character in evidence, and the evidence did not fall into any of the exceptions provided by s.1(f) of the Criminal Justice Act, 1924. Indeed, the 'fact' of Murphy's prior convictions was never proved in court, and the evidence was entirely inadmissible. The issue of the phone records was also relatively straightforward and the CCA determined that they were admissible. An examination of Murphy's personal admissions and the evidence of Morgan will give us a greater understanding of the appeal court's role.

Terence Patrick Morgan testified before the trial court to the effect that Murphy has borrowed his mobile on 14 August 1998 claiming that his own mobile was not working. However, as defence counsel were summing up their case on 11 January 2002 it emerged that the prosecution had received a letter from a solicitor acting on behalf of Mr Morgan in which Morgan withdrew his evidence. Morgan gave fresh evidence to the court in which he completely repudiated his earlier version of events, claiming now that Murphy had not asked for his phone but that he had mislaid it on Friday, 14 August and discovered it again the following Monday. He claimed that he had been induced to give his original evidence by police threats.[19] The Special Criminal Court held that Morgan's original testimony was consistent with the admissions of the accused and decided to accept as truthful Morgan's original evidence. It will be recalled that O'Higgins CJ stated that the role of the appeal courts was 'to consider whether any inferences of fact drawn by the court of trial can properly be supported by the evidence; but otherwise to adopt all findings of fact'.[20] In line with this reasoning, the CCA held that

prosecutors dilema: bargains and punishments', (2003) 72 *Fordham Law Review* 93; Brady 'Just deserts: can a retributivist theory of punishment be justified?' (2004) 12 *Irish Student Law Review*, 86. **16** *The People (DPP) v. Murphy* [2005] IE CCA 1. **17** Ibid. **18** Ibid. **19** Ibid. **20** [1977] IR 336, 340.

> the question of credibility of the evidence given by Mr Morgan, whether in its entirety or in respect of either of the conflicting accounts given by him, was a matter entirely within the competence of the trial court which had the opportunity of hearing and observing Mr Morgan while he was giving evidence.[21]

Therefore, the CCA was unwilling to set aside the inferences drawn by the Special Criminal Court as to the credibility of Morgan's testimony.

The second issue of interest concerns the admissions made by Murphy while in custody. The accused was alleged to have made a number of incriminating statements which amounted to an admission on his part that he had passed the phones to Daly in order to assist him in moving explosives to Northern Ireland for the purpose of causing an explosion there. However, Electrostatic Detection Apparatus (ESDA) evidence established that the Garda notes of interviews conducted with Murphy had been altered. In particular, the original notes included a statement by Murphy that his wife's sister was Sheila Grew, who was known to have republican connections. Sheila Grew was not, in fact, Murphy's wife's sister and defence counsel asked why he would say that she was. The inference drawn by the defence was that Murphy had said no such thing and as a result one could infer that if this fragment of the interview was a fabrication, then the entire interview notes were a fabrication. The trial court held the evidence of two of the six Gardaí who had interviewed Murphy to be inadmissible. The trial court then made an extraordinary assumption, stating that

> Since ... there is no evidence that the error made about Mrs. Murphy's relationship with Ms Grue [sic] and its wrongful inclusion in the original interview note was ever divulged by Gardaí Donnelly or Fahy to any other member of the investigation team either at a case conference or otherwise. It is more likely that Garda Donnelly having discovered the error would not wish to admit to serious misconduct and that he rectified it without the knowledge of other officers except his partner, Garda Fahy ... In the absence of evidence connecting other officers with Garda Donnelly's wrongdoing there is nothing to establish that it might have percolated upwards or outwards and may have tainted the activities of other interrogators.[22]

This is a remarkable leap of faith, and the CCA noted that 'there is absolutely no evidence to support the conclusion ... that "the revised note was then restored to Garda Whelan's custody apparently without his knowledge"'.[23]

21 *The People (DPP) v. Murphy* [2005] IE CCA 1. 22 Ibid. 23 Ibid. This statement by the Special Criminal Court is extremely accommodating toward the Gardaí. It is perhaps the closest

The CCA set aside the conviction as unsafe on the basis that the trial court (that is, the Special Criminal Court) had failed to bring the necessary level of critical analysis to the possibility of the contamination of evidence. The trial court was criticized for making 'findings as a matter of probability about the police evidence which were based on speculation and not on evidence'.[24] The review courts were criticized in the previous chapter for being overly accommodating toward the executive. The CCA appears to be willing to exercise its jurisdiction in a purposeful manner.

9.2 Recent supergrass trials

One of the most striking recent developments in trial by Special Criminal Court has been the emergence of a new breed of Irish 'supergrass'. The need to employ accomplice testimony in the context of terrorism and organized crime is not surprising. 'Given that one of the characteristics of organized crime is that the leaders typically operate through intermediaries, their guilt can rarely be proved by the testimony of victims, eyewitnesses or forensic evidence. Successful prosecution of organized crime leaders therefore normally requires the use of accomplice evidence'.[25] As was noted in Chapter 4, David Rupert, an informer, gave evidence at the trial of Michael McKevitt. The controversial nature of this evidence arose from the fact that Rupert had been paid some $1.25 million (€1,035,000). Similarly, informer evidence has been employed in the series of trials of members of the gang accused of murdering journalist Veronica Guerin.

Accomplice testimony has a long, if not always distinguished, history. 'For centuries the common law has facilitated those who have decided to betray their erstwhile partners in crime by testifying against them. Accomplices who have been induced to turn Queen's ... evidence by the expectation of a reward have been regarded as competent witnesses at least since the seventeenth century.'[26] A supergrass is merely an accomplice who turns Queen's evidence on a 'grand scale'.[27] The modern history of supergrass in England began on 23 December 1972 when Bertie Smalls was arrested. Smalls was a member of a number of gangs responsible for major bank robberies in London. According to the police, after a brief period he offered to name all

Irish equivalent to Lord Denning's declaration in the case of the Birmingham 6 that 'If they won, it would mean that the police were guilty of perjury; that they were guilty of violence and threats; that the confessions were involuntary and improperly admitted in evidence; and that the convictions were erroneous.... That was such an appalling vista that every sensible person would say, "It cannot be right that these actions should go any further"'. Lord Denning MR, 17 January 1980. **24** *The People (DPP) v. Murphy* [2005] IE CCA 1. **25** Fyfe & Sheptycki, 'Facilitating witness co-operation in organised crime cases', 17. **26** Greer, 'Supergrass and the legal system in Britain and Northern Ireland', (1986) 102 *The Law Quarterly Review*, p. 200. **27** Bonner, 'Combating terrorism; supergrass trials in Northern Ireland', (1988) 51 *Modern Law Review*, p. 23.

his accomplices in exchange for his freedom.[28] The Irish experience of supergrass will forever be associated with a two-year period between 1981 and 1983 when 25 supergrasses[29] facilitated the arrest of nearly 600 suspects in Northern Ireland.[30] The history of the supergrass evidence and its fall from grace, in Northern Ireland in particular, have been adequately reviewed elsewhere.[31]

In Irish law, juries have the power to convict on the basis of uncorroborated accomplice evidence; however, there exists a 'very strong, indeed, imperative, rule of practice that the judge should warn the jury of the danger' of so doing.[32] The danger of employing uncorroborated accomplice evidence arises from the fact that

> an accomplice is by definition involved in the offence. Therefore, he 'knows all the details of the crimes and will be able to relate them accurately'; in order to falsely implicate another person, an accomplice 'only has to introduce him into the story which in its main essentials is true'.[33]

The accomplice is a self-confessed criminal with the almost unique ability to falsely implicate another in a convincing manner. The reliability of such witnesses is called into even greater question when one considers that they may have a strong personal motive to implicate others. A review of the recent Irish case law will help to illustrate these points.

Accomplice testimony has played a central role in three cases arising from the prosecutions of those accused of planning and committing the murder of, journalist, Veronica Guerin.[34] The decision in *Ward* is particularly revealing. Importantly, all admissions made by Paul Ward while in custody were held to be inadmissible in evidence by the Special Criminal Court.[35] The accused had remained silent during interrogation; he was then visited by his girlfriend, Ms Meehan, who had been arrested under s.30 of the OAS, Act 1939, and later by his mother. The Special Criminal Court noted that 'the coincidence

28 Greer, 'Supergrass and the legal system', p. 222. 29 Seven loyalist, eighteen republican. 30 Greer, 'The rise and fall of the Northern Ireland supergrass system' (1987) *Criminal Law Review*, pp 664–65. 31 The work of Greer and Bonner, in particular should be considered. 32 *The People (AG) v. Duffy* [1931] IR 144, 149. 33 Egan, 'The emergence of the Supergrass: exposing the inadequacies of the accomplice corroboration warning', (2004) 12 *Irish Student Law Review*, 133, 133. 34 Namely, *DPP v Ward,* Special Criminal Court, 27 November 1998, [1998] IEHC 170; *DPP v. Meehan,* Special Criminal Court, 29 July 1999; and *DPP v. Gilligan,* Special Criminal Court, 15 March 2001. the issues surrounding supergrass testimony in these cases and in Irish law in general, is examined in detail by Egan and Ingoldsby. See generally: Egan, 'The emergence of the Supergrass: exposing the inadequacies of the accomplice corroboration warning'; and Ingoldsby, 'Supergrass testimony and reasonable doubt: an examination of *DPP v. Ward*', (1999) *Trinity College Law Review.* 35 *The People (DPP) v. Ward* [1998] IEHC 170.

that the accused's capitulation after more than 14 hours of silence during interrogations had occurred immediately after the visit by Ms. Meehan [was] a remarkable *volte face* which gives rise to unease and raises a series of pertinent questions'.[36] The Special Criminal Court was satisfied that these visits were a deliberate Garda ploy designed to induce the accused to testify.[37] Since Ward's suspect admissions had been, correctly, excluded the only admissible evidence was the testimony of one Charles Bowden, 'an admitted accessory.'[38]

In assessing the credibility of Bowden,[39] the trial court appears to have been very concerned by the status of the witness. The key issue before the Special Criminal Court was: 'is he no more and no less than a self-confessed accomplice in the murder of Ms. Guerin or is he one of a category of accomplices as found in certain terrorist trials in the Diplock courts of Northern Ireland known as a supergrass?'[40] This has been described as a two-category approach and has been criticized as being overly simplistic.[41] Moreover, Bowden (it has been argued) was wrongly classed by the trial court as being an ordinary accomplice rather than a supergrass.[42] The trial court acknowledged that Bowden was a 'self-serving, deeply avaricious and potentially viscous criminal. On his own admission he is a liar and the court readily accepts that he would lie without hesitation and regardless of the consequences for others if he perceived it to be in his own interests to do so.'[43] Given such an assessment, it appears strange that the court was willing to convict Ward based solely on Bowden's uncorroborated testimony.

Key to the court's acceptance of Bowden's testimony was the assertion that he was an ordinary accomplice rather than a supergrass; I respectfully contend that he was wrongly classified. Bowden was the first witness in the state to be granted protection under the new witness protection scheme.[44] Furthermore, the details of his witness protection programme were still being negotiated.[45] This added feature makes Bowden's testimony particularly unreliable. In Chapter 4 the case of *Mazure*[46] was considered, where the CCA held that the evidence of one Philip Kay was 'more than usually dangerous'[47] because he was an accomplice who, while testifying against the accused, was himself awaiting sentence on a similar charge. Given the court's assessment of the character of Charles Bowden, it would undoubtedly have been wiser to exclude his testimony, at least until his own witness protection deal had been finalized. In fact, on appeal, the CCA held that 'it was doubtful

36 Ibid., para. 7. 37 Ibid., para. 15. 38 Ingoldsby, 'Supergrass testimony and reasonable doubt: an examination of *DPP v. Ward*'. 39 Who also gave testimony in the *Gilligan* and *Meehan* prosecutions. 40 *The People (DPP) v. Ward* [1998] IEHC 170, para. 24. 41 Ingoldsby, 'Supergrass testimony and reasonable doubt'. 42 Ibid. 43 *The People (DPP) v. Ward* [1998] IEHC 170, para. 29. 44 Ingoldsby, 'Supergrass testimony and reasonable doubt'. 45 Egan, 'The emergence of the Supergrass', 140. 46 [1946] IR 448. 47 Ibid., 449.

whether, in light of all the factors which would motivate liars such as Bowden, it would have been possible to reach a conclusion of guilt beyond a reasonable doubt'[48] and in the later case of *Meehan*[49] the Special Criminal Court rejected the testimony of Bowden as unreliable.[50] Ingoldsby suggests that rather than adopting the strict categorical approach of *Ward*, the courts would be better off employing a 'scale of unreliability' test.[51] This scale was employed in the Northern Ireland case of *R v. Crumley*[52] where supergrass testimony was held to be even more unreliable than ordinary accomplice evidence.

One very worrying feature of the Special Criminal Court decision in *Ward* is that the court concluded that Bowden's testimony had a 'strong ring of truth to it'.[53] Egan notes that this is based on 'confirmation' rather than 'corroboration'.[54] The distinction here is a subtle but logical one: since Bowden had participated in the crime he could accurately describe it. As such, it is unsurprising that some evidence existed which could confirm that the crime occurred as Bowden described. Corroboratory evidence is different: it requires evidence that actually supports the account of the witness in establishing the guilt of the accused. In other words, rather than accepting that Bowden's evidence had a general ring of truth to it, the court should have been looking for actual evidence to support Bowden's claims that Ward had been involved. The CCA overruled the Special Criminal Court in *Ward;* however, as Egan notes, the issue of warnings in supergrass cases in Ireland remains somewhat confused.

There are some important objections to the use of supergrass or accomplice testimony: most significantly, from a Kantian perspective 'it is patently unjust ... to punish some offenders less because they are willing to cooperate in some way with the state'[55] because 'punishment is a categorical imperative'.[56] It is not desirable to examine that debate in any detail here; however, Kant's approach excludes all forms of bargain justice regardless of their utility. Ingoldsby notes that 'to exclude accomplice testimony would be to allow criminal gangs profit doubly from their secretive organization'.[57] Bargain justice can only be justified on utilitarian grounds; however, as distasteful as it might appear, this utilitarian approach is both internally consistent and capable of producing the best outcome; it is therefore preferable.[58]

48 *The People (DPP) v. Ward*, Court of Criminal Appeal, 14. See Egan, 'The emergence of the Supergrass', 141. 49 *The People (DPP) Meehan*, Special Criminal Court, 29 July 1999. 50 Egan, 'The emergence of the Supergrass', 142. 51 Ingoldsby, 'Supergrass testimony and reasonable doubt'. 52 (1986) 7 *Northern Ireland Judicial Bulletin*, 1. See Ingoldsby, 'Supergrass testimony and reasonable doubt: an examination of *DPP v. Ward*'. 53 Ibid. 54 Egan, 'The emergence of the Supergrass', 143. 55 Christopher, 'The prosecutor's dilemma: bargains and punishments', 120, citing George Fletcher. 56 Ibid., 119. 57 Ingoldsby, 'Supergrass testimony and reasonable doubt'. 58 For a more in-depth analysis of this point see Christopher, 'The prosecutor's dilemma'.

9.3 'New terrorism'[59] and the Special Criminal Court

The Offences against the State Act, 1939 can operate without any need to declare a state of emergency: all that is required is a declaration that the ordinary courts are inadequate to secure the effective administration of justice. This flexibility has enabled the executive to utilize the Special Criminal Court against a range of different threats – which, as we have seen, has led to much criticism of the court. However, although this adaptability might be seen as a cause for concern it can also be seen as a valuable asset. Terrorism is changing form, and traditional anti-terror responses are, arguably, becoming increasingly less useful.

Ireland has, up to this, faced the threat of the IRA which is organized into a strict cell structure under the leadership of the Army Council.[60]

> The cell has many variants, but the essential principle is simple and effective. Each is part of a hierarchy and is responsible to a single point of contact above. Within each cell, which is typically three to ten persons, a member may not even know all his or her compatriots ... The result is an organization which can act decisively and quickly. Also such an organization cannot easily be 'rolled up' by security forces.[61]

From the point of view of the terrorist organization, such a structure has many advantages; from the point of view of the lawmaker, the important factor is that such a group is hierarchical. The cell structure demands organization; it requires a leadership to direct the various cells who then operate independently but often toward a common purpose. As a result it is possible to target the organization as a whole.

'New' terrorism lacks this sort of organization. A significant development in recent years is the increased 'involvement in terrorism by non-government groups, individuals and, often, "non-group-groups" of individuals who come together for the purpose of committing a terrorist act and then separate'.[62] It is this shift away from organized terrorist groups with identifiable names and cell structures towards a more post-modern terrorism that needs to be considered and legislated for. Such a form of terrorism is better conceived of as involving 'networks' rather than cells or groups. 'A network is a set of independently active nodes ... interconnected by communication pathways. It is a distributed rather than a hierarchical system that can be formal and

59 The phrases 'old' and 'new' are not entirely accurate but they are employed here for the sake of convenience. **60** United States Department of State, *Patterns of global terrorism 2002* (2003), Appendix C, p. 135, henceforth *Patterns of global terrorism 2002*. **61** Harmon, *Terrorism today* (2000), p. 98. **62** Anderson, 'International terrorism & international cooperation' in *Countering suicide terrorism: an international conference* (2001), p. 52.

explicit, or informal and implicit, as long as it is united by common interests and understandings.'[63] Networks have the advantage of being capable of sustaining 'nodal loss' due to their 'mutating structure'.[64] Originally such networks were restricted geographically, but the internet has allowed networks to operate globally.[65]

The most infamous terrorist network operating in the world today is undoubtedly Al-Qaeda; however, the nature of that organization is disputed.[66] It has been suggested that there are essentially two Al-Qaedas – the pre- and post-2001 models. According to this theory, 'Al-Qaeda remains a useful term to describe bin Laden, his close associates and the infrastructure created in Afghanistan between 1996 and 2001'; that organization was effectively demolished by the invasion of Afghanistan and the removal of the Taliban.[67] Burke argues that Al-Qaeda should now be thought of 'as an ideology, an agenda and a way of seeing the world'.[68] This view is supported by a review of the history of the group. Osama bin Ladin developed an organized resistance movement in Afghanistan with the aim of repelling the invading forces of the Soviet Union. To that end he was involved in the establishment of the Maktab-al-Khidarnat (MAK) group which set up an organized conscription service and brought Muslims to Afghanistan for training and fighting. By 1988, bin Ladin split from MAK and formed Al-Qaedaand in 1998 he announced the formation of a new group, the 'Islamic World Front for the struggle against the Jews and the Crusaders'. This organization can accurately be described as an umbrella group for Islamic extremists.[69] The World Front allowed Al-Qaeda to develop into 'a multinational support group which funds and orchestrates the activities of Islamic militants worldwide'.[70] It is in this sense that Al-Qaeda is an ideology or agenda.

While, it might appear that the lack of an organized structure would weaken a terrorist group, that is not the case. The group Jemaah Islamiah (JI) provides a more than adequate example of Al Qaeda post-Afghanistan. JI was responsible for the Bali bombings on 12 October 2002.[71] It has been described as a 'regional Islamic militant network linked to al-Qa'eda'.[72] The use of the

63 The Cambridge Security Seminar, *A new security paradigm: a seminar record*, (2004), pp 30–1, henceforth *A new security paradigm*. 64 Ibid., p.29. 65 Ibid., p. 32. 66 Al-Qaeda suicide hijackers carried out the infamous 11 September 2001 attacks; it directed the attack on the USS *Cole* in the port of Aden, Yemen, on 12 October 2000, and conducted the US embassy bombings in Nairobi, Kenya and Tanzania in August 1998. *Patterns of global terrorism 2002*, p. 119. 67 Burke, 'Al-Qaeda: a meaningless label', *Observer*, 12 January 2003, http:// www.observer.co.uk/ Print/0,3858458I540,00.html accessed 20 April 2003. 68 Burke, 'Terror's myriad faces', the *Observer,* 18 May 2003, http://www. guardian.co.uk/Print/ 0,3858,4671444,00.html accessed 19 May 2003. 69 www.ict.org.il accessed 25 September 2003. 70 Ibid. 71 *Patterns of global terrorism 2002*, p. 110. 72 Spillius, 'Bali bomber greets death sentence with thumbs-up', *Daily Telegraph*, 8 August 2003.

phrase 'network' when referring to JI is interesting, since it implicitly recognizes that the group is not quite an organization. The US State Department notes that 'along with raising its own funds, the JI receives money and logistic assistance from Middle Eastern and South Asian contacts, NGOs, and other groups, including al-Qaida'.[73] It seems obvious that Al-Qaeda is continuing to play a role in international terrorism but its new role is more in the field of consultancy and logistics. This development has not reduced its deadly capability.

When considering this new form of deconstructed terrorist organization, it would be unwise to overstate the novelty of the approach. Terrorist organizations have a long history of cooperation and support for each other. The arrest of Niall Connolly, Martin McCauley and Jim Monaghan in Bogota on 11 August 2001, suggested a link between the IRA and FARC;[74] prior to that the Japanese Red Army, (JRA) had carried out a number of actions on behalf of or in support of other groups.[75] The outstanding feature of the new threat is not just the willingness to share information and logistical support, but rather the loosening of organizational ties. An examination of domestic terrorism in the US should help to further explain the significance of this development. The 'Freedom Club' posted parcel bombs which maimed and murdered scientists and others whom the Freedom Club accused of damaging the environment; the significant factor is that the Freedom Club as a terrorist organization consisted of one member, Theodore Kaczynski.[76] Other ideologies are also employing the internet to spread their message. The American neo-fascist Milton John Kleim Jr has suggested that 'USENET[77] offers enormous opportunity for the Aryan resistance to disseminate our message'.[78] It seems logical to suggest that neo-fascist terrorists would be willing to share logistical information with other, likeminded, individuals. Harmon notes that 'organizationally, the classic cell structure and hierarchy still predominate, but so too flourish their opposites, found in the American militias, eco-terrorists, or autonomous Islamic extremist groups where decentralization may be the prized key'.[79]

73 *Patterns of global terrorism 2002*, p. 111. 74 Stanage, 'Justice denied', *Magill*, August 2003, 26–28, 26. Since then the 'Columbia Three' have been convicted by a Columbian court, they then fled Columbia and are currently residing in Ireland. A statement from the Office of an Tánaiste, states that consideration is being given to the possibility of the three serving their sentences in Ireland. No extradition treaty exists between Ireland and Columbia and no extradition request had been made at the time of publication. See http://www.justice.ie/80256E01003A02CF/vWeb/pcJUSQ6F4MJX-ga accessed 5 September 2005. 75 *Patterns of global terrorism 2002*, p. 137. 76 Harmon, *Terrorism today*, p. 10. 77 'USENET is a collection of user-submitted notes or messages on various subjects that are posted to servers on a worldwide network'. http://searchnetworking.techtarget.com/ sDefinition/0,,sid7_gci213262,00.html accessed 10 September 2004. 78 Harmon, *Terrorism today*, p. 49. 79 Ibid., p. 124.

9.4 New terrorism in the Irish context

As a small, largely neutral state, Ireland can probably assume that it remains off the Islamic terrorists' radar; however, the concept of 'new' terrorism is relevant to Ireland, which has, historically, been to the forefront of these developments. The organization Saor Éire, mentioned previously in this book, operated in the early part of the 1930s and was seen as a communist threat at that time.[80] Saor Éire re-emerged in the 1960s when it was involved in a series of bank raids; and finally in 1975 it made a number of threats against members of the Irish Republican Socialist Party (IRSP) and the Official IRA 'when both organizations were engaged in a feud in Belfast'.[81] Its activities in 1975 aside Saor Éire had effectively disbanded in 1973.[82] A contemporary description of the organization is fascinating:

> Saor Éire was not a homogenous organization. It has no centralized military command, let alone a common political leadership. It was a loose alliance of diverse groups which on occasion co-operated together in joint actions and used the umbrella name Saor Éire. Needless to say, the criminal element used the name as a cover for their own exploits.[83]

This is a textbook definition of new terrorism. A further point of interest is that when Saor Éire re-emerged in the 1960s it was a Trotskyite group with links to the Fourth International but its 'concentration on bank robberies meant that gangsters on the fringes of the republican movement were soon playing a leading role in the organization at the expense of the more politically orientated members';[84] this highlights the difficulties in distinguishing between terrorism and organized crime.

The emergence of dissident republican groups opposed to the current Northern Ireland peace process provides contemporary examples of new Irish terrorism. Irish republicanism has always been prone to schisms: the 1920s divide was between Treatyites and die-hards; the 1960s saw the Official and Provisional IRA split; and the Northern Ireland peace process of the 1990s witnessed the emergence of a veritable alphabet soup of paramilitary

80 See chapter 2.7. 81 http://cain.ulst.ac.uk/othelem/organ/sorgan.htm accessed on 2 August 2005. 82 'While Saor Eire had been formed to struggle against imperialism … "during the last two years, owing to political weaknesses … undesirable elements have been able to operate around its fringes and carry out actions … which had nothing in common with the stated objectives of that organization".' O'Ruaric, 'A little known republican military group: Saor Éire', *Blanket*, 13 January 2005. http://lark.phoblacht.net/lor1401051g.html accessed on 2 August 2005, quoting a statement issued by Saor Éire prisoners in Portlaoise jail on 18 May 1973. 83 'Militatnts leave Saor Éire' (June 1973), the *Plough*, vol. 2, no.2, http://lark.phoblacht.net/lor1401051g.html accessed 2 August 2005. 84 Ibid.

organizations.[85] The Continuity IRA (CIRA) and Real or True IRA (RIRA) are structurally 'new' terrorist networks. The RIRA is a group of some 100 to 200 members and emerged in 1998 as the armed wing of the 32 County Sovereignty Movement. It opposes the Northern Ireland peace process and has been linked to the 1998 Omagh bombing.[86] The CIRA formed in 1994 as the paramilitary wing of Republican Sinn Féin, is smaller than the RIRA.[87] Their shared ideology and lack of strict hierarchical structures allows both groups to cooperate without being overly concerned by organizational coherence or status.

The OAS, 1939 was drafted as a response to the original IRA[88] and employs the proscription model of counter-terrorism. (Arguably this model was never very well suited to loyalist terrorism which tended to be less organized; this may explain why only the IRA and INLA were ever officially proscribed in Ireland.) The problem with proscription is that new organizations are unlikely to give advance warning of their intention to commit offences; the first we hear of any new organization is after it has committed its first act. As a result the proscription approach can only ever be reactive. Alternatively, the legislature could define terrorism. The Criminal Justice (Terrorism Offences) Act, 2005[89] incorporates the EU Council's 13 June 2002, Framework Decision on Combating Terrorism into Irish law,[90] and defines terrorist activity as including an act committed in or outside the state which is committed with the intention of –

(i) seriously intimidating a population,
(ii) unduly compelling a government or international organization to perform or abstain from performing an act, or
(iii) seriously destabilizing or destroying the fundamental political, constitutional, economic or social structures of a state or international organization.

This appears to be a useful working definition but we will have to wait and see how the courts interpret it; in the meantime, it might be possible to argue that new organizations are already covered by existing list of proscribed organizations.

The issue of dissident republicanism has been directly addressed by the courts. In *Murphy*[91] the Gardaí believed that the accused was a member of the CIRA, while the arresting officer mistakenly believed that he was a member

85 The Continuity IRA, the Real IRA, on the republican and the Red Hand Defenders on the loyalist side have emerged as dissident groups opposed to the peace process. 86 *Patterns of global terrorism 2002*, p. 120. 87 Ibid., p. 132. 88 See chapter 3.4. 89 Hereinafter the CJTO Act, 2005 90 s.4 Criminal Justice (Terrorism Offences) Act, 2005. 91 *The People (DPP) v. Murphy* [2005] IE CCA 1.

of RIRA. The court held that 'this error, if error it be, seems to us ... to be of no significance having regard to the courts findings that both organizations were terrorist organizations within the generic concept of IRA or Óglaigh na hÉireann'.[92] The CCA and Special Criminal Court both clearly accept that 'IRA' can be construed as including both the CIRA and RIRA. This issue was addressed in more detail by the decision in *Campbell.*[93] Campbell was convicted by the Special Criminal Court of membership of an 'unlawful organization, to wit: an organization styling itself the Irish Republican Army'.[94] During police questioning the accused had repeatedly denied membership of such an organization. Following his conviction an appeal was lodged, the sole ground for appeal being that 'the court had erred in holding that the Real IRA was a prescribed [sic] organization within the terms of a suppression Order published pursuant to s.19 of the Offences against the State Act, 1939'.[95] In previous hearings the Special Criminal Court ruled that

> labels such as 'official', 'provisional', 'continuity' or 'real' are irrelevant ... The so-called 'Real IRA' are on all fours with the original IRA as it existed in 1939 in terms of its philosophy, objectives and structure and members of that group are within the ambit of the Suppression Order of 1939.[96]

The CCA upheld that ruling on 19 December 2003. Thus, so far, the approach of the Irish courts has been to assume that these dissident groups are in fact covered by the proscription of the IRA. The logic of the Special Criminal Court is supported by the fact that these dissident groups retain the title IRA but with the addition of a prefix (indeed, the use of the title IRA provides these groups with a link to the history of that older organization, which they presumably see as legitimizing their actions). While such an approach may be suitable for dissident organizations which 'are on all fours with the original IRA', the case would be more complicated if an alternative title were employed. I suggest that a more long-term strategy is required. The definition of terrorist activity contained within s.4 of the CJTO Act, 2005 may form the basis of that new long-term strategy.

A further difficulty surrounds the issue of de-proscription: what should be done with a group which no longer poses a threat? Saor Éire remains proscribed, in the UK, despite the fact that it has not been active since the 1970s.[97] This issue is particularly pertinent when consideration is given to the current IRA ceasefire and acts of decommissioning. In *The Kurdish Workers' Party*[98] case, the High Court of England and Wales considered the

92 Ibid., judgment of Kearns J. 93 *The People (DPP) v. Campbell* [2005] IE CCA 27. 94 Ibid. 95 Ibid. 96 Ibid. 97 Schedule 2, The Terrorism Act 2000. 98 *R v. Secretary of State for the Home Department, ex parte the Kurdistan Workers' Party & others*, [2002] EWHC 644.

proscription of three organizations. Most relevant was the ongoing proscription of the PKK,[99] a group that had been involved in terrorist activities since 1984 but had been on ceasefire since 1999 when its leader Abdullah Ocalan had been captured and convicted by the Turkish authorities.[1] The UK Home Secretary refused an application to have the organization de-proscribed on the basis that

> the organization retains its capacity for terrorist acts and has not renounced terrorism. He is aware furthermore of recent statements made by the organization's presidential council and individual members of that council hinting at a return to armed conflict. On the basis of these declarations, and other information available to him, such as knowledge of fundraising on behalf of the organization in the United Kingdom, the Home Secretary remains satisfied that as an organization the PKK is 'concerned in terrorism' as defined by the Terrorism Act 2000.[2]

Therefore, the organization remained a terrorist organization while not being actively engaged in terrorism. However, the substantive issue appears to have been that the PKK retained the ability to engage in terrorism and had hinted that it might re-engage in such actions.

On 28 July 2005 the IRA declared that

> the leadership of Óglaigh na hÉireann has formally ordered an end to the armed campaign ... All IRA units have been ordered to dump arms. All volunteers have been instructed to assist the development of purely political and democratic programmes through exclusively peaceful means. Volunteers must not engage in any other activities whatsoever.[3]

The Minister for Justice has made it clear that the IRA will remain illegal because the 'constitution of the IRA [is] treasonable to the Irish state'.[4] However, if we employ the reasoning of *Kurdish Workers' Party*, it is logical to assume that if the IRA were to alter and become a solely social or political movement committed to a United Socialist Republic of Ireland, then at some stage it would have to be de-proscribed. While s.20 of the OAS, 1939 provides for a right of appeal against a Suppression Order declaring an organization to be unlawful, the Act states that such an appeal must be brought within thirty days of the publication of the Order in *Iris Oifigiúil*.[5] The legislation does not

99 Kurdistan Workers' Party. 1 Ibid., para. 38. 2 Ibid., para. 39. 3 http://news.bbc.co.uk/1/hi/northern_ireland/4724599.stm accessed on 7 September 2005. 4 http://www.rte.ie/news/2005/0828/mcdowellm.html accessed on 7 September 2005. 5 Offences against the State

provide a means by which a member of the IRA could appeal against the existing Suppression Order. It has been recommended that this thirty-day restriction should be removed.[6] If the IRA was de-proscribed, the courts could not rely on the view that the RIRA and CIRA were on 'all fours with the original IRA' since that organization would no longer be proscribed. Furthermore, if an organization were removed from the proscribed list its title would again become available for use.

Act, 1939 s.20(1). 6 *Committee to review the Offences against the State Acts, 1939–1998*, para. 6.38.

10

Conclusion – The Special Criminal Court: 1922–2005

> The Tribunal[1] was clearly established for the purpose of dealing more effectively than the ordinary courts ... with an extraordinary situation which makes the ordinary administration of justice peculiarly difficult. Consequently the Tribunal is a practical compromise between military efficiency and the ordinary desirable methods of administering justice. Such a compromise is naturally distasteful – extremely distasteful – but the legislature has recognized that it may be necessitated by circumstances ... The alternative to such a compromise would doubtless be something more unwelcome.[2]

Meredith J's description of the Constitution (Special Powers) Tribunal is undoubtedly accurate; indeed, all emergency powers involve this distasteful compromise. As President Lincoln asked rhetorically upon abolishing the right to habeas corpus, 'Are all laws but one to go unexecuted, and government itself go to pieces lest that one be violated?'[3] The Special Criminal Court is a distasteful compromise; but it is a constitutional compromise between the desire to maintain the right to trial by jury in the majority of cases and the need to deliver the effective administration of justice.

10.1 Justifying interference with the right to trial by jury

In Chapter 1 I stated that the primary purpose of any trial process is to secure a fair trial. I emphasized that the right to a fair trial is the primary right and that the right to trial by jury is merely one means of securing that right. Historically, as we have seen, trial by jury has not always been capable of securing a fair trial; furthermore, international experience has shown that alternative trial procedures are capable of delivering a fair trial without a jury. I am not advocating the abolition of the jury system; the jury has a long tradition within the common law and it has, by and large, proved to be a positive development; what I am saying is that the absence of a jury does not, in and of itself, indicate a lack of justice. I recognize the 'democratizing' benefits of the jury, as outlined by de Tocqueville; however, if the justification

1 That is the Constitution (Special Powers) Tribunal established by the Constitution (Amendment No. 17) Act, 1931 also known as Article 2A; see chapter 2. 2 *The State (Hughes) v. Lennon & Others* [1935] IR 128, 148. 3 Katyal & Tribe, 'Waging war, deciding guilt: trying the military tribunals' (2002) 111 *Yale Law Journal* 1259–1310, 1273

for trial by jury is largely political, then it should be kept in place only so long as it is able to fulfil its primary, judicial role. Important as the involvement of the community in the judicial process may be, if that involvement jeopardizes the right to a fair trial then it is legitimate to remove the jury and replace it with a system which is able to effectively administer justice.

10.2 Non-jury trials during states of emergency

Bunreacht na hÉireann explicitly provides for military trial in cases of war or armed rebellion[4] and the Special Criminal Court was augmented by military tribunal during the Emergency. As we have seen, this 'curious and sinister' court[5] made huge inroads into the ordinary laws of evidence through the Emergency Powers Orders (Nos. 41F and 139), 1941. Controversy surrounding military tribunals has recently resurfaced due to President Bush's Military Order of 13 November 2001 which 'directed the secretary of defence to create military tribunals and to take into custody at once anyone the president names as subject to the Order'.[6] The order has been criticized because:

> military officers ... lack the insulation [from the executive branch of government] of Article III judges, being wholly dependent on the discretion of their military superiors for promotions and indeed for their livelihood. Furthermore, the Order does not guarantee an appeal from any conviction or sentence to judges independent of the executive branch.[7]

This US tribunal is in many respects similar to the Irish wartime military tribunal. Despite the significant criticisms levelled at the independence of the US tribunals it has been argued that 'in a time of declared war, or in a place where no other form of justice can be administered', they are acceptable.[8] The main doubt regarding the legitimacy of the US tribunals is that they were established without the consent of Congress.

> The [US] Constitution sets up a structure whereby the concurrence of all three branches is normally needed in order to authorize a decisive departure from the legal status quo ... But in the absence of an emergency that threatens truly irreparable damage to the nation or its Constitution, that Constitution's text, structure, and logic demand approval by Congress if life, liberty, or property are to be significantly curtailed or abridged.[9]

4 Article 38.4 Bunreacht na hÉireann. 5 Kelly, *Fundamental rights*, p. 274. 6 Katyal & Tribe, 'Waging war', 1260–61 7 Ibid., 1262. 8 Katyal & Tribe, 'Waging war', 1259. 9 Ibid., 1266

Military tribunals in the US are not, necessarily, unacceptable, but the means by which they were established is; it is a matter of process, not form.

Both the International Covenant on Civil and Political Rights and the European Convention of Human Rights secure the right to a fair trial; however, the Human Rights Committee in *Landinelli v. Uruguay*[10] and the European Court of Human Rights in *Lawless v. Ireland*[11] have accepted the concept of a proportionality test. Such a test accepts the proportionate interference with the rights guaranteed. I have argued that if detention without trial and trial by military tribunal are, in certain circumstances, proportionate then a trial procedure before a modified, but independent court can also be proportionate. Trial by Special Criminal Court incorporates an appeal to the ordinary courts and, since 1972, the court has been made up of three members of the judiciary; it is a proportionate response to times of emergency.

10.3 Non-jury trials and terrorism

The 'core business' of the Special Criminal Court has always been combating terrorism. The establishment of the Court in 1939, 1960 and 1972 was a direct response to IRA activities. The majority of the recent Committee to Review the Offences against the State Acts was 'that the security risk is sufficiently high to justify the retention of the Court' on the grounds of terrorism alone.[12] They were also of the view that this issue should be kept under review.[13] However, a significant dissenting opinion was expressed by, amongst others, the chairman of the review group. Despite their misgivings, the dissenters recognized the need for non-jury trial in certain circumstances; for example, Professor Walsh in his personal dissent states that,

> I can accept that from time to time exceptional measures will be needed to combat threats to the stability of the state and its institutions. I am firmly of the view however, that the nature of such measures and their inherent potential to be used as powerful instruments to crush political opposition, trade union activity, the promulgation of unconventional views are such that they must be framed in very clear and precise terms.[14]

The concerns expressed by the minority cannot simply be dismissed. The potential misuse of any emergency power is grounds for concern and it should be recalled that previous governments have been willing to use special

10 Communication No. 34/1978, 8 April 1981. 11 *Lawless v. Ireland (no. 3)*, (1979) 1 EHRR. The case was decided on 1 July, 1961 but was not reported until 1979. 12 *Committee to review the Offences against the State Acts, 1939–1998*, para. 9.29. 13 Ibid., para. 9.39. 14 Ibid., 'General Dissenting Views of Professor Dermot Walsh', p. 275.

powers in the most alarming ways. In Chapter 5 we saw that on 16 May 1947, the government decided 'as a matter of urgency' to amend the Protection of the Community (Special Powers) Act, 1926 in order to provide for 'the prohibition of a strike or lock-out of workers of any class; to prohibit any person from inciting, maintaining or subsidising such strike and to provide that, where a trade union is involved, a financial penalty may be imposed on the trade union funds'.[15] Furthermore, in April 1947 ministers considered amending the Offences against the State Act, 1939 in order to enable

> offences, such as contraventions of the control and rationing of commodities, to be made scheduled offences for the purposes of Part V of the Offences against the State Act, 1939, in circumstances and subject to a procedure to be specified, without a declaration that the ordinary courts are inadequate to secure the effective administration of justice.[16]

The purpose of these changes was to avoid having to make the required declaration that the ordinary courts were inadequate. As such, history shows us that the potential for abuse of these powers does exist.

There are three main responses to these concerns. Firstly, although the government considered amending the Schedule in 1947 (an act which would have given rise to concern and would have clearly signalled the 'normalization' of the court) it did not in fact do so. However, it would be naïve to simply trust the government not to abuse its' powers.[17] The recommendations of the Committee to Review the OAS[18] and the decision in *Eviston*[19] provide the possibility of meaningful judicial review; the ordinary courts have already displayed the willingness to overrule the Special Criminal Court on appeal; and annual review of the use of the Special Criminal Court by the Oireachtas would ensure scrutiny. The combination of these factors go some way to alleviating concerns of the minority of the Committee.

The final response to the concerns of the minority arises from their

15 Attorney General's Office file 22/47, from Department of Industry and Commerce, to The Attorney General, signed (illegible), 17 May 1947. 16 Department of An Taoiseach, file S14068, *Extract From Cabinet Minutes, G.C. 4/252, 25.4.1947, item 3*, Pr. Sec. M.I.& C., Finance, Justice advised 26/4/1947. 17 As Katyal & Tribe note in the context of the US Attorney General's assurance that military tribunals would be conducted in public except where the urgent requirements of national security prevented them from being so held, 'it is, to be sure, nice to have White House Counsel's personal guarantee that this is so, but "trust me" has never been enough for the American people when their rights have been at stake'. Katyal & Tribe, 'Waging war', 1263, footnote 16. 18 See Chapter 7, the Committee to Review the OAS proposed review of the decision of the Director of Public Prosecutions, to send a case for trial before the Special Criminal Court, by a judge of the Supreme Court. *Committee to review the Offences against the State Acts, 1939–1998*, para. 9.76. 19 [2002] 3 IR, 260, see Chapter 8.

outlook on the importance of trial by jury. The dissenting opinion is largely based on the premise that

> trial by jury is the cornerstone of the criminal justice system. It ensures that the innocence or guilt of a person charged with an offence is determined by twelve randomly chosen members of the community, each of whom brings to the process the benefit of his or her life-experience and individual perspective.[20]

They offer no evidence to support this contention. Indeed, the minority note that the Special Criminal Court is advantageous since 'the risk of possible jury intimidation is reduced; the members of the Court can be relied on not to be swayed by political views from convicting where the offence was politically inspired; and the prospects of conviction may be considered more likely';[21] and in the same breath they assert that 'jury trial is valuable, in spite of its inconvenience, because of deeper values relating to a liberal democracy'.[22] These values are not identified. I have argued that it is possible to conduct a fair trial, in line with the principles of liberal democracy, in the absence of a jury. Given the evidence in support of the view that jury intimidation by terrorists and others[23] has occurred, it would seem wise to adopt a means of trial which avoids such complications. There is a 'Catch 22' with regard to the Special Criminal Court; it is impossible to prove that such a threat of intimidation exists (because the law prevents us from questioning jurors) and in the absence of such evidence, the legitimacy of the court may be questioned. On this point I concur with the majority of the Committee; the threat of jury intimidation remains sufficient to justify the retention of trial by Special Criminal Court.

10.4 Non-jury trials and non-subversive cases

The most controversial aspect of the court's use has been in the field of non-subversive cases. Chapter 5 detailed the court's use in economic cases. These cases are closest to the 'emergency' scenario, since although not directly associated with a terrorist threat it was associated with maintaining order and the maintenance of supplies during an emergency. Thus, the court's use in black market cases during the 1940s can be understood. Although the court was established to combat a terrorist threat the legislation allowed for its extension to other cases in which the ordinary courts were deemed to be inadequate. As was noted, although the use of a non-jury court in cases

20 *Committee to review the Offences against the State Acts, 1939–1998*, para. 9.88. **21** Ibid., para. 9.90. **22** Ibid. **23** see for example Ó Donnchadha, 'Witness intimidation: criminal justice in crisis?' (2004) *Cork On-line Law Review*, VI, http://colr.ucc.ie/2004vi.html accessed on 29 June 2005.

concerning the supply of flour might at this distance appear unjustifiable during the emergency the maintenance of supply of such an essential product can be explained. The modern equivalent of these cases are the organized crime cases. The view of the minority of the Committee to Review the OAS was that although Ireland had experienced a growth in organized crime this was not comparable to the existence of organized crime in other jurisdictions, jurisdictions where no equivalent to the Special Criminal Court exists.[24] The use of the Special Criminal Court in such cases could, therefore, be seen as either an overreaction on the behalf of the Irish government or a 'normalization' of the court. The decision of the HRC in *Kavanagh v. Ireland*[25] was also critical of the court's use in such cases.

The use of the Special Criminal Court in organized crime cases does give rise to concern that this exceptional measure is being normalized however, a few points are worth re-iterating. It is not unusual for anti-terror measures to be adopted to the fight against organized crime. In Continental Europe the use of some forms of accomplice evidence, initially designed to combat terrorism have been adapted to fight organized crime groups.[26] Indeed, a majority of the Committee to Review the OAS 'was of the view that the threat posed by organized crime was sufficiently serious to justify the continuation of the Special Criminal Court'.[27] It should also be noted that the main criticism of the HRC in *Kavanagh* was that the decision of the director of public prosecutions (DPP) to certify that the ordinary courts were inadequate was not open to review.[28] Again, it is contended that the adoption of the recommendations of the Committee to Review the OAS would alleviate such difficulties. While it is tempting to see the court's use in organized crimes cases as heralding a new era in its evolution, such an analysis is a gross oversimplification. The court was employed in a series of high-profile cases emerging from the murder of Veronica Guerin; however, it has not been over employed in such cases since then.[29] For example, during the Liam Keane murder trial, despite difficulties surrounding witness and jury intimidation[30] there was no attempt by the prosecuting authorities to transfer that trial to the Special Criminal Court.

The fear of normalization gives rise to two possible courses of action: firstly, the use of the Court in these cases could be abolished, with the attendant risk of jury intimidation and miscarriages of justice through

24 *Committee to review the Offences against the State Acts, 1939–1998*, para. 9.93. 25 CCPR/C/71/D/819/1998, 26 April 2001, para. 4.4. 26 Passim, Fyfe & Sheptycki, 'Facilitating witness co-operation in organised crime cases'. 27 *Committee to review the Offences against the State Acts, 1939–1998*, para. 9.37. 28 *Kavanagh v. Ireland* CCPR/C/71/D/819/ 1998, 26 April 2001, para. 10.2. 29 A reliable source has informed the author that there are no immediate plans to continue the Court's use in such cases. 30 'Keane trial adjourned over jury difficulties', http://www.rte.ie/news/2003/1022/keane.html accessed on 16 November, 2005.

acquittal; alternatively, reform of the procedure by which the DPP certifies the ordinary courts to be inadequate could be instituted. Given this choice, the prudent course of action is to adopt a scheduling-in procedure whereby the DPP must certify the ordinary courts inadequate in each individual case. Following the implementation of the reforms mentioned earlier, the certificate should then be open to meaningful judicial and parliamentary review.

10.5 Final conclusions

The Special Criminal Court is the result of an evolutionary process which began before the creation of the state. It is undeniably preferable to the PSA, 1927 and Article 2A. It is interesting to note that the US has chosen to employ a system of trial by military tribunal in its current war on terror.[31] These military commissions have attracted considerable criticism because they lack independent judicial review and provide for military trial of civilians and (more disturbingly) because they place restrictions on the defendant's right to counsel.[32] If the OAS, 1939 is amended to remove the possible appointment of members of the Defence Forces to the court, none of these allegations could be levelled at the Special Criminal Court; in which case trial by Special Criminal Court would be preferable to the current system employed by the Bush administration.

While the democratizing effect of jury trial is valuable, in circumstances where a juror is intimidated the overriding concern must be to ensure that justice is done. The difficulty in ascertaining the existence of jury intimidation makes this decision problematic. Terrorist organizations are able to intimidate jurors: for example, in November 2003 Kurdish protestors took a number of judges hostage in Istanbul;[33] and the Real IRA allegedly threatened to kill the family of David Rupert who testified in the McKevitt trial.[34] If terrorists are capable of such acts, they can also intimidate juries. Organized crime groups possess similar capabilities. In such circumstances the interference with the right to trial by jury is acceptable.

There remains only one principled objection to prosecution by Special

31 Military Order: detention, treatment, and trial of certain non-citizens in the war against terrorism, s.4(a) states that 'any individual subject to this order shall, when tried, be tried by military commission for any and all offenses triable by military commission that such individual is alleged to have committed, and may be punished in accordance with the penalties provided under applicable law, including life imprisonment or death'. This Order was promulgated by President George W. Bush on 13 November 2001 as a legislative response to the events of 11 September 2001. http://news.findlaw.com/hdocs/docs/terrorism/bushtribunalord111301.html accessed 20 April 2004. 32 Human Rights Watch, 'Military commissions shouldn't be used: pentagon rules shortchange justice', (June, 2003), http://hrw.org/press/2003/06/us062503.htm accessed 28 September 2005. 33 Zaman, 'Police free hostage judges' (filed, 19/11/2003) www.telegaph.co.uk accessed 13 August 2004.

Criminal Court: that is the absence of a jury. I have concluded that the jury is not indispensable. This is not a call for the abolition of the jury system; it is a recognition of the fact that circumstances exist in which maintaining the right to trial by jury can be detrimental to the interests of justice. The Special Criminal Court may be an 'extremely distasteful' compromise, but it is also moderate, legitimate and proportionate.

34 Foggo, 'Real IRA threatened to kill trial witness's family in US' (filed, 10/08/2003) www.telegraph.co.uk accessed on 13 August 2004.

Appendix 1

Department of An Taoiseach file S S9249[1]

Murders since 1927 arising directly or indirectly from political motives, labour disputes or rent agitation. In no case has anybody been convicted.[2]

Year	*Name & Description*	*Hour/Date/ Place*	*How*	*Trial?*	*Comment*
1927	Kevin O'Higgins Min. for Justice	12pm 10/7/27[3] Booterstown Co. Dublin	Shot	No	–
1929	Albert H. Armstrong	7.15pm 20/2/29 Dublin	Shot	No	Gave evidence in a case of tearing down a GB flag
	Tim O'Sullivan, Detective Officer	10.10pm 11/6/29 Clare	Opened trap mine	No	–
1931	Patrick J. Carroll Motor Driver	7pm 31/1/31 Crumlin Dublin	Bomb exploded	No	Suspected of being a police agent
	John Curtin Superintendant Garda Siochana	10.20pm 20/3/31 Tipperary	Shot	No	Active against local IRA
	John Ryan Labourer	1.45pm 20/7/31 Tipperary	Shot	No	Suspected of being a police agent
1933	J. Patterson Railway Clerk	10.15am 1.2.33	Train derailed	No	Industrial murder probably not directly intended but undoubtedly murder in law.
	J. McWilliams Engineer	"	"	"	"
	Hugh Reilly (No Business)	5am 29/10/33	Beaten with sticks and guns	No	A 'Blueshirt martyr'

1 The following is based on the author's transcript of the relevant file available in the National Archive of Ireland. 2 A handwritten note on the file states: 'except in Egan's case, Conway has now been convicted'. 3 The dates in this table should be read as day, month year; thus 10/7/27 should be read as 10 July 1927.

Year	Name & Description	Hour/Date/ Place	How	Trial?	Comment
1934	Mrs Frances McGory Dundalk	8pm 11/3/34	Death on 18/3/34 accelerated by a bomb explosion on 11/2/34	Yes. 5 men were charged before the Military Tribunal and were acquitted.	The IRA blew up the house in revenge for the son's giving police information: they didn't directly intend to murder the woman.
1935	Richard More O'Farrell Clerk	9pm 9/2/35 Edgeworthstown Co Longford	Shot	Yes. 4 men were put on trial but were acquitted.	The IRA intervened on the tenant's side in a rent dispute and sent an armed party to tar and feather father (Land Agent): son shot whilst struggling with attackers.
1936	Henry Boyle Sommerville Vice-Admiral, British Navy	9.30pm 24/3/36	Shot		Helped local boys to join British Navy.
	John Egan Labourer	11.20pm 26/4/36 Co. Waterford	Shot		Suspected of being a police agent (had joined the IRA and then left it).

Appendix 2

Department of an Taoiseach file S 8211[1]

Extract from Constitution Committee Report, 1934

7. We have given special consideration to Article 2A, and in doing so we have borne in mind the statement made by you in the Dáil on Committee Stage of the Constitution (Amendment No. 24) Bill on 26th April last, column 2480, viz:

   'that it is necessary to ensure, in cases of real urgency and real public emergency, that an Executive would not be prevented from taking the action that might be considered necessary to safeguard public interests'.

8. We are of opinion that Article 2A in its present form is not a proper one for retention in the Constitution. We suggest that it should be replaced by a simple Article which would enable the Oireachtas, by ordinary legislation, to empower an Executive to take any measure necessary to deal effectively with a state of public emergency not amounting to armed rebellion or state of war, including, when necessary, the temporary suspension of many Articles of the Constitution which under normal conditions are rightly regarded as fundamental.
9. We realise the great importance of providing safeguards to prevent such drastic powers being resorted to except in the abnormal circumstances for which they are designed, and at the same time to secure that an Executive which has real occasion to use them will not be in danger of finding its efforts to cope with a serious situation hampered or defeated by appeals to the Courts based on normal constitutional rights.
10. A suggested scheme which might meet the position is briefly outlined in Appendix B.

APPENDIX B
EMERGENCY POWERS

SUGGESTIONS OF THE COMMITTEE:

1. What may be regarded as the first serious phase in the development of a grave state of disorder throughout the country is the failure of the ordinary Courts, either through intimidation of jurors and/or witnesses, or lack of civic spirit on the part of either or both, to secure the conviction of a semi-political nature.
2. The resultant immunity of offenders from punishment leads inevitably to the spread of offences of this character, resulting sometimes in a serious situation with which the ordinary processes of law are unable to cope.
3. We are of the opinion that the development of a situation of this nature could in most cases be arrested by the application of suitable measures in the early stages, and we think that, to this end, the Constitution should contain a permanent provision to supplement the operation of the ordinary Courts.

1 The following is based on the author's transcript of the relevant file available in the National Archive of Ireland.

4. Our suggestion, which for convenient reference we call Scheme A. is as follows:

SCHEME A

(a) Power should be provided in the Constitution for the enactment of legislation to provide, as part of the permanent judicial machinery of the State, for the trial by Special Courts of persons accused of a crime, in respect of whom the appropriate ordinary Judge or Justice certifies, at any stage of the proceedings, either on his own initiative, or on the application of the Attorney General, that it is desirable, in the interests of justice, that the trial should be removed to a special court set up under this scheme.

(b) The exact constitution and powers of these special courts would remain to be settled by legislation, but what we have in contemplation is something in the nature of the Constitution (Special Powers) Tribunal, with such changes as experience has shown to be desirable.

5. In addition to the Scheme A. outlined above, which may be regarded as a preventive measure, aimed at stopping, where possible, the development of a state of public emergency, we consider it essential that the State should be in a position to deal effectively with such an emergency in the event of its occurring, and for that purpose, we suggest Scheme B. which is outlined hereunder.

SCHEME B

(a) In substitution for the present Article 2A, a new Article should be inserted in the Constitution which would authorise the Oireachtas to provide by ordinary legislation such powers as the Oireachtas might consider necessary (including power to suspend temporarily any Article of the Constitution), to meet the requirements of any period during which the ordinary laws are not adequate for the preservation of public order, such legislation to come into effect at the times and in the manner set out hereunder.

(b) The Article should provide that nothing in the Constitution or in any Act should be capable of being invoked or cited as invalidating anything in the Article or in any legislation enacted or any other action taken under it.

(c) All such legislation should, by way of title or preamble state expressly that its object is to carry out the provisions of the said Article.

(d) The Article should provide that, if and whenever the Executive Council is of opinion that it is desirable to do so, they may request the president, or the senior available Judge, of the High Court (hereinafter called the summoning officer) to summon all Judges or Justices exercising criminal jurisdiction, but not including Judges of the Supreme or High Court nor any person acting only as a temporary Judge or Justice, to meet at a stated place and time, (not being sooner than three days or later then seven days after the issue of such summons) for the purpose of advising the Executive Council as to whether the state of the country is such that the ordinary laws are not adequate for the preservation of public order.

(e) The said Judges shall meet accordingly under the Chairmanship of the summoning officer, and shall, after such discussion as they shall think fit, decide, by way of majority vote, on secret ballot, on the question referred to them by the Executive Council, and the summoning officer shall report to the Executive Council in writing (attested by the signatures of all present at the meeting) as to the result of the votes, without specifing [sic] the names or numbers or persons voting for or against.

(f) To provide against wilful abstention from the meeting the judges and justices, severe penalties, amounting if necessary to automatic removal from office, should be provided. In case of unavoidable absence, a certificate from the summoning officer setting out the reasons for such absence would be essential.

(g) If and whenever the Executive Council receives from the summoning officer a report in the affirmative, they may by Order declare that the provisions of all such legislation as is mentioned in paragraph (a) above shall come into operation on a day which shall be appointed in such order and the said provisions shall come into operation on such day.

(h) The Order of the Executive Council should, inter alia,

(1) cite that the report referred to in the preceding paragraph has been duly received;

(2) be so worded and operate as to summon the Dáil forthwith if not already in session;

(3) be published in Iris Oifigiuil not later then the day preceding the appointed day;

(4) be laid before the Dáil forthwith, and unless and until a resolution annulling such Order is passed by the Dáil within the next subsequent twenty-one days on which the Dáil has sat after such order is laid before it, such order shall have full force and effect, but no such resolution shall operate to prejudice the validity of anything previously done under such Order.

(i) The effect of the Order and the operation of all legislation brought into effect under it shall cease, without prejudice to anything done under it:

(a) six months after the appointed day, or

(b) on an earlier date named in an ad hoc Order, by the Executive Council, or

(c) on an earlier date named in an express resolution passed by Dáil Éireann for that purpose.

(j) If the Executive Council consider it is desirable that the period of six months should be extended, they may at any time, either during the operation of the Order, or after its termination, take steps as provided in paragraph (d) et seq. above with a view to the making of a new Order to bring the scheme into operation for a further period.

6. With regard to the meeting of Judges and Justices provided for in paragraph (d) of Scheme B. above, our proposal to exclude the High Court and Supreme Court Judges is deliberate, on the grounds

(a) that their jurisdiction is in practice almost exclusively civil, that they function in Dublin only, and that they are accordingly not in the same position as District Justices and Circuit Court Judges to assess the general condition of the country from the point of view of maintenance of law and order;

(b) that these judges may have to decide Constitutional questions arising out of the operation of the Article.

Appendix 3

Part I: Persons Sentenced in the District Courts[2]

Name	*Offence*[3]	*Sentence*
Peter Pringle	Possession of firearms and ammunition *and* Refusal to account for movements	6 months *and* 6 months (consecutive)
Malachy McGurran	Possession of firearms and ammunition *and* Refusal to account for movements	6 months *and* 6 months (consecutive)
Séamus McCann	Possession of ammunition *and* Refusal to account for movements	6 months *and* 6 months (consecutive)
Alphonsus Ryan	Refusal to account for movements *and* Refusal to give name and address	6 months *and* 3 months (consecutive)
William Folan	Possession of firearms and ammunition *and* Refusal to account for movements	6 months *and* 6 months (consecutive)
James Hayde	Possession of firearms and ammunition *and* Refusal to account for movements	6 months *and* 6 months (consecutive)
Patrick O'Regan	Refusal to account for movements	6 months
James Joseph Roche	Possession of firearms and ammunition *and* Refusal to account for movements (4 counts).	6 and 6 months (consecutive). Three other sentences of 6 months each concurrent with foregoing (12 months in all).
Seán Tracey	Possession of firearms and ammunition *and* Refusal to account for movements (4 counts).	6 and 6 months (consecutive). Three other sentences of 6 months each concurrent with foregoing (12 months in all).

2 Dáil Éireann, *Parliamentary Debates*, 15 February 1962, vol. 193, cols. 377–8. 3 *Possession (or carrying) of firearms (or ammunition)* refers to possession or carrying without a firearm certificate, contrary to section 2 of the Firearms Act, 1925. Possession of firearms, etc. 'with intent' refers to their possession: (a) with intent to endanger life or cause serious injury to property, or (b) with intent to enable any other person by means of such firearms or ammunition to endanger life or cause serious injury to property, contrary to section 15 of the Firearms Act, 1925. *Refusal to account for movements or to give information* refers to a refusal contrary to section 52 of the Offences against the State Act, 1939. *Refusal to give name and address* refers to a refusal contrary to section 30 of the Offences against the State Act, 1939. *Membership of an unlawful organization:* this refers to section 21 of the Offences against the State Act, 1939. *Possession of incriminating documents:* this refers to section 12 of the Offences against the State Act, 1939.

Patrick Murphy	Refusal to account for movements *and* Membership of unlawful organization *and* Possession of incriminating documents	6 months *and* 3 months *and* 3 months (concurrent)
Joseph Maguire	Refusal to account for movements	6 months
Lorcan Bergin	Possession of firearm *and* Refusal to account for movements	6 months *and* 6 months (concurrent)
Michael Murtagh	Refusal to account for movements (2 counts)	6 months *and* 6 months (concurrent)

Part II: Persons Sentenced by the Special Criminal Court[4]

Name	*Offence*	*Sentence*
Cathal Goulding	Refusal to account for movements	6 months
Seán Cronin	Refusal to account for movements	6 months
Thomas Nixon	Refusal to account for movements	6 months
Éamon Thomas	Refusal to account for movements	4 months
Hugh Hutchinson	Refusal to account for movements	4 months
Éamon McNulty	Refusal to account for movements	4 months
Tomás MacGiolla	Refusal to account for movements *and* Refusal to give information	6 months *and* 6 months (concurrent)
Séamus Ó Doráin	Refusal to account for movements	6 months
Líam Mac Aogain	Refusal to account for movements	6 months
Líam Boylan	Refusal to account for movements	4 months
Séamus McCollum	Refusal to account for movements *and* Refusal to give information	6 months *and* 6 months (concurrent)
Patrick Mulcahy	Membership of unlawful organization *and* Possession of incriminating documents *and* Refusal to account for movements and failing to give information (2 counts).	12 months *and* 4 months *and* 4 months (all concurrent)
Matthew Murray	Possession of firearms and ammunition *and* Membership of unlawful organization *and* Possession of incriminating documents *and* Refusal to account for movements *and* Refusal to give information	2 years *and* 2 years *and* 6 months *and* 6 months *and* 6 months (concurrent)
Thomas O'Sullivan	Possession of firearms *and* Membership of unlawful organization *and* Possession of incriminating documents *and* Refusal to account for movements *and* Failing to give information.	2 years *and* 6 months *and* 6 months *and* 6 months *and* 6 months (concurrent)

4 Dáil Éireann, *Parliamentary Debates,* 15 February 1962, vol. 193, cols. 377–80.

Name	*Offence*	*Sentence*
Walter Dunphy	Possession of ammunition with intent *and* Possession of ammunition *and* Refusal to account for movements	4 years *and* 18 months *and* 6 months (concurrent)
Denis O'Riordan	Possession of ammunition with intent *and* Possession of ammunition *and* Refusal to account for movements	3 years *and* 1 year *and* 4 months (concurrent)
Patrick Ryan	Refusal to account for movements *and* Refusal to give information (2 counts)	6 months *and* 6 and 6 months (all concurrent)
Thomas F. Smith	Refusal to account for movements *and* Refusal to give information (2 counts)	4 months *and* 6 and 6 months (all concurrent)
Patrick J. Tierney	Refusal to account for movements *and* Refusal to give information (2 counts)	6 months *and* 6 and 6 months (all concurrent)
Alphonsus Larkin	Possession of firearms and ammunition with intent *and* Possession of firearms and ammunition (concurrent)	7 years *and* 12 months
Michael McEldowney	Possession of firearms and ammunition with intent *and* Possession of firearms and ammunition	8 years *and* 12 months (concurrent)
Richard Nagle	Possession of firearms and ammunition with intent *and* Possession of firearms and ammunition	7 years *and* 12 months (concurrent)
John J. McGirl	Carrying of ammunition *and* Refusal to account for movements	2 years *and* 6 months (concurrent)
John P. Mulvihill	Refusal to account for movements	4 months
Nicholas Swanton	Refusal to account for movements	4 months
Michael F. Hennessy	Refusal to account for movements	6 months
James McCabe	Refusal to account for movements	4 months
Richard Walsh	Refusal to account for movements	4 months
Peadar Doyle	Possession of firearms and ammunition with intent *and* Possession of firearms and ammunition *and* Possession of explosive substance	5 years *and* 18 months *and* 5 years (concurrent)
Thomas O'Neill	Possession of firearms and ammunition with intent *and* Refusal to account for movements	5 years *and* 4 months (concurrent)

Bibliography

ARCHIVE FILES

Irish National Archive Files

Attorney General's Office files as detailed in footnotes.

Department for Justice file JUS 8/1040.

Department of An Taoiseach files as detailed in footnotes.

US Department of Justice Files

US Department of Justice 'Ten Year program to Compensate Japanese Americans Interned During World War II Closes its Doors' (February 19, 1999), http://www.usdoj.gov/opa/pr/1998/June/276.htm.html, accessed 16 August 2004.

U. S. Department of Justice, 'Memorandum for Deval Patrick, Asst. Attorney General Civil Rights Division',(May 10, 1994), http://www.usdoj.gov/olc/14815mem.htm, accessed 16 August 2004.

DÁIL ÉIREANN PARLIAMENTARY REPORTS

Dáil Éireann, *Parliamentary Debates*.

SECONDARY SOURCES

Aitken, Ian, 'New laws will tighten net on terrorists', *The Guardian*, 21 December 1972.

Amnesty International, 'Israel/Occupied Territories, administrative detention: despair, uncertainty and lack of due process' (April 1997), 3.

Anderson, Frank, 'International terrorism & international cooperation' in *Countering suicide terrorism: an international conference* (Herzilya, 2001), pp 47–57.

Auld, Lord Justice Robin, *Review of the criminal courts of England & Wales* (London: 2001), http://www.criminal-courts-review.org.uk/ccr-00.htm, accessed 4 August 2005.

The *BBC* 'IRA statement in full', http://news.bbc.co.uk/1/hi/northern_ireland/4724599.stm accessed on 7 September 2005.

Bell, J. Bowyer, *The gun in politics: an analysis of Irish political conflict, 1916–1986* (New Brunswick, NJ, 1987).

Bell, J. Bowyer, *The secret army: the IRA* (3rd ed. Dublin, 1989).

Bell, J. Bowyer, *The Irish troubles: a generation of violence, 1967–1992* (Dublin, 1993).

Bell, John, *French constitutional law* (Oxford, 1992).

Bew, P., & G. Gillespie, *Northern Ireland: a chronology of the troubles, 1968–1993* (Dublin, 1993).

Bloom, Robert M. 'Jury trials in Japan' (March 16, 2005), Boston College Law School Research Paper No. 66, http://ssrn.com/abstract+688185, accessed 17 August 2005.

Bloomfield, Sir Kenneth, *We will remember: report of the Northern Ireland victims commissioner* (Belfast, 1998).
Boland, Kevin, *We won't stand (idly) by* (Dublin, 1973).
Boland, Kevin, *The rise & decline of Fianna Fáil* (Dublin, 1982).
Bonner, David, 'Combatting terrorism: supergrass trials in Northern Ireland' (1988) 51 *Modern Law Review*, 23–53.
Boyle, Andrew, *The riddle of Erskine Childers* (London, 1977).
Brady, Paul, 'Just deserts: can a retributivist theory of punishment be justified?' (2004) 12 *Irish Student Law Review*, 86–100.
Burke, Jason, 'Al-Qaeda: a meaningless label', *The Observer*, 12 January 2003, http://www.observer.co.uk/Print/0,38584581540,00.html, accessed 20 April 2003.
Burke, Jason, 'Terror's myriad faces', *The Observer*, 18 May 2003, http://www.guardian.co.uk/Print/0,3858,4671444,00.html, accessed 19 May 2003.
Byrne, Raymond, 'Judicial reviewability of a prosecutorial discretion" (1981) 16 *Irish Jurist*, 86–94.
Byrne, Raymond, 'The director of public prosecution's power to refer cases to the Special Criminal Court' (1984) 6 *Dublin University Law Journal*, 177–84.
The Cambridge Security Seminar, *A new security paradigm: a seminar record* (Cambridge, 2004).
Campbell, Colm, *Emergency law in Ireland, 1918–1925* (Oxford, 1994).
Carroll, Joseph T., *Ireland in the war years* (Newton Abbot, 1975).
Christopher, Russell L. 'The prosecutors dilemma: bargains and punishments' (2003) 72 *Fordham Law Review*, 93–168.
Chubb, Basil, *The constitution & constitutional change in Ireland* (4th ed.) (Dublin, 1978).
Comerford R.V. 'The land war & the politics of distress, 1877–1882' in W.E. Vaughan (ed.), *A new history of Ireland*, vi: *Ireland under the Union, ii: 1870–1921* (Oxford, 1996) pp 26–52.
Coogan, Tim Pat, *De Valera: long fellow, long shadow* (London, 1993).
Coogan, Tim Pat, *The troubles: Ireland's ordeal 1966–1995 and the search for peace* (London, 1995).
Corker, David, 'Trying fraud cases without juries' (2002) *Criminal Law Review*, 283–94.
Cornish, W.R., *The Jury* (London, 1968).
Curran, Joseph M., *The birth of the Irish Free State 1921–1923* (2nd ed. Tuscaloosa, AL, 1981).
Curtis, L. Perry, *Coercion & conciliation in Ireland, 1880 – 1892: a study in conservative unionism* (Oxford, 1963).
Davis, Fergal, 'Extra-Constitutionalism, the Human Rights Act and the 'Labour rebels': applying Prof. Tushnet's theories in the UK' (2006) 4 *Web Journal of Current Legal Issues*, http://webjcli.ncl.ac.uk/2006/issue4/davis4.html, accessed 4 October 2006.
de Vere White, Terence, *Kevin O'Higgins: strong man in the Free State government, 1922–27: his eventful life and mysterious violent death* (Tralee, 1966).

Dershowitz, Alan, *Why terrorism works: understanding the threat, responding to the challenge* (New Haven, 2002).

de Tocqueville, Alexis, *Democracy in America & two essays on America*, trans. G.E. Bevan (London, 2003).

Devlin, Sir Patrick, *Trial by jury* (London, 1966).

Diplock, Lord Kenneth, *Report of the commission to consider legal procedures to deal with terrorist activities in Northern Ireland*, Cmnd. 5185 (London, 1972).

Doolan, Brian, *Lawless v Ireland (1957–1961): the first case before the European Court of Human Rights: an international miscarriage of justice?* (Aldershot, 2001).

Dworkin, Ronald, *Taking rights seriously* (London, 1978).

Egan, Emily, 'The emergence of the supergrass: exposing the inadequacies of the accomplice corroboration warning' (2004) 12 *Irish Student Law Review*, 133–52.

Elazar, Dahlia S., *The making of Fascism: class, state, and counter-revolution, Italy 1919–1922* (New York, 2001).

Fanning, Ronan, '"The rule of order": Eamon de Valera & the IRA 1923–1940' in J.P. O'Carroll & J.A. Murphy (eds), *De Valera & his times* (Cork, 1983), pp 160–72.

Fanning , Ronan, 'Mr de Valera drafts a constitution' in Farrell (ed.), *De Valera's constitution & ours* (1988), pp 33 45.

Farrell, Brian (ed.), *De Valera's constitution & ours* (Dublin, 1988).

Farrell, Brian 'From First Dáil through Irish Free State' in Farrell (ed.), *De Valera's constitution & ours* (Dublin, 1988), pp 18–32.

Finn, John E., *Constitutions in crisis: political violence & the rule of law* (Oxford, 1991).

Fitzgibbon C., & G. Morrison, *The life and times of Eamon de Valera* (Dublin, 1973).

Foggo, Daniel, 'Real IRA threatened to kill trial witness's family in US', *Daily Telegraph*, 10 August 2003, http://www.telegraph.co.uk/news/main.jhtml?xml=/news/2003/08/10/nira10.xml, accessed 13 August 2004.

Frewen, Gerard L., *Judgments of the Court of Criminal Appeal 1924–1978* (Dublin, 1983).

Fyfe, Nicholas & James Sheptycki, 'Facilitating witness co-operation in organized crime cases: an international review' (Home Office Online Report 27/05) http://www.homeoffice.gov.uk/rds/pdfs05/rdsolr2705.pdf, accessed on 22 September 2005.

Ganor, Boaz, 'Defining terrorism: is one man's terrorist another man's freedom fighter?', http://www.ict.org.il/articles/define.htm accessed 28 April 2003.

Gardiner, Lord Gerald Austin, *Report of a committee to consider, in the context of civil liberties and human rights, measures to deal with terrorism in Northern Ireland*, Cmnd. 5847 (London, 1975).

Garvin, Tom, *The evolution of Irish nationalism* (New York, 1981).

Garvin, Tom, *1922: the birth of Irish democracy* (Dublin, 1996).

Gearty, Conor, 'Reflections on civil liberties in an age of counterterrorism' (2003) 41 *Osgoode Hall Law Journal*, 185–208.

Gewirth, Alan, *Reason & morality* (Chicago, 1978).

Goodhart A.L., 'The legality of the Nuremberg trials', *Juridicial Review*, April 1946, http://www.nizkor.org/hweb/imt/, accessed 8 August 2005.

Greer, Steven, 'Supergrass and the legal system in Britain and Northern Ireland' (1986) 102 *Law Quarterly Review*, 198–249.

Greer, Steven, 'The rise and fall of the Northern Ireland supergrass system' (1987) *Criminal Law Review*, 663–70.

The Guardian, 'Keeping some law in Ulster', 21 December 1972.

Gwynn, Denis R., *The Irish Free State, 1922–1927* (London, 1928).

Haaretz, 'Israel seeks international support for a treaty against suicide bombers', http://www.haaretzdaily.com/hasen/objects/pages/Print/ArticleEn.jhtml?itemNo=269141, accessed 5 March 2003.

Hachey, Thomas E., *Britain & Irish separatism: from the Fenians to the Free State, 1867–1922* (Chicago, 1977).

Harding, Thomas, 'The butcher of Omagh faces life: families hail Real IRA conviction', *Daily Telegraph,* 7 August 2003, http://www.telegraph.co.uk/news/main.jhtml?xml=/news/2003/08/07/wira07.xml, accessed 17 July 2006.

Harmon, Christopher C., *Terrorism today* (London, 2000).

Hermon, Sir John, *Holding the line: an autobiography* (Dublin, 1997).

Hofnung, Menachem, *Democracy, law & national security in Israel* (Aldershot, 1996).

Hogan, Gerard, 'Offences against the State (Amendment) Bill, 1940' (2000) 35 *Irish Jurist*, 238–79.

Hogan, Gerard, 'A desert island case set in the silver sea: *The State (Ryan) v. Lennon* (1934)' in E. O'Dell (ed.) *Leading cases of the twentieth century* (Dublin, 2000), pp 80–103.

Hogan, Gerard, 'The constitutional review group of 1934' in F. Ó Muircheartaigh (ed.), *Ireland in the coming times: essays to celebrate T.K. Whitaker's 80 years* (Dublin, 1997) pp 342–369.

Hogan, Gerard, 'Hugh Kennedy, the Childers habeas corpus application and the return to the Four Courts' in C. Costello (ed.), *The Four Courts: 200 years* (Dublin, 1996), pp 177–219.

Hogan G., & David G. Morgan, *Administrative law in Ireland* (Dublin, 1998).

Hogan G., & C. Walker, *Political violence & the law in Ireland* (Manchester, 1989).

Hogan G., & G. Whyte, *Kelly: the Irish Constitution* (4th ed. Dublin, 2003).

Home Office, *One step ahead; a 21st century strategy to defeat organized crime*, Cmnd. 6167 (London, 2004).

House of Commons Science & Technology Committee, *Forensic science on trial, seventh report of sessions 2004–05*, HC 96–1 (London, 2005).

Human Rights Committee, *Concluding observations of the Human Rights Committee: Ireland. 03/08/'93*. CCPR/C/79/Add.21, 3 August 1993 http://www.unhchr.ch/tbs/doc.nsf/(Symbol)/10cef6e66dedc39e41256324003c32cc?Opendocument, accessed 9 September 2004.

Human Rights Watch, 'Military commissions shouldn't be used: Pentagon rules short-change justice", 25 June 2003, http://hrw.org/press/2003/06/us062503.htm accessed 24 July 2006.

Ingoldsby, Caitríona, 'Supergrass testimony and reasonable doubt: an examination of *DPP v. Ward*' (1999) *Trinity College Law Review*, http//:www.csc.tcd.ie/~law/tcle/articles/1999/1999art3.htm accessed 31 May 2005.

Irish Times, 'Prisons bill signed by President', 26 May 1972.
Irish Times, 'Special Criminal Courts now being considered', 25 May 1972.
Irish Times, 'Very active consideration', Editorial Comment, 25 May 1972.
Irons, Peter, *Justice at war* (Oxford, 1983).
Izenberg, Dan, 'Supreme Court orders Lebanese hostages freed', the *Jerusalem Post,* 13 April 2000.
Jackson J. & S. Doran, 'Diplock & the presumption against jury trial: a critique', [1992] *Criminal Law Review*, 755–66.
Jackson J., & S. Doran, *Judge without jury: Diplock trials in the adversarial system* (Oxford, 1995).
Joseph, S., J. Schultz & M. Castan, *The International Covenant on Civil & Political Rights: cases, materials & commentary* (Oxford, 2000).
Katyal, N.K. & L.H. Tribe, 'Waging war, deciding guilt: trying the military tribunals' (2002) 111 *Yale Law Journal*, 1259–1310.
Kearney, Vincent, 'Bloody Sunday soldiers "allowed to change stories"', *Sunday Times,* 8 August, 1999.
Kelly, John M., *Fundamental rights in the Irish law & Constitution* (2nd ed. Dublin, 1967).
Kohn, Leo, *The Constitution of the Irish Free State* (London, 1932).
Korff, Douwe, *The Diplock courts in Northern Ireland: a fair trial?* (Utrecht, 1983).
Lee, Joseph J., *Ireland, 1912–1985: politics & society* (Cambridge, 1989).
Lee, Joseph J., 'Séan Lemass' in J.J. Lee (ed.), *Ireland 1945 –70* (Dublin, 1979) pp 16–26.
Lord Lloyd of Hampstead, *Introduction to jurisprudence* (4th ed. London, 1979).
Lyon, Ann, *Constitutional history of the United Kingdom* (London, 2003).
Lyons, F.S.L. 'The developing crisis, 1907–1914' in W.E. Vaughan (ed.), *A new history of Ireland,* vi: *Ireland under the Union, ii: 1870–1921* (Oxford, 1996) pp 123–44.
Lyons, F.S.L. 'The new nationalism, 1916–1918' in W.E. Vaughan (ed.), *A new history of Ireland,* vi, pp 224–39.
Lyons, F.S.L., *Ireland since the Famine* (London, 1973).
MacDermott , Eithne, *Clann na Poblachta* (Cork, 1998).
MacEoin, Uinseann, *The IRA in the Twilight Years: 1923–1948* (Dublin, 1997).
McCartney, Donal, 'From Parnell to Pearse (1891–1921)' in T.W. Moody & F.X. Martin (eds), *The course of Irish history* (Cork, 1967) pp 294–312.
McDermot, Paul A., *Res judicata & double jeopardy* (Dublin, 1999).
McGoldrick, Dominic, *The Human Rights Committee: its role in the development of the International Covenant on Civil & Political Rights* (Oxford, 1991).
McInerney, Michael, 'Special court now established', *Irish Times,* 27 May, 1972.
McInerney, Michael, 'Government gets plans for special courts ready, *Irish Times,* 25 May 1972.
McLoughlin, Michael (ed.), *Great Irish speeches of the twentieth century* (Dublin, 1996).
Macardle, Dorothy, *The Irish Republic* (London, 1968).
Manning, Maurice, *The Blueshirts* (Dublin, 1987).

Matthews, R., L. Hancock & D. Briggs, 'Juror's perceptions, understanding, confidence and satisfaction in the jury system: a study in six courts' (Home Office Online Report 05/04), http://www.homeoffice.gov.uk/ rds/pdfs2/rdsolr0504.pdf, accessed on 22 August 2005.

Merino-Blanco, Elena, *The Spanish legal system* (London, 1996).

Mitchell A., & P. Ó Snodaigh (eds), *Irish political documents, 1869–1916* (Dublin, 1989).

Morgan, David G., *Constitutional law of Ireland* (Dublin, 1985).

Murphy, John A., *Ireland in the twentieth century* (Dublin, 1989).

Netanyahu, Benjamin, *Fighting terrorism: how democracies can defeat the international terrorist network* (New York, 2001).

Ó'Donnachadha, Colmán P. '"The likes of which has never been encountered before". Witness intimidation: criminal justice in crisis?' (2004) *Cork On-line Law Review VI*, http://colr.ucc.ie/2004vi.html, accessed 29 June 2005.

O'Donnell, John L. 'The jury on trial: reflections on *DPP v. Haugh*' (July, 2000) *Bar Review*, 470–75.

O'Donoghue, David, *Hitler's Irish voices: the story of German radio's wartime Irish service* (Belfast, 1998).

O'Halpin, Eunan, *Defending Ireland: the Irish State & its enemies since 1922* (Oxford, 1999).

O'Leary, Cornelius, *Irish elections 1918–1977, parties, voters & proportional representation* (Dublin, 1979).

O'Mahony, T.P., *Jack Lynch: a biography* (Dublin, 1991).

O'Ruaric, Liam, 'A little known republican military group: Saor Eire', the *Blanket*, 13 January 2005, http://lark.phoblacht.net/lor1401051g.html, accessed 2 August 2005.

O'Sullivan, Donal, *The Irish Free State & its Senate* (New York, 1972).

Oraá, Jaime, *Human rights in states of emergency in international law* (Oxford, 1992).

Packard, Jerrold M., *Neither friend nor foe: the European neutrals in World War II* (New York, 1992).

Packenham, Frank (earl of Longford) & T.P. O'Neill, *Eamon de Valera* (London, 1970).

Patterson, Henry, *The politics of illusion: a political history of the IRA* (London, 1997).

The *Plough*, 'Militants leave Saor Éire', http://lark.phoblacht.net/lor1401051g.html, accessed 2 August 2005.

Pye, Stephen, 'Judicial review of discretionary powers under Part V of the Offences against the State Act 1939' (1985) 3 *Irish Law Times*, 65–73.

Quinn, Katie, 'Jury bias and the European Convention on Human Rights: a well kept secret?', [2004] *Criminal Law Review*, 998–1014.

Rawls, John, *A theory of justice* (Oxford, 1973).

Report of the Committee to Review the Offences against the State Acts, 1939–98 and Related Matters (Dublin, 2002).

Robinson, Mary, *The Special Criminal Court* (Dublin, 1974).

Rostow, Eugene V. 'The Japanese American cases: a disaster' (1945) 54 *Yale Law Journal*, 489–533.

RTE, 'McDowell insists IRA will remain illegal', http://www.rte.ie/news/2005/0828/mcdowellm.html accessed on 7 September 2005.

Schaffer, Robert, 'Opposition to internment: defending Japanese American rights during World War II', Historian (Spring, 1999), http://www.findarticles.com/p/articles/mi_m2082/is_3_61/ai_55426755, accessed 16 August 2004.

Scherman, Rabbi Nosson (trans.), *The complete artscroll siddur: ashkenaz* (2nd ed. New York, 2001).

Schmid, A.P., & A.J. Jongman, *Political terrorism: a new guide to actors, authors, concepts, data bases, theories and literature* (Amsterdam, 1988).

Secretary of State for the Home Department & the Secretary of State for Northern Ireland, *Legislation against terrorism*, Cmnd. 4178 (London, 1998).

Sharfman, Daphna, *Living without a constitution: civil rights in Israel* (New York, 1993).

Sherrin, Ned (ed.), *The Oxford dictionary of humorous quotations* (Oxford, 1995).

Spillius, Alex, 'Bali bomber greets death sentence with thumbs-up', *Daily Telegraph*, August 8 2003, http://www.telegraph.co.uk/news/main.jhtml?xml=/news/2003/08/08/wbali08.xml, accessed 17 July 2006.

Spjut, R.J. 'Executive detention in Northern Ireland: the Gardiner Report and the Northern Ireland (Emergency Provisions) (Amendment) Act 1975' (1975) 10 *Irish Jurist*, 272–99.

Spjut, R.J. 'Internment and detention without trial in Northern Ireland 1971 – 1975: ministerial policy & practice' (1986) 49 *Modern Law Review*, 712–740.

Stanage, Niall, 'Justice Denied', *Magill* (August 2003), 26–28.

Tapper, Colin, *Cross & Tapper on evidence* (8th ed. London, 1995).

Telushkin, Rabbi Joseph, *Jewish literacy: the most important things to know about the Jewish religion, its people, and its history* (New York, 2001).

Ten Broek, J., E.N. Barnhart & F.W. Matson, *Prejudice war & the constitution: causes & consequences of the evacuation of Japanese Americans in World War II* (5th ed. Berkeley, 1975).

Thomas, Rosamund M. 'The British Official Secrets Acts 1911–1939 and the Ponting case' (1986) *Criminal Law Review*, 491–510.

Thornton, Peter, 'Trial by jury: 50 years of change', [2004] *Criminal Law Review*, 683–701.

Townshend, Charles, *Political violence in Ireland: government & resistance since 1948* (Oxford, 1983).

Tushnet, Mark, 'Defending Korematsu?: reflections in civil liberties in wartime' (2003) *Wisconsin Law Review*, 273–307.

Tushnet, Mark, 'Replies: controlling executive power in the war on terrorism' (2005) 118 *Harvard Law Review*, 2673–82.

Twining, W.L. 'Emergency powers & criminal process: the Diplock Report', [1973] *Criminal Law Review*, 406–417.

United States Department of State, *Patterns of Global Terrorism 2002* (Washington D.C., 2003).

Vaughan, W.E. (ed.), *A new history of Ireland*, vi*: Ireland under the Union, ii: 1870–1921* (Oxford, 1996).

Walker, Brian, *Dancing to history's tune: history, myth & politics in Northern Ireland* (Belfast, 1996).
Walker, Clive, 'The commodity of justice in states of emergency' (1999) *Northern Ireland Legal Quarterly*, vol.50, no.2, 164–185.
Walsh, Dermot, *Criminal procedure* (Dublin, 2002).
The *Washington Post,* 'Israel seeks to codify detention of hostages', April 18, 2000, http://washingtonpost.com/wp-dyn/articles/A37757-2000Apr18.htm, accessed 15 November, 2000.
Wigmore, John Henry, *A treatise on the Anglo-American system of evidence in trials at common law: vol. 17* (3rd ed. Boston, 1940).
Wilson, Thomas, *Ulster: conflict & consent* (Oxford, 1989).
Zaman, Amberin, 'News in brief: police free hostage judges', the *Daily Telegraph,* 19 November 2003, www.telegaph.co.uk, accessed 13 August 2004, http://www.telegraph.co.uk/news/main.jhtml?xml=/news/2003/11/19/wbul19.xml, accessed 17 July 2006.
Zamir, I. & A. Zysblat, *Public law in Israel* (Oxford, 1996).

Miscellaneous

'Meretz', http://www.fact-index.com/m/me/meretz.html accessed 30 July, 2004.
'Prosecution on the same charge after entering a nolle prosequi, *The State (Walsh) v. Lennon*' (1942) 6 *Journal of Criminal Law,* 205.

Index

Constitutional documents, table of statutes and table of cases

CONSTITUTIONAL DOCUMENTS

Irish

Other

International treaties

TABLE OF STATUTES

Irish Statutes

Irish Statutory Instruments

Other Statutes

TABLE OF CASES

A